E-DISCOVERY
A Guide for Corporate Counsel
Second Edition

Including Proposed Changes to Federal Rules of Civil Procedure

Sills Cummis Epstein & Gross P.C.

Newark, New Jersey

Copyright © 2004 Sills Cummis Epstein & Gross P.C.

- Second Edition -

www.sillscummis.com

All rights reserved. No reproduction of any portion of this book is permitted without express written consent from Sills Cummis Epstein & Gross P.C.

The information in this book is for informational purposes only. It is not intended as legal advice or any other professional service. Persons seeking legal advice should consult with an attorney.

ISBN 0-9754730-1-8

ACKNOWLEDGEMENTS

Sills Cummis Epstein & Gross P.C. gratefully acknowledges the contributions of the following persons:

Managing Editors: Barry M. Epstein
Stuart J. Glick
Jeffrey J. Greenbaum
Mark S. Olinsky

General Editors: Kenneth F. Oettle
James M. Hirschhorn

Chapter Authors and Editors:
Linda B. Katz, Arlene E. Mirsky, Trent S. Dickey,
A. Ross Pearlson, Mark E. Duckstein, Thomas S. Novak,
Karen J. Krause, Michele C. Lefkowitz, Kenneth Hayes,
Deborah M. Heindl, Karina D. Fuentes

The Firm also acknowledges Peter Calhoun, Hanna Schwartz and Ken Calhoun for proofreading, Jacques Pierre for drafting the Index and Glossary, Keith Murphy and Megan Clark for cite checking, and Joseph Sandomeno for his work on cover and layout. Special thanks is given to Eric Friedberg of Stroz Friedberg, LLC, a consulting and technical services firm, 15 Maiden Lane, Suite 1208, New York, NY 10038, (212) 981-6540 (main), (212) 981-6545 (fax), for his input on Chapter 1.

TABLE OF CONTENTS

Introduction 1

- The challenges of e-discovery, including the cost, can be formidable because of the exponential growth of information in electronic format and the difficulty of recovering it. With judicious use of expert help, most issues can be resolved in familiar ways. This book is intended to help you understand how.

Chapter 1:   Your Company's Computer System 3

- E-discovery has its own developing vocabulary, such as "metadata," "tiffing," and "harvesting protocols." Counsel and clients looking to participate in the brave new world of e-discovery need to know the terms.

   A. Types of Networks. 3
   B. Types of Software. 6
   C. Types of Data. 7
      1. Active Data. 7
         a. Readily Available Data. 8
         b. Metadata. 9
         c. Embedded Data. 12
      2. Back-up Data. 12
      3. Residual Data. 16

Chapter 2:   Your Company's Document Management and Retention Program (DMRP) 19

- Document discovery begins with document retention. When litigation is imminent, you may need to interrupt your normal cycle of data deletion and destruction.

   A. The Need for a Document Management and Retention Program. 19
      1. Satisfy business/operational needs. 20
      2. Meet retention periods required by law. ...20
      3. Preserve documents for litigation. 22
      4. Respond to obstruction of justice concerns under Sarbanes-Oxley. 28

    B. Establishing an Effective Document Management and Retention Program. 31
       1. Overview: Your touchstones are reasonableness, good faith, and effective implementation. 31
       2. Cover all records within the meaning of Fed.R. Civ. P. 34. 33
       3. Implement effectively. 35
       4. Store documents centrally in organized fashion. 36
       5. Establish reasonable retention schedules. . .38
       6. Develop litigation hold procedures. 39
       7. Audit and adjust your DMRP. 42
       8. Develop your DMRP in light of the above. 43
    C. A Recent Guide: The Sedona Principles. 45

Chapter 3: Discovery of Electronic Data Under the Federal Rules of Civil Procedure 47

- Like paper discovery, electronic discovery is governed by Rules 26 and 34 of the Federal Rules of Civil Procedure and their state analogs and by the concepts of cooperation, relevance and reasonable burden.

    A. The Basic Structure of Discovery. 47
    B. The Obligation To Produce Documents in Electronic Form. 50
    C. Evolving Court Rules. 56
    D. Proposed Changes to the Federal Rules of Civil Procedure. 58
       1. Definition of Electronically Stored Information. 58
       2. Electronic Discovery as Part of Early Discovery Planning. 59
       3. Form of Production. 60
       4. Privilege Waiver. .60
       5. Two-Tiered Discovery – Discovery of Data that Is Not Reasonably Accessible 62
       6. Safe Harbor from Sanctions. 63
    E. August 2004 Changes to the ABA Civil Discovery Standards on Electronic Discovery. .64

Chapter 4: Non-Party Electronic Discovery 67
- Identifying, harvesting and analyzing electronic data from non-parties follows the same protocols as obtaining discovery from parties, but the cost-benefit analysis is more protective of the non-party.
  - A. Introduction. 67
  - B. Tasks in Obtaining Electronic Discovery from Non-Parties. 68
    - 1. Identify non-parties possessing relevant information. 69
    - 2. Harvest the information. 70
  - C. Non-Parties' Rights and Duties when Served with a Discovery Demand. 75
  - D. Cost Issues. 78
  - E. Conclusion. 79

Chapter 5: Spoliation of Evidence 81
- Parties should preserve electronic documents that may be relevant to litigation.
  - A. The Duty To Preserve Evidence. 82
  - B. When the Duty To Preserve Arises. 82
  - C. Who Has the Duty To Preserve. 85
  - D. What Must Be Preserved. 87
  - E. How Preservation Can Be Accomplished. 89
  - F. Spoliation of Evidence. 91
  - G. The Elements of Spoliation. 93
  - H. The Consequences of Spoliation. 94
  - I. Conclusion. 101

Chapter 6: Matters of Privilege and Confidentiality 103
- Protection against disclosure of privileged and confidential electronic information requires special procedures because of the sheer volume of information and the ease with which inadvertent disclosures can occur.
  - A. Production by the Respondent. 105
  - B. Production by Intervention of an Expert Not Under Respondent's Direct Control. 112

Chapter 7: Cost-Shifting 121
- Though the general rule is still that the responding party bears the cost of production, the difficulty and expense of recovering and producing electronic data may justify cost-shifting.
  - A. The General Rule Regarding Cost-Shifting...121
  - B. The Factors Governing Cost-Shifting. 125
    - 1. The Accessibility Threshold...........127
    - 2. Cost Allocation Factors. 129
  - C. Review for Privileged or Confidential Material. 134

Chapter 8: The Role of Experts in Electronic Discovery 137
- One often needs an expert to help harvest electronic information, select what is relevant and protect what is privileged and confidential.
  - A. Why You Need an Expert. 137
    - 1. Offensive Reasons. 137
      - a. Discovering a Basis for Suit. 137
      - b. Shaping Discovery Requests. 139
      - c. Recovering Electronic Data. 143
      - d. Authenticating Discovery. 148
    - 2. Defensive Reasons. 151
      - a. Creating Document Retention Programs. 151
      - b. Responding to Discovery Requests. ..154
  - B. Who the Experts Are. 155
  - C. Selecting a Testifying Expert. 156
  - D. Cost of Experts. 158
  - E. Court-Appointed Experts. 159

Glossary 167

Appendix A (Federal Rules) 175

Table of Authorities 219

Index 237

INTRODUCTION

This is a primer on electronic discovery for in-house counsel. It is useful to anyone whose client maintains electronic records and to any litigator who needs to shape demands for electronic documents or respond to them. If you have designed a document retention program or litigated electronic discovery issues, much of the material in this text may be familiar to you.

A comforting truth about electronic discovery is that the legal issues are not unlike the issues one faces with discovery of paper documents. Litigants must share information voluntarily and produce what is reasonably requested, given the cost of recovery in relation to the perceived value of the information. They can withhold privileged material and seek protection for what they deem confidential. If they conceal, alter or destroy evidence, they may pay dearly. All this is true for electronic documents as it is for hard copy.

On the other hand, electronic evidence is different from paper evidence in many ways, including the following: (1) electronic documents are easy to save, duplicate and distribute, resulting in their proliferation; relevant records can be found in innumerable places, and the cost of recovering them can be extraordinary; (2) electronic documents are easy to lose or alter, exposing the company to possible regulatory or litigative sanctions; (3) electronic documents contain information normally omitted from the paper version, such as data showing edits and by whom; (4) an electronic document may continue to exist even after we think we have deleted it, making it potentially a spy within our own camp; (5) we can search millions of electronic records in minutes with well-chosen search terms, which makes electronic information an extremely efficient vehicle for discovery; and (6) at least for the time being, we need experts to help us preserve, recover and review electronic documents because they are stored not in boxes and file cabinets but as integrated bits of data inside machines.

We don't look inside these machines. We take on faith that the machines retain true copies of what we create or scan in, just as we take on faith that TV produces a true version of what is happening miles away. Because the technology of document storage has, for most of us, outstripped our capacity to understand and manipulate it, we need the assistance of experts, whether from our own MIS department or from the outside.

This book addresses the principal questions to which persons involved in the preservation and production of electronic information seek answers. Topics include the design of records management programs (Chapter 2); the use of forensics experts to locate, analyze and produce electronic evidence (Chapter 8); terms and concepts in the field of electronic information (Chapter 1); and the relevant rules of court (Chapter 3). The book also addresses privilege and confidentiality (Chapter 6); cost-shifting in discovery (Chapter 7); documents in the hands of non-parties (Chapter 4); and the potentially serious consequences of losing or destroying electronic evidence (Chapter 5).

We assume you will open the book to seek answers to specific questions rather than read it through like a novel. With this in mind, each chapter is an integrated presentation and may touch on material covered in other chapters, such as seminal judicial opinions or definitions of key terms. As you read through the chapters, you will realize that courts confronted with disputes over electronic evidence are resolving classic issues of discovery: Are the documents true versions? Are they the only versions? Were any documents lost or destroyed? Is the benefit of recovering the data worth the cost?

Though the questions are familiar, the means of developing answers are new. With guidance from this book and the assistance of good advisors, you will be well on your way to mastering the brave new world of electronic discovery.

YOUR COMPANY'S COMPUTER SYSTEM

YOUR COMPANY'S COMPUTER SYSTEM

To respond to electronic discovery or to formulate it, counsel needs to understand computer systems, which may consist of large computers serving many users or personal computers working individually or linked through a network, or both. Counsel should have a basic knowledge of the servers, data storage devices, desktop computers and other hardware that make up the network; the operating system(s) that run the computers; the applications software, such as word processing and spreadsheet programs; and the back-up procedures and media.

The best source for this information is the company's management information system ("MIS") or information technology ("IT") department – the technicians who have day-to-day responsibility for designing and administering the company's computer system. Counsel for smaller companies without MIS or IT departments may have to rely on their computer system consultant, their vendors, or outside counsel to gain an understanding of their computer system. The technicians and other advisors should be consulted early on and throughout the process of electronic discovery to prevent serious problems later.

A.   Types of Networks.

The term "network" refers to the hardware and software that connects computers and allows them to share data. The most common computer networks are "local-area networks" (LANs), which are basically computers located close together, and "wide-area networks" (WANs), which are computers farther apart, connected by telephone, cable lines or radio waves. Networks provide many services, including file, e-mail, web and database. These services can be provided by computers designated as servers (the "client/server model") or by any workstation within a network (the "peer-to-peer model"). In a peer-to-peer network, any workstation can act as a file server. For electronic discovery purposes, this means that counsel should expect to find on any such workstations the scope of documents one would find on a file server.

A client-server network normally has file servers to which users can save documents they create or receive. File servers are centrally located repositories of data containing one or more hard drives. Typically, each user has some private space on those hard drives (a "home directory") to which to save files. The space is private in that other users cannot access documents in a user's home directory. Sometimes the network is set up such that by default, a user's documents are saved to the user's home directory. In other networks, the user may have the option of saving documents "locally," that is, to the hard drive in the user's desktop or laptop computer, often called the "c:/ drive."

Lawyers experienced in electronic discovery no doubt have learned that users don't use home directories just for storing documents. Not infrequently, they archive gigabytes of their old e-mail there as well. Though a company may have only the last sixty days of e-mail on its servers, and though it may have only one year of e-mail back-up tapes, a user may have archived the last four years of e-mail in the user's home directory.

Further complicating electronic discovery, most corporate networks have other file servers, or areas on the file servers that house their home directories, where users can post documents for others to see and work on. These are sometimes called "shared drives" or "group shares." One of the challenges to compliance in electronic discovery is

YOUR COMPANY'S COMPUTER SYSTEM

1

filtering the documents of the relevant users out of the group shares, which often contain hundreds of thousands of documents and are normally organized, if at all, by subject, not user. Tiffing[1] the entire group share so that it may be searched can be prohibitively expensive, and using the file server's operating system to search for the relevant users is often too slow. Normally, tailored Perl scripts or other network-forensic tools can be deployed to cull out documents of the relevant users.

In complying with electronic discovery requests, lawyers should also be cognizant that users within a network can save documents to many forms of removable media and external devices such as CD-ROMs, floppy disks, USB thumb drives, jaz drives, PDAs and external hard drives.

Counsel must also consider Internet-based file servers. In some industries, the company's business model, or issues of data storage, require that corporate documents be posted on file servers housed not by the company but by a third party, as on *xdrive.com*. Documents stored in such fashion are subject to document requests just like documents on servers housed by the company.

Finally, with remote access to computers having blurred the line between home and work, users often store documents on their home computers, sometimes exclusively. Thus, compliance with a document request – whether voluntary or court-ordered – may require that data be harvested from home computers.

---

[1] Tiffing and PDF'ing are technologies that create an image file, which is a snapshot of the surface of a document and does not include any hidden data. Tiffs and PDFs can be opened only in specialized viewers such as Microsoft Imaging and Adobe Acrobat.

E-DISCOVERY
A Guide for Corporate Counsel

To sum up, in the mushrooming field of electronic discovery, the lawyer's responsibility now extends to multiple sources of documents:

- Laptops/desktops
- Home directories
- Group shares
- Removable media
- Home computers
- Internet-based file servers
- PDAs

The inconvenience and cost of gathering, reviewing and producing data from all these sources can be enormous, and the burden can be amplified where the server-based data has been captured in different forms on periodic back-up tapes. One way to reduce the potential burden is to negotiate the scope of compliance with the adversary, whether opposing counsel or a regulator. For example, if you agree to produce only server and desktop/laptop-based documents, you need not worry about the documents resident on Blackberries, Palm Pilots or floppy disks. In civil litigation, where what is good for the goose is good for the gander, an adversary may be content to limit discovery in this manner.

B.   Types of Software.

Software is divided into two broad categories: systems software and applications software. The operating system is the master program that runs the computer – it allows the other software programs to function. Windows, Netware, UNIX, Linux, Macintosh OS X and DOS are examples of operating systems. Systems software interacts with the computer at a very basic level. Applications software, also known as "end-user programs," carries out the tasks desired by the users. Word processing, spreadsheets and database

YOUR COMPANY'S COMPUTER SYSTEM

management programs are examples of applications software. Virtually all requests for electronic discovery require the responding party to specify operating system and applications software so the requesting party can consider the format in which files and data will be produced.

C. Types of Data.

The three basic types of data are: (1) active data; (2) back-up data; and (3) residual data. Residual data is not visible or accessible to end-users, but it may still exist on the system and be recoverable. Most prominent of the forms of residual data for electronic discovery purposes is the data cached to desktop and laptop hard drives after a document or e-mail is deleted, or after a document or e-mail is drafted, opened or viewed, even if it is not intentionally saved to a hard drive. Discoverable electronic data can also be present in the buffers (memories) of the company's printers, fax machines and copy machines. The destruction or even the inadvertent loss of such data after notice of a claim could result in sanctions.

1. Active Data.

Active data is the information stored either on a network server or locally on a hard drive and currently available and readily accessible to end-users through a desktop or other computer connection. It includes information needed for daily tasks, such as word-processing documents, calendars, memo pads, task lists, addresses, e-mail and databases – that is, the data to which you have access when you turn your computer on in the morning. Such data is the primary, most obvious source of active data, but it comprises only a part of it. Also included in active data is hidden information called "metadata" or "embedded data," regarding, among other things, when documents were created, accessed and modified and how they were changed (*See* "b" and "c" below).

a.   Readily Available Data.

Extracting e-mail from e-mail servers is fairly straightforward, but collecting other active data is not. Consider the desktop environment. If users placed all their relevant files in their My Documents folder (and placed nothing else there), harvesting those folders would be simple. But users can and often do place documents in unpredictable places on their hard drives. Therefore, all hard drive directories must be searched. In that search, the examiner may encounter thousands of irrelevant program and system files. Accordingly, a protocol must be drafted (a "harvesting protocol") to sort each computer's files by file extension and then to extract only the files with those extensions, *e.g.*, .doc, .xls, .ppt, .wpd and .pdf. This takes some sophistication because scores of file extensions are potentially relevant. Some are unique to the client's environment, and the list is ever-expanding with the emergence of new applications.

A number of other wrinkles must also be handled. What if the user compressed all the user's .xls files with Winzip, a popular compression program? Then all the .zip files need to be exploded and analyzed pursuant to the harvesting protocol. The problem is that more than fifty types of compressed file formats exist, each with its own extension.

Or what if the user wrote word processing documents with software that saved them as .txt files (stripped-down word processing files with little formatting functionality)? The problem with harvesting all the .txt files is that thousands of system files also have .txt file extensions. In the end, a very careful protocol informed by all these considerations must be structured and then scrupulously followed. These same issues exist when harvesting data from file servers and group shares.

Similar issues arise when dealing with e-mail archived to local hard drives. The local hard drive must be profiled to determine how many e-mail programs the user has used. It may not be just the corporate e-mail application. Often, users transact company business over Internet mail accounts such as AOL, Yahoo! or hotmail and have archives of such mail on their c:/ drives. AOL creates a separate archive for every version of AOL installed, so all such folders must be checked. In addition, certain e-mail programs create hidden files that – unbeknownst to the user – contain e-mail. For example, when a user is synchronizing mail between a corporate Exchange server and a local Outlook client, an ".ost" file will be saved to the user's hard drive. Although the user cannot access that file, the file can forensically be converted to a .pst file, and large caches of past e-mail, calendar items and tasks can be found therein. Accordingly, be careful about representing that you've produced all the e-mail from a corporate environment. There may be more somewhere.

b.   Metadata.

Metadata is sometimes described as "data about data." It includes information recording, among other things, when a document was created, last accessed, last modified, and last printed, and who created the document (sometimes defined by the name of the person to whom the application suite that created the document is registered or the name of the person logged onto the computer on which the document is created). Metadata can exist not only at the file system level but also within documents themselves. Windows-based file systems maintain file allocation tables ("FATs") (called master file tables ["MFTs"] in certain Windows systems) that enable the computer to know where saved documents are stored so they can be retrieved. FATs and MFTs also contain metadata that chronicles when a document was created, last modified and last accessed.

The documents themselves – such as Word documents and WordPerfect documents and Excel and Access files – also contain similar metadata, but the metadata that exists within the files may be different from that contained in the FAT or MFT. For example, if a Word document is created and modified in Windows-based network A on January 1, 2004 and e-mailed to a user in network B on January 4, 2004, and the network B user copies the document and saves it to network B on January 4, 2004, the metadata at the FAT/MFT level in user B's network will show a "created date" of January 4, 2004. But the act of saving the document will not change the embedded Word metadata, which will still show a "created date" of January 1, 2004. Also, Word draws all its information regarding created, last accessed and last modified dates from the file system; but Word documents contain other metadata such as last printed, last ten "authors," and last-saved-by that do not depend on the file system, and thus do not change as the document is moved from one file system to another.[2] Different file systems, such as those used by Linux and Solaris, present other metadata issues.

Requests for electronic discovery may require the preservation and production of metadata. A lawyer

---

[2] The metadata displayed in the Word Properties box (revealed by selecting File on the standard Word toolbar and then electing Properties) includes both the file system metadata (under the General tab) and Word metadata (under the Statistics tab). Other Word metadata – such as last saved time and last ten authors – are not even reported in this view. They are discoverable only through the use of forensic tools such as Metadata Assistant.

YOUR COMPANY'S COMPUTER SYSTEM

1

attempting to comply with such a request may wish to clarify which level of metadata is being requested: FAT/MFT, application-level metadata or both. Compliance with a request to preserve and produce "metadata" must be handled with care because many methods of copying electronic data can change the data regarding last access and even the creation date of the documents being copied. For example, if, after a preservation request, documents are opened in their native applications for lawyers to review for relevance or privilege, the last accessed date will change (both at the FAT/MFT and application levels) to the date the document is opened. Even if documents are copied from a desktop or server in an appropriate fashion, the act of burning copies of those documents to CD can cause new creation dates to appear, and last-accessed dates to completely disappear, on the CD-resident copies. When such data is requested, technical tools and methodologies for preserving metadata should be put in place at the beginning of counsel's electronic document collection. This may require the involvement of a computer forensics expert.

E-mails received from outside a company's network also have metadata in the form of hidden "Internet headers." These headers can normally be revealed by an operation within the e-mail program on a user's machine, such as Outlook or Outlook Express. The headers contain esoteric information not normally relevant to litigation, including the name of the e-mail server from which the e-mail was sent, the name of the e-mail server receiving the mail, the Internet protocol addresses of those servers, and time stamps for when the e-mail passed through those servers. This information is likely to be useful only in a dispute whether a particular e-mail was sent or received. A native-format preservation of e-mails automatically secures this metadata, and, unlike the preservation process for documents, it poses no risk that the metadata will be altered. On the other hand, if only the visible text of an e-mail is preserved, as through a tiffing process, the embedded Internet headers will be lost.

c. Embedded Data.

Substantive information created by the user and hidden within the file itself (*i.e.*, not displayed in the default view of the document) is commonly known as "embedded data." Such data includes, for example, the substance of previous edits, formatting commands, links to other files, hidden rows or columns in spreadsheets, or 'electronic stickies,' which are notes or reminders that authors and reviewers leave for each other. Because embedded data can embody lawyer-client communications, work product and other confidential communications, it can be the subject of difficult negotiations in determining what data must be produced. Although electronic discovery productions are sometimes made in a form that strips both metadata and embedded data – such as tiffing or PDF'ing the documents – the metadata and embedded data still exist in the original, "native" documents. In appropriate cases, courts may order the production of files in native form so that such metadata and embedded data can be examined.[3]

2. Back-up Data.

Anyone who has worked with computers has likely heard the cardinal rule, "*Back up your files regularly.*" The institutionalized adherence to this rule has resulted in a

---

[3] Metadata is sometimes defined to include embedded data, or aspects of it such as prior edits, because such data can be considered "meta" to what the end-user sees on the screen or what the end-user can easily access with a click of the mouse.

YOUR COMPANY'S COMPUTER SYSTEM

proliferation of sources in which files and e-mails can be located, and it has drastically increased the complexity, uncertainty and cost of responding to discovery requests.

Typically, back-up data is copied by network administrators from a network drive, such as an e-mail server, a file server or a group share, to removable or remote media, such as a disk or a tape, to provide data redundancy in the event of a system failure. Less frequently encountered are a user's own back-ups from hard drives to media such as jaz drives, CD-ROMs, DVDs or other external hard drives. Network back-ups are usually generated on a regular schedule.

Each server environment will likely have a different back-up policy, and the administrator for that particular environment will be aware of the policy. The CIO may have no clue about such specifics. Typically, on smaller servers, the data on the server is backed up in full each day for several weeks, collectively called a "rotation." Each back-up is made to a separate tape. When the rotation is over, the back-up process continues, except that tapes from the prior rotation are re-used, beginning with the earliest tape. In a three-week rotation, tape one is overwritten on day twenty-two, which is the first day of the second rotation.

Larger servers may have too much data for the system to be backed up in full each night. Accordingly, administrators can make one full back-up (usually on a weekend day) and six "incremental" back-ups in which only the files that have changed since the previous day are backed up. To restore system data in case of a server failure, the administrator must restore the most recent full back-up and all subsequent incremental back-ups and add them together.

E-DISCOVERY
A Guide for Corporate Counsel

1

Companies often retain full end-of-month, end-of-six-month, and/or end-of-year back-up tapes for several years. Regulated businesses do so pursuant to statute or rule. Recently, companies have begun to minimize the number of back-up tapes they maintain to avoid the cost and inconvenience of litigation-related restoration and analysis.

Counsel relying on either written or informal rotation policies should be mindful that back-up tapes slated for discard may actually be retained or that, unbeknownst to the administrator, the back-up process on a particular day failed, leading either to a useless tape or to tape containing older data that was not overwritten. In this regard, practice and policy may be quite different.

One of the greatest challenges for counsel is the volume of data on back-up tapes and the enormous levels of duplication among tapes. The closer that back-up tapes are in time, the greater the level of duplication. For example, if the user is a pack rat and has thousands of e-mails in the mailbox, a three-week rotation of "full" back-ups could produce a 95% duplication rate from one day to the next. The cost of restoring and de-duplicating all three weeks of that e-mail would be enormous.

Accordingly, counsel should negotiate with opposing counsel to make the production responsive but cost-effective. For example, if the subject events preceded the rotation period, then perhaps only the earliest back-up tape needs to be restored. Because e-mail attachments can increase the size of production by many multiples, producing just e-mails first can make sense, with selected attachments in a second round.

A company's back-up or preservation protocols will not ensure that every file is backed up at least once. The system will have gaps because a file can be received, reviewed and

YOUR COMPANY'S COMPUTER SYSTEM

1

deleted before it is captured by a regularly scheduled network back-up. For instance, if an e-mail was received in the early morning and deleted immediately, and the company backs up e-mails at the end of the day, such an e-mail would not have been backed up. Thus, a company's back-up system may be under-inclusive as well as duplicative.

Several variables impact the accessibility of back-up data. One such variable is the method of storage. Back-ups are frequently stored on tapes that contain large quantities of data arranged in linear fashion and therefore not easily searched. Types of such tapes include the older reel-to-reel tapes that afford high capacity and are often used in conjunction with large mainframes; digital audio tapes (DAT); QIC tapes; and the newer format Travan tapes often used on smaller computers and networks. Optical drives and archival optical disks are also used as back-up media and present fewer problems in electronic discovery because the data on optical drives and disks does not have to be accessed in linear fashion and does not have to be restored to be searched.

Another variable that impacts the accessibility of back-up data is whether the data has been "compressed." To fit as much data as possible on a storage device, back-up programs normally compress the data, fitting more data into a smaller space but requiring the data to be decompressed and restored to a host drive for accessing. This is not difficult, but it can be time-consuming.

One of the most dangerous pitfalls in electronic discovery is the failure to remove relevant back-up tapes from rotation after a duty to preserve arises. As a result, relevant information can be overwritten, possibly subjecting the company to sanctions. The relevant tapes should be taken out of rotation and placed in a secure location, with the

1 E-DISCOVERY
A Guide for Corporate Counsel

administrator substituting clean, blank tapes for the ongoing rotation.

In sum, to navigate the universe of back-up data effectively in connection with electronic discovery, one must have a comprehensive understanding of a company's back-up procedures and protocols. This includes the intervals at which back-ups are generated, the media used and the retention period.

3.   Residual Data.

It is a common misconception that deleting a document removes it from the computer, or more accurately, the hard drive. When data is "deleted," the space on the storage device on which the data was stored is made available by the file system to store other data. Although the deleted data is not readily retrievable through normal end-user operations, it is not actually erased until it is overwritten by new data. Whatever portion of the deleted data is not overwritten remains recoverable for as long as the hard drive functions.

Only through the use of forensic utilities can this residual data be recovered. The odds that an item of deleted data will be overwritten increase with the volume and frequency of use of the computer. This is why it rarely makes sense to forensically image computer servers, as opposed to desktops and laptops. Servers often run at near-capacity, and even where substantial capacity remains, it is quickly consumed by a high level of use. In addition, compression techniques that fit more data on servers also result in overwriting. For all these reasons, remnants of deleted and unsaved data are quickly overwritten and rendered unrecoverable.

YOUR COMPANY'S COMPUTER SYSTEM

1

Even if data is not intentionally saved by the user to a c:/ drive, the computer's operating system can save documents or e-mails that the user merely opens, views, or drafts without saving. This "cached" material can be recovered only forensically. But as with deleted material, these forensically recovered fragments can be – and have not infrequently been – the "smoking guns" that resolve a litigation.

The effort of forensic utilities to recover this deleted or unsaved material may be frustrated by using "wipe" programs that overwrite the "unallocated free space" and "slack space" (the portions of the drive where deleted and unsaved data reside) with zeros, ones or other junk data. These programs, especially the free ones, are not foolproof, and sometimes they do not fully accomplish their overwriting agenda. Even if they do, forensic utilities can usually establish the date of their use. If a company has used a wipe utility after the company's duty to preserve arose, issues regarding sanctions may be raised.

An unresolved issue at the cutting edge of electronic discovery is whether a litigant in a routine civil litigation has any duty to preserve the unallocated free space and slack space on hard drives so that forensic analysis can later retrieve deleted and unsaved items. This would impose a great burden on companies and would require full forensic images of each such desktop and laptop computer. The current wisdom is that such a burden is not required, but the law in this area is evolving.

YOUR COMPANY'S DOCUMENT MANAGEMENT AND RETENTION PROGRAM (DMRP)

A. The Need for a Document Management and Retention Program.

Companies create and maintain increasingly large volumes of electronic records, including e-mail messages.[1] More than ninety percent of all business documents are now created electronically, and only thirty percent are ever printed into paper copies.[2] By one estimate, the average office worker in the U.S. sends or receives between 60 and 200 e-mail messages each day.[3] In 2001, businesses in North America sent an estimated 2.5 trillion e-mails, which was expected to increase to 3.25 trillion for 2002.[4] Retaining unnecessary electronic documents or, conversely, deleting documents that should have been preserved can lead to a host of costly problems, especially when a company is faced with litigation or a government investigation. As a result, the development and implementation of a reasonable and effective document management and retention policy (DMRP) has become a necessity. A DMRP governs the review, retention and destruction of the paper and electronic documents that a company creates or receives. A company developing a DMRP should keep in mind four principal goals: facilitating the company's ongoing operational needs; complying with

---

[1] DMRPs apply to paper as well as electronic records. The subject of this publication is electronic discovery, and this chapter focuses primarily on electronic records under DMRPs.

[2] *See* Michelle C.S. Lange, *New Act Has Major Impact on Electronic Evidence; Several Provisions of Sarbanes-Oxley Govern Document-Retention Policies*, 26 N.J.L.J. 11, Nov. 4, 2002, at C8.

[3] *See Market Statistics* at http://www.krollontrack.com/eEvidence/eDiscovery/MarketStatistics/ (citations omitted).

[4] *Id.*

specific retention periods under applicable law; minimizing the cost and risk of sanction in litigation; and avoiding violations of the newly enhanced federal obstruction of justice laws under the Sarbanes-Oxley Act of 2002 (SOX).

1.　Satisfy business/operational needs.

This goal is self-explanatory. Effective maintenance of records facilitates the retrieval of information that supports a company's operations.[5] A well-developed and applied DMRP will enhance efficiency by improving access to information, such as active contracts, that employees need in day-to-day operations.[6]

2.　Meet retention periods required by law.

State and federal statutes and a myriad of agency regulations require that particular businesses keep records for specified periods. The United States Code of Federal Regulations alone contains more than 1,200 separate sections relating to when and how documents or property may be stored or destroyed. For example, the Americans with Disabilities Act requires personnel and employment records to be kept for one year from the date of creation[7]; ERISA requires all plan documents to be kept for six years[8]; and the Family and Medical Leave Act requires that records containing dates of leave, leave notices, premium payments and disputes be kept for three years.[9]

---

[5]　Christopher V. Cotton, *Document Retention Programs for Electronic Records: Applying a Reasonableness Standard to the Electronic Era*, 24 Iowa J. Corp. L. 417, 417-418 (Winter 1999) (citations omitted).
[6]　*Id.* at 420.
[7]　29 CFR § 1627.3 (2004).
[8]　Employee Retirement Income Security Act, 29 U.S.C. §§ 1027, 1059 (2003).
[9]　29 CFR § 825.500 (2004).

YOUR COMPANY'S DOCUMENT MANAGEMENT AND RETENTION PROGRAM (DMRP)

2

Adding to the already substantial list of federal statutes and regulations mandating document retention, federal law now imposes separate criminal sanctions for an accountant's failure to retain audit workpapers. Under § 802 of SOX, an accountant's audit workpapers must be retained for five years from the end of the fiscal period in which the audit was concluded (applicable SEC rules increased this retention period to seven years). An accountant who "knowingly and willfully" violates the retention period is subject to fine or imprisonment for not more than twenty years, or both.[10] The retention statutes and regulations that apply to a company should be included in the company's DMRP.

A company may incur significant fines or suffer other consequences for destroying documents before the expiration of the legally required retention period. For example, in December 2002, five major Wall Street banking firms were each fined $1.65 million for failing to retain e-mail records as prescribed by applicable rules. The actions brought jointly by the Securities and Exchange Commission, the New York Stock Exchange and the National Association of Securities Dealers charged that the firms violated Section 17(a) of the Securities Exchange Act of 1934; Rule 17a-4 under the Exchange Act; NYSE Rule 440; and NASD Rule 3110 by failing to preserve electronic communications for three years and/or preserve them in an accessible place for two years. This included interoffice memoranda and other communications. The actions also charged violation of rules requiring the firms to establish, maintain and enforce a supervisory system to ensure compliance with NASD and NYSE rules and federal securities laws relating to retention of electronic communications.

---

[10] Section 802 of the Sarbanes-Oxley Act (Corporate and Criminal Fraud Accountability Act of 2002), 15 U.S.C. §§ 7201-7266 (2002).

The regulators found that each of the five firms had inadequate procedures and systems to retain e-mail communications and make them accessible. In those instances in which the firms did retain e-mail communications, the e-mail was often stored in unorganized fashion on back-up tapes or other media as part of disaster-recovery or business-continuity measures, and the tapes were often discarded or recycled and overwritten a year or less after back-up. Sometimes the e-mails were stored on individual employee computer hard drives, which in some instances were erased when individuals left the firm. No systems were in place to ensure that employees were actually preserving the records. The regulators required the Wall Street firms to review their procedures to ensure compliance with record-keeping statutes and rules.[11]

3.   Preserve documents for litigation.

Skyrocketing costs and judicial sanctions can result from a company's careless retention of too many documents or, conversely, its ad hoc destruction of potentially relevant documents. Companies that implement and consistently follow reasonable DMRPs can reduce production costs by paring down the volume of stored information and can mitigate the risks of sanctions for spoliation of evidence or other failure to produce. Courts have ruled that the existence of a DMRP may be a mitigating factor when documents are destroyed pursuant to such policy, and the failure to

---

[11]   *See* Securities and Exchange Commission Press Release 2002-173, dated December 3, 2002, available at http://www.sec.gov/news/press/2002-173.htm.

YOUR COMPANY'S DOCUMENT MANAGEMENT AND RETENTION PROGRAM (DMRP)

implement a coherent policy or to follow an existing policy may be an aggravating factor.[12]

The problem with saving everything. If a company is not routinely destroying unnecessary electronic information, it is creating enormous volumes of records to be searched, sorted and reviewed in response to discovery requests, which greatly increases the cost of responding to discovery. Sources estimate that a company that retains e-mail for one year could spend "six to seven figures" in complying with discovery requests, even before counsel reviews any documents.[13] Implementing and following a DMRP reduces the amount of stored electronic information and organizes it coherently,

---

[12] *See* Willard v. Caterpillar Inc., 40 Cal. App. 4th 892, 921, 48 Cal. Rptr. 2d 607, 625 (1995), *citing* Carlucci v. Piper Aircraft Corp., 102 F.R.D. 472, 481-82 (S.D. Fla. 1984). *See also Moore's Federal Practice 3d*, § 37A.12[5][d] ("In general, the destruction of a document does not raise an adverse inference of spoliation if it is done in accordance with a routine housekeeping records retention and disposition policy and without knowledge that the destroyed document is relevant to the claim or defense of any party in pending or imminent litigation. Conversely, destroying documents in a manner inconsistent with a record-disposition policy may be persuasive evidence that the destruction was not done in good faith."), *citing* Vick v. Texas Employment Comm'n, 514 F.2d 734, 737 (5th Cir. 1975) (no adverse inference when records destroyed under routine procedures without bad faith and before service of interrogatories); Coates v. Johnson & Johnson, 756 F.2d 524, 551 (7th Cir. 1985) (court found inference of bad faith unwarranted because employee responsible for disposition of personnel records destroyed documents after consultation with union officials and under misguided belief that records were duplicates); In re Prudential Ins. Co. of Am. Sales Practices Litig., 169 F.R.D. 598, 615 (D.N.J. 1997), *rev'd on other grounds* 133 F.3d 225 (3d Cir. 1998)(adverse inference drawn from destruction of relevant computer records pursuant to haphazard and uncoordinated document retention policy); and Capellupo v. FMC Corp., 126 F.R.D. 545, 549 n.9 (D. Minn. 1989) (party deviated from accepted corporate practice by not making list of documents being destroyed).

[13] *See* Frank C. Morris, Jr., *The Electronic Platform: E-mail and Other Privacy Issues in the Workplace*, 20 NO. 8 Computer & Internet Law. 1 (August 2003), summarizing *Beware Workplace E-mail: Survey Says Expert Tells How to Reduce Risk and Avoid Court Dates*, 2001 Electronic Policies & Practice Surveys, available at http://www.epolicyinstitute.com/survey/index.html.

thereby streamlining the production process and reducing discovery costs (often substantially) in the event of litigation.

One case in point is *Murphy Oil U.S.A. v. Fluor Daniel, Inc.*, where the court noted that if defendant Fluor had followed its own document retention policy, the e-mails subject to the discovery dispute would have been purged, and the discovery issue would have been moot.[14] Instead, Fluor spent considerable time and money disputing the production of e-mails. The disputes could have been avoided if the e-mails had been rightfully destroyed pursuant to the company's DMRP.

Cost-Shifting. Courts do engage in cost-shifting analyses when faced with voluminous electronic records and extensive electronic discovery requests, but the general presumption is still that the expense of production is a cost of doing business for the producing party, who controls how its documents are retained and stored. Courts tend to lack sympathy for a company that complains of having to search and restore old back-up tapes at significant cost in response to a document request, adopting a "you designed it – you're stuck with it" approach.[15]

In the recent, widely-cited *Zubulake* case,[16] the United States District Court for the Southern District of New York applied a test for shifting costs from the producing party to the requesting party. In that gender discrimination action, the

---

[14] No. Civ.A. 99-3564, 2002 WL 246439, *2 (E.D. La. 2002).
[15] *See* Virginia Llewellyn, *Planning With Clients For Effective Electronic Discovery,* 14 NO. 4 Prac. Litigator 7, 17 (July 2003).
[16] Zubulake v. UBS Warburg, LLC, 216 F.R.D. 280, 284 (S.D.N.Y. July 24, 2003) ("Zubulake III"); Zubulake v. UBS Warburg LLC, 217 F.R.D. 309, 316 (S.D.N.Y. May 13, 2003) ("Zubulake I"); *see also* Zubulake v. UBS Warburg LLC, No. 02 Civ. 1243 (SAS), 2003 WL 22410619 at *2 (S.D.N.Y. Oct. 22, 2003) ("Zubulake IV"), and Zubulake v. UBS Warburg LLC, No. 02 Civ. 1243 (SAS), 2004 WL 1620866 (S.D.N.Y. July 20, 2004) ("Zubulake V"). *See* discussions of the Zubulake cases in Chapters 5 and 7, *infra*.

court ultimately ordered plaintiff Zubulake to share twenty-five percent of the costs of restoring the back-up tapes that plaintiff sought, but defendant UBS Warburg was required to bear not only seventy-five percent of the restoration costs but also the cost of reviewing the documents once they were restored from an "inaccessible" to an "accessible" format.

The court first analyzed the modes used by defendant in storing the subject e-mail communications: back-up tapes, which require a lengthy and costly restoration process, and optical disks, which are more easily searchable and retrievable. The court then considered whether cost-shifting would be appropriate. The parties agreed that the governing standard for shifting discovery costs was the eight-factor *Rowe* test.[17] Though acknowledging that the *Rowe* test had "unquestionably become the gold standard for courts resolving electronic discovery disputes,"[18] the *Zubulake* court noted that the *Rowe* factors, as applied, consistently favored cost-shifting, thereby undercutting the presumption that the producing party pays. The court then restricted the number of situations in which cost-shifting should even be considered to those cases in which the electronic data to be searched is maintained in an "inaccessible format," as on back-up tapes. In cases where the data to be searched is contained in a relatively accessible format, such as off-line archived data on optical disks, the judge held that courts should not even entertain requests to shift costs to the requesting party.[19]

---

[17] The eight factors set forth in Rowe Entm't, Inc. v. William Morris Agency, Inc., 205 F.R.D. 421, 429 (S.D.N.Y. 2002) are: (1) the specificity of the discovery requests; (2) the likelihood of discovering critical information; (3) the availability of such information from other sources; (4) the purposes for which the responding party maintains the requested data; (5) the relative benefits to the parties of obtaining the information; (6) the total cost associated with production; (7) the relative ability of each party to control costs and its incentive to do so; and (8) the resources available to each party.

[18] Zubulake I, 217 F.R.D. at 320.

[19] *Id.* at 320, 324.

The *Zubulake* court held that once the factual determination is made that the electronic data subject to the discovery dispute is maintained in an inaccessible format, the following cost-shifting test is applied, modifying the *Rowe* factors to correct the imbalance that in the court's view disfavored the presumption that the producing party pays. The seven *Zubulake* factors are, (1) the extent to which the request is specifically tailored to discover relevant information; (2) the availability of such information from other sources; (3) the total cost of production, compared to the amount in controversy; (4) the total cost of production, compared to the resources available to each party; (5) the relative ability of each party to control costs and its incentive to do so; (6) the importance of the issues at stake in the litigation; and (7) the relative benefits to the parties of obtaining the information.[20] In applying the test, courts should assign weight to the factors in descending order, such that the first two factors are the most important, followed by factors three through five. Factor six will come into play only rarely, in cases of high public importance, such as toxic tort class actions, environmental actions and social reform litigation, but when it applies, it may outweigh factors one through five. The seventh factor should be given the least weight.[21]

The *Zubulake* court ordered UBS Warburg to produce all responsive e-mails on its optical disks or its active servers (both accessible formats) at its own expense. The court ordered UBS Warburg to produce, at its own expense, responsive e-mails from a sample of five back-up tapes (out of ninety-four) selected by plaintiff for the court's review so the court could determine the kinds of information the tapes contained and the costs involved in restoring them. After

---

[20] *Id.* at 322.
[21] *Id.* at 321.

production of the five sample tapes, plaintiff moved for production of the remaining back-up tapes, and in *Zubulake III*, the court engaged in the cost-shifting analysis outlined in *Zubulake I*. The *Zubulake III* court ruled that UBS Warburg must restore the remaining tapes and pay for seventy-five percent of such costs, as well as all the costs incurred in reviewing the restored documents for privileged information. Plaintiff Zubulake was ordered to pay for twenty-five percent of the cost of back-up tape restoration.

The problem with destroying documents haphazardly. Carelessly destroying documents may give rise to spoliation of evidence accusations, leading to sanctions such as unfavorable jury instructions and, in extreme cases, adverse judgments.[22] "Spoliation" is the destruction or significant

---

[22] *See, e.g.*, Metro. Opera Ass'n v. Local 100, Hotel Employees & Rest. Employees Int'l Union, 212 F.R.D. 178, 231 (S.D.N.Y. 2003) (court entered a finding of liability against defendant and awarded attorneys' fees to plaintiff because of discovery abuses in which defendant and its counsel willfully and in bad faith failed to comply with discovery in failing to preserve and produce documents, including disposing of computers after receipt of plaintiff's notice to have computers examined); P & G Co. v. Haugen, 179 F.R.D. 622, 632 (D. Utah 1998), *aff'd in part, rev'd in part* 222 F.3d 1262 (10th Cir. 2000) (Procter & Gamble sanctioned $10,000 for failure to preserve e-mail, despite company's knowledge that the e-mail would be relevant to the action); Linnen v. A.H. Robbins Co., Inc., No. 97-2307, 1999 WL 462015, at *11 (Mass. Super. June 16, 1999) (court orders that at time of trial, jury be instructed that it may infer that documents were destroyed by defendant [by continuing to recycle back-up tapes] because of defendant's realization that the documents were unfavorable); In re Prudential, 169 F.R.D. 598, 615 (D.N.J. 1997), *rev'd on other grounds* 133 F.3d 225 (3d Cir. 1998) ("Prudential") (among other findings, court imposed $1 million fine against defendant Prudential where "haphazard and uncoordinated approach to document retention indisputably" denied plaintiff potential evidence to establish facts, and Prudential was found to have violated court order to preserve documents); Applied Telematics, Inc. v. Sprint Communications Co., No. Civ. A. 94-4603, 1996 WL 539595, at *10 (E.D. Pa. Sept. 18, 1996) (defendant ordered to pay plaintiff's costs and attorneys' fees where defendant failed to preserve electronically stored routing plans); Capellupo v. FMC Corp., 126 F.R.D. 545, 551 (D. Minn. 1989) (defendant ordered to pay twice the amount of plaintiff's attorneys' fees and costs incurred in investigating, researching, preparing and presenting all motions related to the issue of

E-DISCOVERY
A Guide for Corporate Counsel

2

alteration of evidence or the failure to preserve evidence for use by another person in pending or future litigation. Under the spoliation doctrine (*see* Chapter 5, *infra*), when evidence is destroyed or simply not retained, an adverse party may be entitled, for example, to a jury instruction in the form of a presumption that the evidence was not preserved because it was unfavorable to the party that failed to preserve it.[23]

Evolving court rules governing discovery of electronic data. Court rules being implemented in many jurisdictions now require a company and its counsel to review and understand the methods of storage for, and location of, the company's electronic data. Failure to have implemented a DMRP may substantially impede a party's ability to comply with court rules regarding electronic discovery and can place a company at a litigative disadvantage before the substantive litigation even begins. *See* Chapter 3, *infra*, regarding proposed changes to the Federal Rules of Civil Procedure.

4. Respond to obstruction of justice concerns under Sarbanes-Oxley.

In the wake of the massive destruction by Arthur Andersen of documents relating to the Enron audit, the U.S. Congress took

---

document destruction and additional fees for unnecessary consumption of the court's time where court found defendant intentionally destroyed documents after it was put on notice of potential gender-based employment discrimination action); Telectron, Inc. v. Overhead Door Corp., 116 F.R.D. 107, 126 (S.D. Fla. 1987) (court enters default judgment where discoverable documents were destroyed under counsel's direction on the day counsel was served with complaint and document production request); Carlucci v. Piper Aircraft Corp., 102 F.R.D. 472, 486 (S.D. Fla. 1984) (default judgment granted against defendant where stated purpose of records destruction was elimination of documents that might be harmful to defendant in litigation).

[23] Ian C. Ballon, *Spoliation of E-mail Evidence: Proposed Intranet and Extranet Policies and a Framework For Analysis*, American Bar Association Pretrial Practice & Discovery Committee, Vol. IX, No. 1 (Winter 2001).

significant steps to strengthen and expand the reach of the federal obstruction of justice laws. These steps are codified as Sections 802 and 1102 of SOX.

Section 802 creates a new criminal statute – 18 U.S.C. § 1519 (2003).[24] This statute expands the scope of federal obstruction of justice provisions by imposing a maximum twenty-year prison sentence on any person who knowingly destroys, alters or conceals documents with the intent to "impede, obstruct or influence the investigation or proper administration of any matter within the jurisdiction of any department or agency of the United States . . . or *in relation to or in contemplation of any such matter*" (emphasis added).[25]

With this new statute, Congress eliminated any requirement that the action constituting the obstruction of justice be linked to a pending or imminent government proceeding. Congressional debate on the provision supports this broad interpretation. According to the Senate Report, the statute is specifically meant not to include any technical requirement – which some courts had read into existing federal obstruction of justice statutes – to tie the obstructive

---

[24] Section 802 also creates new 18 U.S.C. §1520, which requires accountants to retain their audit workpapers for public companies. Section 1102 amends 18 U.S.C. § 1512 to cover persons who themselves corruptly alter, destroy, mutilate or conceal documents with the intent to impair the documents' integrity or availability for use in an official proceeding, closing the loophole in the prior statute, which applied only to those who "corruptly persuade" others to do the same.

[25] 18 U.S.C. § 1519 is called "Destruction, alteration or falsification of records in Federal investigations and bankruptcy" and reads in full: "Whoever knowingly alters, destroys, mutilates, conceals, covers up, falsifies, or makes a false entry in any record, document, or tangible object with the intent to impede, obstruct, or influence the investigation or proper administration of any matter within the jurisdiction of any department or agency of the United States or any case filed under title 11, or in relation to or contemplation of any such matter or case, shall be fined under this title, imprisoned not more than 20 years, or both."

conduct (*e.g.*, the destruction, falsification or alteration) to a pending or even imminent proceeding.[26]

The new federal obstruction of justice laws create significant uncertainties regarding what documents must be retained and what documents may be legitimately destroyed. Some commentators contend that the new laws "precipitously enhance the criminal penalty provisions of statutes that now provide even less guidance on when otherwise ordinary and legitimate corporate activities may become suspect."[27] Because a federal investigation need not be pending, or even imminent, for criminal liability to attach to document destruction, the best way for a company to reduce the risk of prosecution for destroying corporate records is to implement, and consistently apply throughout the company, a reasonable DMRP.

In drafting a DMRP, companies may wish to consider adding language such as the following to help bolster compliance with the new federal obstruction of justice laws:

> NO COMPANY EMPLOYEE MAY DESTROY, ALTER, FALSIFY, MUTILATE, CONCEAL, COVER UP OR MAKE A FALSE ENTRY IN ANY RECORD OR DOCUMENT (WHETHER IN ELECTRONIC FORMAT OR OTHERWISE) BASED ON THE CONCERN THAT THE DOCUMENT COULD BE HARMFUL IN ANY PENDING, IMMINENT OR POTENTIAL FUTURE INVESTIGATION OR LITIGATION. FAILURE TO ADHERE TO THESE INSTRUCTIONS OR THE

---

[26] Sen. Rep. No. 107-146 at 14.
[27] Stanley S. Arkin and Charles S. Sullivan, *Document Destruction Under Sarbanes-Oxley*, N.Y.L.J., September 15, 2003, at T6.

COMPANY'S DOCUMENT PRESERVATION PROCEDURES CAN CARRY SEVERE CIVIL AND/OR CRIMINAL PENALTIES AND MAY SUBJECT THE EMPLOYEE TO COMPANY DISCIPLINARY ACTION, INCLUDING BUT NOT LIMITED TO TERMINATION OF EMPLOYMENT.

B.   Establishing an Effective Document Management and Retention Program.

1.   Overview: Your touchstones are reasonableness, good faith, and effective implementation.

To help mitigate a company's liability for spoliation of evidence in the litigation context, the DMRP must be reasonable, adopted in good faith, communicated to all employees and consistently applied. As the Eighth Circuit stated in the oft-cited case of *Lewy v. Remington Arms Co.*, "[A] corporation cannot blindly destroy documents and expect to be shielded by a seemingly innocuous document retention policy."[28]

To determine whether a DMRP is "reasonable," a court should consider not only the elements of the policy but also the nature of the information at issue and the circumstances of the particular case. *Lewy* involved a products liability suit against a gun manufacturer for injuries sustained when plaintiff's gun accidentally discharged. Defendant Remington destroyed complaints and gun examination reports after three years under its then-longstanding record retention policy. The court explained that if the trial court on remand was asked to give a jury instruction adverse to defendant for failure to produce, the court should first determine whether three years is reasonable for retention of complaints and gun reports. "A three year retention policy may be sufficient for documents

---

[28]   836 F.2d 1104, 1112 (8th Cir. 1988).

such as appointment books or telephone messages, but inadequate for documents such as customer complaints."[29]

In making the reasonableness determination, the court should also consider "whether lawsuits concerning the complaint or related complaints have been filed, the frequency of such complaints and the magnitude of the complaints."[30] Presumably, if the destroyed information would likely be material to a dispute, discarding it would be unreasonable.

A court should also determine whether the policy was adopted in bad faith.[31] A DMRP is adopted in bad faith if it appears to have been implemented solely to limit the amount of damaging evidence in a foreseeable litigation. If a DMRP is adopted in bad faith, an instruction to the jury that it may infer that the destroyed evidence is unfavorable to defendant may be proper.[32] Finally, the *Lewy* court commented that even if a policy is reasonable given the nature of the documents subject to the policy, the court may find that the documents should be retained notwithstanding the policy "if the corporation knew or should have known that the documents would become material at some point in the future."[33]

---

[29] *Id.* at 1112.
[30] *Id.*
[31] *Id.*
[32] *Id.* The instruction to the jury given by the trial court was: "If a party fails to produce evidence which is under his control and reasonably available to him and not reasonably available to the adverse party, then you may infer that the evidence is unfavorable to the party who could have produced it and did not." *Id.* at 1111, *citing* E. Devitt, C. Blackmar & M. Wolff, 3 *Federal Jury Practice and Instructions* § 72.16 (4th Ed. 1987).
[33] *Id.* at 1112; *see, e.g.,* Rambus, Inc. v. Infineon Technologies AG, 220 F.R.D. 264, 281 (E.D. Va. 2004) (once a party reasonably anticipates litigation, it has duty to suspend any routine purging system and put in place a litigation hold).

YOUR COMPANY'S DOCUMENT MANAGEMENT AND RETENTION PROGRAM (DMRP)

2

To be effective, the DMRP should be communicated and consistently applied across the entire organization. All employees should be informed of the policy regularly.[34] "One of the best enforcement procedures is to issue a well-documented periodic reminder to employees about the retention policy. [C]opies should be retained of all reminders, internal audit records and inspections for compliance with the policy. With this documentation in hand, if there is ever a questionable destruction of records, the company will have ample evidence that its document retention program is valid, reasonable and consistently enforced."[35]

An unreasonable or unenforced DMRP is likely to be just as harmful to a company as the failure to have any policy at all. Such was the case in *Prudential*, where Prudential had a written DMRP but could not convince the court that its employees were actually aware of the policy, much less following it consistently. As a result, Prudential was hit with a $1 million fine and other sanctions related to its destruction of documents. *See* Subsection 3 below.

2. Cover all records within the meaning of Fed. R. Civ. P. 34.

A company's DMRP should cover all documents within the meaning of Rule 34 of the Federal Rules of Civil Procedure. Under Rule 34, a party may request discovery of any document, "including writings, drawings, graphs, charts, photographs, phonorecords and other data compilations from which information can be obtained, translated, if necessary,

---

[34] Joseph P. Messina and Daniel B. Trinkle, *Document Retention Policies After Anderson*, Boston Bar Journal, September – October 2002, at 20.
[35] Ladd A. Hirsch, *Document Retention and Destruction: Issues in a Post Sarbanes-Oxley World*, University of Houston Law Foundation, November 2002, at 15.

by the respondent through detection devices into reasonably usable form."[36] Electronic records fall under the rubric of "data compilations."

By way of comparison, the Uniform Rules of Evidence define "record" as "information that is inscribed on a tangible medium or that is stored in an electronic or other medium and is retrievable in perceivable form." This includes items created on a computer, as through word processing or spreadsheet programs; records sent or received, such as e-mail; data stored through scanning or image processing of paper originals; and information compiled into data bases.[37]

It is well settled that Rule 34 applies to electronic documents, including e-mails, whether currently in use or "deleted" and housed only on back-up disks.[38] Nevertheless, before granting a plaintiff's request that a defendant be required to produce deleted or "residual" data (data that is deleted from the system but that continues to reside on the hard drive until overwritten by another file, which could take weeks or months), a court may require the plaintiff to show that the need to conduct such a search and the relevance of the deleted information outweigh the burden and cost of retrieving the data.[39]

---

[36] Fed. R. Civ. P. 34(a) (2004).
[37] See Uniform Rules of Evidence (1999), Rule 101 and comment.
[38] Zubulake I, 217 F.R.D. at 317, citing Antioch Co. v. Scrapbook Borders, Inc., 210 F.R.D. 645, 652 (D. Minn. 2002), and Simon Property Group L.P. v. mySimon, Inc., 194 F.R.D. 639, 640 (S.D. Ind. 2000).
[39] See McPeek v. Ashcroft, 212 F.R.D. 33, 35-37 (D.D.C. 2003)("McPeek II") (court that in prior decision "rejected the notion that the mere possibility that data exists justifies forcing the government to search backup tapes irrespective of the cost," refused to order certain back-up tape searches where burden on defendant would be great, and plaintiff did not demonstrate a likelihood of obtaining relevant information).

YOUR COMPANY'S DOCUMENT MANAGEMENT AND RETENTION PROGRAM (DMRP)

Discoverable electronic information is stored not only on computer laptops, desktops, centralized servers, back-up servers and storage media (such as CD-ROMS, floppy disks, magnetic tape and .zip disks), but also on personal data assistants, cell phones and pagers, and even digital cameras.[40]

3. Implement effectively.

A committee that includes a mix of legal, IT, administrative, human resources, library and executive personnel should be assembled to develop, implement and enforce the company's DMRP.[41] The range of people included will depend on the size of the company.

Demonstrable implementation of a DMRP is critical in defending against spoliation of evidence charges. For example, in *Prudential*, the insurance company had adopted a document retention policy but could not show that the policy was effectively implemented and communicated to all employees. As a result, the court essentially disregarded Prudential's policy and imposed evidentiary sanctions for the destruction of documents. In addition to inferring that the destroyed documents would have proved the plaintiff's claim, the court ordered Prudential to pay plaintiff's attorneys' fees associated with the discovery issues, pay the court $1 million, mail the court's order to every Prudential employee, and submit a written DMRP to the court.

---

[40] Kenneth K. Dort and Roger R. Spatz, *Discovery in the Digital Era: Considerations For Corporate Counsel*, 20 NO. 9 Computer & Internet Law. 11, September 2003, at 11.

[41] *See* Ruth A. Tressel & Daniel J. Noonan, *Using Technology To Fend Off Future Legal Crises*, ACCA Docket 21, NO. 7, July/August 2003, at 90.

As instructed by one commentator:

> Email retention and destruction policies must be clearly communicated to all employees. Posting a notice on a corporate intranet or transmitting it multiple times by email should provide sufficient notice of a policy, but only where employees actually read their email and pay attention to notices posted on an intranet. In *Prudential*, the company's dissemination of its policy through multiple emailings was deemed insufficient because a number of employees did not have access to computers and others did not routinely read their email.
>
> To avoid the problems experienced by Prudential, a document policy should be communicated during new employee orientation and circulated to existing employees by department heads or other managerial-level employees. A higher burden may arise when particular categories of documents appear likely to be relevant to reasonably anticipated litigation. An even higher burden of preservation exists when documents have been expressly requested. Once a court order prohibiting destruction has been entered, a party's failure to take even more extreme measures to ensure compliance may result in the entry of severe sanctions.[42]

Employees should be provided with a copy of the company's DMRP and periodically receive training on the application of the DMRP. In this regard, a company's DMRP should be treated similarly to the company's policies covering sexual harassment.

4. Store documents centrally and in organized fashion.

Organization. Care should be taken to ensure that stored electronic documents are organized in coherent categories. Such organization will make it easier to determine what is and

---

[42] Ian C. Ballon, *E-Commerce and Internet Law: Treatise with Forms* (Glaser Legal Works 2001), photo reprint in part, *Email and Electronic Communications*, Advanced Corporate Compliance Workshop 2003, San Francisco, CA (July 10-11, 2003).

what is not responsive to a discovery request. In addition, the producing party is in a better position to argue that the requesting party is engaged in a prohibitively broad fishing expedition where the producing party can demonstrate that it has implemented and follows a systematic electronic filing system.[43]

Of equal concern is the segregation of privileged and confidential information.[44] If a company commingles its stored confidential communications with those of a routine nature, a judge is less likely to be sympathetic when company lawyers complain about the expense of having to examine documents for privilege before producing them to opposing counsel.[45] If privileged communications are appropriately segregated, the company will not be required to sort through volumes of information to weed out privileged or confidential data.[46]

Location. To serve a company's business and potential litigation needs, electronic documents archived under a DMRP should be stored not on back-up tapes but in a central depository using media designed for archiving and should be searchable and retrievable. According to the Sedona Principles, "An effective document retention program, combined with a preservation approach triggered by the reasonable anticipation of litigation, would establish the principal source of discovery material, thus reducing the need to routinely access and review multiple sources of likely

---

[43] Kenneth K. Dort & George R. Spatz, *supra* note 40, at 17.
[44] *Id.*
[45] *Id.*
[46] *Id.*

duplicative data, including back-up tapes."[47] Archival systems maintain data for long-term storage and recordkeeping purposes, whereas back-up systems are designed to store data on portable media to permit recovery in the event of a disaster.[48] Archival data is considered "accessible," and back-up data is "inaccessible."[49]

The practice of using back-up tapes for archiving purposes is likely to cause the company to incur substantially higher costs for document preservation and production in connection with litigation. The preservation of data for business or litigation purposes should be performed by means other than disaster recovery back-up tapes.[50]

5. Establish reasonable retention schedules.

Company counsel participating in the development of a DMRP should work with appropriate company personnel to apply the following factors in formulating the retention periods for company documents: (1) the company's business requirements; (2) the technical aspects of the company's information systems; (3) regulatory or other governmental requirements; and (4) the historical value of the documents.[51] The retention period for a given document should be based on the longest period suggested by these requirements.[52]

---

[47] See Principle 1, Comment 1.a, *The Sedona Principles: Best Practices, Recommendations & Principles for Addressing Electronic Document Production* (Sedona Conference Working Group Series 2004), available at http://www.sedonaconference.org. The Sedona Conference is a nonprofit research and education institute dedicated to the advancement of law and policy in the areas of antitrust, complex litigation, and intellectual property rights.
[48] *Id.* at 51.
[49] *See id.* at Cmt. 13.a.
[50] *Id.* at Cmt. 5.h.
[51] Kenneth K. Dort and George R. Spatz, *supra* note 40, at 16-17.
[52] *Id.* at 17.

YOUR COMPANY'S DOCUMENT MANAGEMENT AND RETENTION PROGRAM (DMRP)

2

Some commentators advocate retaining documents for the length of the statute of limitations for potential claims, even if such time exceeds that for which the documents must be retained under applicable regulations.[53]

6. Develop litigation hold procedures.

A DMRP that is reasonable when litigation is not underway or threatened may, if adhered to in the context of the litigation, result in destruction of potentially discoverable evidence and subject the company to spoliation of evidence sanctions, adverse judgments or, in some cases, obstruction of justice charges. An effective DMRP must contain adequate procedures to suspend, or put on "hold," regular document destruction once litigation has begun or is even anticipated.

It is settled law that parties have an affirmative duty to preserve evidence.[54] The duty applies to electronic documents on a company's servers, back-up tapes, network drives, e-mail directories, e-mail archives and local hard drives. The following oft-cited standard for preserving evidence was articulated by a California district court:

> While a litigant is under no duty to keep or retain every document in its possession once a complaint is filed, it is under a duty to preserve what it knows, or reasonably should know, is relevant to the action, is reasonably calculated to lead to the discovery of admissible evidence, is reasonably likely to be

---

[53] *See, e.g.*, Michael E. Arruda, Margaret R. Prinzing and Shruti A. Rana, *Documents? What Documents? Some Guidelines About a Document Retention Policy and Its Implementation*, ABA's Business Law Today, Vol. 12, Number 3 (January/February 2003), available at http://www.abanet.org/buslaw/blt/2003-01-02/arruda.html.

[54] *See, e.g.*, Shamis v. Ambassador Factors Corp., 34 F. Supp. 2d 879, 888-889 (S.D.N.Y. 1999) (parties are required to preserve relevant information when litigation is pending, imminent or reasonably foreseeable); In re Prudential, 169 F.R.D. at 615, *rev'd on other grounds* 133 F.3d 225 (3d Cir.1998) ("The obligation to preserve documents that are potentially discoverable materials is an affirmative one that rests squarely on the shoulders of senior corporate officers").

requested during discovery and/or is the subject of a pending discovery request.[55]

No definitive standard states when the duty is triggered to suspend routine destruction of electronic documents under a DMRP and preserve potentially discoverable data. The duty to preserve clearly arises once litigation begins, but the duty prior to litigation remains unclear. In one case, the court found that the duty arises when the corporation receives notice of potential litigation or shortly thereafter. The court found that the defendant corporation's receipt of pre-litigation correspondence from plaintiff, among other items, constituted such notice, triggering the duty to preserve.[56] In the much publicized Arthur Anderson/Enron scandal, the government charged that Andersen obstructed justice by destroying documents relevant to the SEC investigation that it knew was underway, even though Andersen had yet to be served with a subpoena.[57]

A key component of a DMRP, therefore, is a quick and effective mechanism to stop document destruction once litigation or a government investigation is pending, threatened, or even reasonably foreseeable, especially in light of the enhanced federal obstruction of justice laws under SOX. The failure to discontinue routine document destruction pursuant to a DMRP can result in sanctions even if such

---

[55] Ian C. Ballon, *supra* note 42, *quoting* William T. Thompson Co. v. General Nutrition Corp., 593 F. Supp. 1443, 1455 (C.D. Cal. 1984).

[56] *William T. Thompson Co.*, 593 F. Supp. at 1446; *see also* Stevenson v. Union Pac. R.R., 354 F.3d 739 , 748-749 (8th Cir. 2004) (trial court was within discretion to impose sanction of adverse inference against defendant for its pre-litigation destruction of tape-recorded voice radio communications between train crew and dispatchers on date of collision, but trial court abused its discretion by imposing adverse inference for defendant's pre-litigation destruction of track maintenance inspection records).

[57] Ultimately, the jury found that the corruption supporting the obstruction of justice claim related to accounting practices, rather than Andersen's shredding of potentially discoverable evidence. *See* Arruda, *supra* note 53.

YOUR COMPANY'S DOCUMENT MANAGEMENT AND RETENTION PROGRAM (DMRP)

2

conduct was not intentional.[58] The DMRP should include a mechanism to alert a company's IT department to freeze automatic e-mail purges, at least until appropriate personnel can review and catalogue relevant electronic records and appropriate employees are notified of the need to archive electronic records on a going-forward basis. The IT department may also need to cease routine recycling of back-up tapes temporarily. In some cases, it may be prudent to obtain court orders for the resumption of automatic deletion programs and routine recycling or to stipulate to procedures in discovery or pre-discovery conferences.

The policy should provide guidance on effectively communicating the "legal hold" on document destruction to the company's employees once a company is on notice that litigation is likely. A party's culpability encompasses its employees, and the company has an affirmative obligation to inform its employees of the beginning of litigation and direct them to preserve records relevant to the proceeding. It may be no defense if company employees destroy relevant materials inadvertently because responsible officers failed to alert them to the litigation.[59]

In all events, the company should document the process implementing the "legal hold" procedures.

Whether routine back-up tape recycling should be suspended during or in anticipation of litigation is an issue.

---

[58] *See, e.g.*, In re Prudential, 169 F.R.D. at 615 (in imposing $1 million fine and other sanctions for document destruction, court acknowledged that there was no proof that Prudential employees acted with the purpose of destroying evidence to thwart discovery but noted that Prudential's ad hoc approach to document retention denied plaintiffs potential evidence with which to establish their case).

[59] *See Moore's Federal Practice 3d*, §37A.12[5][d]; the duty to inform probably includes a duty to remind. *See* Zubulake v. UBS Warburg, No. 02 Civ. 1243 (SAS) 2004 WL 1620866 ("Zubulake V") at *9.

Some commentators argue that the preservation obligation should be balanced against a party's right to continue to manage its electronic information in the best interests of the enterprise.[60] But authority exists for the preservation of back-up tapes once litigation has begun.[61] One commentator suggests the "conservative approach" of temporarily suspending back-up recycling at the outset of litigation and requesting permission from the court to resume normal practices.[62]

Failure to have legal hold procedures and to follow them can lead to spoliation of evidence sanctions, including entry of adverse judgments, and possibly to obstruction of justice charges.

7. Audit and adjust your DMRP.

A company's DMRP should be reviewed regularly by the oversight committee or the legal department and should be updated to reflect changes in document retention laws and changes in the company's business. As stated by one commentator:

---

[60] *See* Sedona Principles, *supra* note 47, at Principle No. 5 and Cmt 5a.

[61] *See, e.g., Moore's Federal Practice 3d*, §37A.12[5][e] ("The routine recycling of magnetic tapes that may contain relevant evidence should be immediately halted on commencement of litigation."); Linnen, 1999 WL 462015, at *10 ("During the period of time when the ex parte order requiring the defendants to preserve all documents relating to this action was in effect, the customary recycling of backup tapes for the electronic mail system should have been suspended."). *But see* McPeek I, 202 F.R.D. at 33 ("There is certainly no controlling authority for the proposition that restoring all back-up tapes is necessary in every case. The Federal Rules of Civil Procedure do not require such a search, and the handful of cases are idiosyncratic and provide little guidance."); Sedona Principles (2004), *supra* note 47, at Principle No. 5, Cmt 5.h. ("Absent specific circumstances, preservation obligations should not extend to disaster recovery backup tapes created in the ordinary course of business.").

[62] *See* Virginia Llewellyn, *supra* note 15, at 13.

> YOUR COMPANY'S DOCUMENT MANAGEMENT AND RETENTION PROGRAM (DMRP) — 2

> Case law suggests that any document retention policy . . . should be adjusted over time. Counsel may need to override a document destruction policy when lawsuits are filed or appear likely to be filed, and should periodically revise the policy when new case law or statutes impose additional record retention requirements, or when a category of documents relates to matters which have been the subject of significant or repeated non-frivolous complaints by customers or third parties.[63]

It is easier to convince a court that a DMRP is reasonable if the policy is regularly examined and if requisite adjustments are regularly made.

8. Develop your DMRP in light of the above.

Counsel assisting in the development of a company's DMRP should address the following questions and considerations:

- Determine the required retention periods in state and federal laws affecting the company.
- Based on a review of the company's history of litigation and government investigations, determine whether the company is subject to repetitive claims or complaints such that documents pertaining to these matters should be retained.
- Determine the make-up of the committee charged with guiding the development, enforcement and implementation of the DMRP, ensuring adequate representation from legal, IT, administrative, human resources and management personnel.
- Has management designed a quick and effective means to halt regular document destruction, including a way to communicate the "hold" to all employees, in the event of a pending, threatened or foreseeable litigation or investigation?

---

[63] Ian C. Ballon, *supra* note 23.

- Is there an audit process for regular checks of the DMRP to ensure that employee retention and destruction practices conform to the DMRP and that the DMRP is being consistently implemented?
- Consider whether the company may need to add one or more technology solutions to implement the DMRP.
- Consider how and where electronic records will be stored, including cataloging the stored information in a central location and ensuring that documents are stored so they can be easily retrieved.
- Has IT established a schedule for backing up the system, including e-mail, and for recycling back-up tapes, each in accordance with the business and IT needs of the company?
- Has IT established a system for the automatic deletion of e-mails that are not otherwise saved and stored?
- Consider establishing guidelines to assist employees in determining what documents must be retained to satisfy applicable law and to comply with a legal hold in the event of litigation or government investigation.
- Does the DMRP cover all electronic records, including those created or received on company computers, home computers, PDAs, hand-held devices and other portable electronic devices? Consider including in the policy an inventory of the company's electronic framework, including documentation of all electronic hardware and software in use throughout the company, the locations and storage formats of archived electronic data, and methods in which electronic data can be transferred to and from the company.
- Include a statement of the purpose of the DMRP, which should be the creation, maintenance and

destruction of records in a timely, efficient and cost-effective manner, tailored to the operational needs of the company and the applicable retention periods mandated by law.

C. A Recent Guide: The Sedona Principles.

In March 2003, the Sedona Conference published a set of principles creating best practices for electronic document production.[64] The Sedona Principles have been widely cited by commentators and courts, including the *Zubulake* court. The Sedona Principles were updated and refined in January 2004. According to the Sedona Principles, an "appropriate" electronic document preservation program would involve the following:

- Establishing a thorough but practical records management program, including training of individuals to manage and retain business records created or received in the ordinary course of business;
- Helping business departments establish practices and customs, tailored to their specific business needs, to identify the business records they need to retain;
- Implementing a system of presumptive limits on the retention of e-mails and other communications that are not business records, such as instant messaging and voicemail, and developing policies to promote the appropriate use of company systems;
- Determining the recycle time applicable to back-up tapes based on disaster recovery needs;

---

[64] *See* The Sedona Principles, *supra* note 47.

- Developing and implementing procedures to identify and notify the applicable employees and departments of the need to preserve electronic records in connection with reasonably anticipated or pending litigation; and
- Establishing and maintaining awareness of the importance of preserving potential evidence in the case of threatened litigation, and training legal and business personnel on when how to carry out their responsibilities.[65]

Any records management program should also be guided by developing case law and rules of court. For a discussion of evolving rules, *see* Chapter III, *infra*, Sections C and D.

As the laws relating to electronic discovery continue to evolve, the maintenance, retention and destruction of electronic records pursuant to a valid records policy will enhance a company's ability to comply with developing rules. Without a policy in place, or one that is followed consistently, a company may encounter difficulty – as well as significant cost – in conducting electronic document review and in attempting to reach agreement with opposing parties regarding electronic discovery.

---

[65] *Id.* at Principle 1, Cmt 1.a.

3

DISCOVERY OF ELECTRONIC DATA UNDER THE FEDERAL RULES OF CIVIL PROCEDURE

A. The Basic Structure of Discovery.

This chapter discusses electronic discovery under the Federal Rules of Civil Procedure for two reasons. First, most state procedural systems mirror the Federal Rules, with local variations. Second, the great bulk of the case law on electronic discovery has arisen under the Federal Rules. Recently published proposed changes to the Federal Rules are discussed at the end of this Chapter.

A party's obligation under the Federal Rules to produce electronic data in discovery is premised in two sources: Fed. R. Civ. P. 26, which governs the general scope of discovery, and Fed. R. Civ. P. 34, which governs document discovery.[1] The master principle for electronic as well as paper discovery is set forth in Fed. R. Civ. P. 26(b)(1). Subject to the court's discretion to limit cumulative, uneconomical or burdensome discovery,[2] and without court order, a party may obtain discovery "regarding any matter, not privileged, that is relevant to the claim or defense of any party." Upon a showing of good cause, a court can order discovery of any matter relevant to the subject matter of the action.[3]

---

[1] For examples of state rules addressed to electronic discovery, *see* Note 30, *infra*.

[2] Fed. R. Civ. P. 26(b)(2) authorizes the court to limit otherwise permissible discovery if (i) it is unreasonably cumulative, or the information can be obtained from a more economical source; (ii) the proponent has already had "ample opportunity" to obtain the information sought; or (iii) the burden of the proposed discovery outweighs its benefit, taking into account the magnitude of the case, the parties' resources, and the importance of the information to the case. The application of Rule 26(b)(2) to electronic discovery is discussed in Part B of this chapter.

[3] Fed. R. Civ. P. 26(b)(1) (2004).

3

E-DISCOVERY
A Guide for Corporate Counsel

It is beyond question that information stored in electronic form, if it falls within the scope of Rule 26(b)(1), is discoverable.[4] It is equally beyond question that information does not become discoverable merely because it exists and can be recovered in electronic form. As with paper discovery, a party is required, without court order, to search and produce its electronic records to the extent they contain information "relevant to the claim or defense of any party."[5]

The discovery process begins with the obligation of each party, under Fed. R. Civ. P. 26(a), to make initial disclosure of specified information "without awaiting a discovery request." These disclosures must be supplemented during the case if the disclosing party learns that the information disclosed is

---

[4] See, e.g., Crown Life Ins. Co. v. Craig, 995 F.2d 1376, 1382-83 (7th Cir. 1993) (electronic data used to compute commissions was "document" subject to discovery; respondent sanctioned for willful failure to produce); Anti-Monopoly, Inc. v. Hasbro, Inc., No. 94 Civ. 2121 (LMM) (AJP), 1995 WL 649934 at *2 (S.D.N.Y. Nov. 3, 1995) ("black letter law" that relevant electronic data is discoverable); see Fed. R. Civ. P. 34, Advisory Committee Notes, 1970 Amendment (Rule 34 applies to "electronic data compilations" either as printouts or in electronic form). The 1970 Amendments were promulgated, if not in the infancy of the computer age, then at its toddler stage, before the development of the desktop personal computer. The very general language of the Advisory Committee note does not anticipate the broad variety of modern electronic data or the facility by which it may be transmitted and read in electronic form. See generally Hon. Shira A. Scheindlin & Jeffrey Rabkin, Electronic Discovery In Federal Civil Litigation: Is Rule 34 Up To The Task? 41 B.C. L. Rev. 327, 368-78 (2000) (asserting insufficiencies in, and suggesting revisions to, Fed. R. Civ. P. 34 to cover electronic evidence).

[5] See, e.g., Wright v. AmSouth, 320 F.3d 1198, 1205 (11th Cir. 2003) (indiscriminate request for electronic copies of all word processing files created, modified or accessed by five named employees over 30 months denied as overbroad; proponent provided no theory of relevance); McPeek v. Ashcroft, 212 F.R.D. 33, 35 (D.D.C. 2003) ("McPeek II") (respondent required to search back-up e-mail tapes only for probably relevant periods). The Magistrate Judge in McPeek II reviewed in detail the nature of the proponent's factual claims in the suit to determine the likelihood that relevant information would be available on back-up tapes covering particular periods.

incomplete or incorrect.[6] For purposes of electronic discovery, the most important disclosure is required by subsection (a)(1)(B) of the rule, which directs disclosure of:

> a copy of, or a description by category and location, of all documents, data compilations and tangible things which are in the possession, custody or control of the party, and that the disclosing party may use to support its claims or defenses, unless solely for impeachment.

This includes a description of those documents in electronic form that the party intends to use to support its position.[7] In addition, Rule 26(f) requires the parties to meet early in the litigation and to attempt, in good faith, to agree to a discovery plan. The subjects discussed at that conference should include the scope and availability of information in electronic form and the allocation of the cost of producing it. As one court has said, "[T]he production of electronic information should be at the forefront of any discussion of issues involving discovery and trial, including the fair and economical allocation of costs."[8]

Specific requests to produce documents beyond those produced in voluntary disclosure are governed by Fed. R. Civ. P. 34(a),[9] which provides that any party may request the production of any relevant document, including:

---

[6] Fed. R. Civ. P. 26(e)(1) (2004).

[7] See Super Film of Am. Inc. v. UCB Films, Inc., 219 F.R.D. 649, 656 (D. Kan. 2004); In re Bristol-Meyers Squibb Sec. Litig. 205 F.R.D. 437, 441 (D.N.J. 2002) ("Bristol-Meyers Squibb"); Fed. R. Civ. P. 26(a), 1993 Revision, Advisory Committee Notes.

Bristol-Meyers Squibb held that Fed. R. Civ. P. 26(a)(1)(B) required disclosure only of information already in electronic form, as opposed to the disclosure of information that the party was placing in electronic form for purposes of the litigation. Id. But the case also held that paper documents scanned into electronic form for the litigation were discoverable in electronic form upon request under Fed. R. Civ. P. 34. Id.; 205 F.R.D. at 442-43.

[8] Bristol-Meyers Squibb, 205 F.R.D at 444.

[9] "Reasonable particularity" has been interpreted to mean that a person of

writings, drawings, graphs, charts, photographs, phonorecords, and other *data compilations* from which information can be obtained, translated, if necessary, by the respondent through detection devices into reasonably usable form, or to inspect and copy, test, or sample any tangible things. [Emphasis added].

The request must describe the items "with reasonable particularity" and "shall specify a reasonable time, place, and manner of making the inspection."[10] The responding party must produce the documents either "as they are kept in the ordinary course of business" or organized and labeled "to correspond with the categories in the request."[11] Fed. R. Civ. P. 33(d) allows a party to respond to written interrogatories by producing business records, indexed in such a manner as to allow the proponent to determine which documents are responsive to which interrogatory.[12]

B. The Obligation To Produce Documents in Electronic Form.

As noted above, information recorded in electronic form is a "data compilation" discoverable under Fed. R. Civ. P. 34.[13]

---

ordinary intelligence would understand what documents must be produced, and a court would be able to determine whether all requested documents have been produced. *See, e.g.,* Mallinckrodt Chem. Works v. Goldman, Sachs & Co., 58 F.R.D. 348, 353-54 (S.D.N.Y. 1973); Camco Inc. v. Baker Oil Tools, Inc., 45 F.R.D. 384, 387 (S.D. Texas 1968).

[10] Fed. R. Civ. P. 34(b).

[11] *Id.* The purpose of this requirement is to prevent the sharp practice of attempting to bury critical documents among a mass of less significant information. Fed. R. Civ. P. 34 (c), Advisory Committee Note, 1980 Amendment. *See* Bd. of Educ. of Evanston Tp. High Sch. Dist. No. 202 v. Admiral Heating and Ventilating, Inc., 104 F.R.D. 23, 36 (N.D. Ill. 1984).

[12] *See generally* T. N. Taube Corp. v. Marine Midland Mortgage Corp., 136 F.R.D. 449, 451-56 (W.D.N.C. 1991).

[13] *See* note 4, *supra*.

DISCOVERY OF ELECTRONIC DATA UNDER THE FEDERAL RULES OF CIVIL PROCEDURE

Data compilations may include "e-mail, telephone/voice-mail messages, information stored on the hard drives of desktop and laptop computers, palm pilots, computer discs, computer servers, internet, electronic archives, magnetic stripes on ATM and credit cards."[14] The language of Rule 34 was written at a time when the desktop personal computer had not been developed, and the only computers were large, expensive mainframes that could be used only by specialists. In current conditions, computers that can access files in the common formats for applications software are widely available, and the use of such software is an element of the everyday practice of law. The computer is the "detection device" of which Rule 34 speaks, and an electronic file readable through available applications software has been produced in "reasonably usable form."

Production specifically in electronic form may be required when demanded because electronic files may contain significantly more information than paper documents and because the electronic data can be retrieved and sorted with far greater facility. As one federal judge has pointed out,[15] data in electronic form has the following significant characteristics:

- It can easily be subject to perfect duplication.
- It can be altered in ways that are invisible on the paper printout.
- It contains information that does not ordinarily appear on the paper printout, such as data showing prior changes and data showing what users accessed a file at what times.

---

[14] A. Klein, *Federal Rules of Civil Procedure: Depositions and Discovery, Commentary* (National Institute for Trial Advocacy 2003).
[15] *See* Scheindlin & Rabkin, *supra* note 4, at 362-67.

- It includes data of which the ordinary user may not be aware, or which are not retrievable by the ordinary user, such as duplicate copies in the form of temporary and back-up files.
- It is not destroyed by the ordinary practice of deletion and can sometimes be recovered in whole or part after the user believes it has been disposed of.
- It often contains proprietary information, such as software code or database formats, that is built into the structure of the data.[16]
- It can be stored, sorted, searched, compared and analyzed with much greater speed and facility than paper data.[17]

---

[16] *See, e.g.,* Jones v. Goord, No. 95 Civ. 8026 (GEL), 2002 WL 1007614 at *12 (S.D.N.Y. May 16, 2002) (production of Department of Corrections databases would intrinsically "provide access not merely to the data themselves, but also to the techniques used to record and store data," which is analogous to trade secrets). *But cf.* York v. Hartford Underwriters Ins. Co., 2002 WL 31465306, at *2 (N.D. Okla. 2002) (claim that insurer failed to settle claim in bad faith; insurer's claim evaluation software relevant; insufficient evidence that software was trade secret).

[17] *See* Black & Veatch Int'l Co. v. Foster Wheeler Energy Corp., No. 00-2402 – JAR, 2002 WL 1071932, at *4 (D. Kan. May 10, 2002) (respondent's "input files" would allow proponent to recreate paper "interim design calculations" that respondent had discarded); Anti-Monopoly, Inc., 1995 WL 649934 at *2 (computerized sales and price data facilitate analysis in antitrust case).

But see Jones, 2002 WL 1007614 at *3-*4 in which plaintiffs contended that the New York State Department of Corrections' electronic data bases of violent incidents were not only relevant but essential to their attack on the Department's practice of "double celling," a practice where, because of overcrowding, two prisoners are held in a cell designed for one person. Plaintiffs claimed that they would prove their case by a statistical analysis of the Department's data, using their own software. The Department had created no such statistics and lacked the capacity to do so. Plaintiffs' attempt to discover the data bases failed, in part because they did not provide expert evidence of what statistical analysis they intended to conduct, the method they would use, or the evidence it would produce. *Id.* at *13.

- It exists in tremendous volume.[18]

These distinctive characteristics are relevant both to the question of whether the information must be produced in electronic form at all, and, if so, how the cost of search and production must be allocated between the proponent and the respondent.

As a general proposition, data kept in electronic form is discoverable in electronic form.[19] This could include data that has been deleted but is still retrievable.[20] It could also include data that has already been produced in paper form.[21]

---

[18] As one Magistrate Judge explained the impact of volume:
"E-mails have replaced other forms of communication besides just paper-based communication. Many informal messages that were previously relayed by telephone or at the water cooler are now sent via e-mail. Additionally, computers have the ability to capture several copies (or drafts) of the same e-mail, thus multiplying the volume of documents. All of these e-mails must be scanned for *both relevance and privilege.*" Byers v. Illinois State Police, No. 99 C 8105, 2002 WL 1264004, at *10 (N.D. Ill. June 3, 2002) (emphasis added).

[19] *See, e.g.,* Super Film of Am., Inc., 219 F.R.D. at 656-57; Zubulake I, 217 F.R.D. at 316-17; Rowe Entm't Inc. v. William Morris Agency, 205 F.R.D. 421, 428 (S.D.N.Y. 2002) ("Rowe"); Playboy Enterprises, Inc. v. Welles, 60 F. Supp. 2d 1050, 1053 (N.D. Cal. 1999).

[20] *See, e.g.,* Antioch Co. v. Scrapbook Borders, Inc., 210 F.R.D. 645, 652 (D. Minn. 2002); Simon Property Group, L.P. v. mySimon, Inc., 194 F.R.D. 639, 640 (S.D. Ind. 2000); Playboy Enterprises, Inc., 60 F. Supp. 2d at 1050. Because of the unusual cost of the forensic retrieval of such data, and the fact that it is not available in the ordinary course of business, these cases often involve orders shifting a portion of the cost to the proponent. *See* Chapters 7 and 8, *infra.* The technical aspects of how supposedly deleted data can be retrieved from a computer's hard drive or from back-up media are discussed in Chapter I.

[21] *See* Bristol-Meyers Squibb, 205 F.R.D. at 442-43; Anti-Monopoly, Inc., 1995 WL 649934 at *1.

In Bristol-Meyers Squibb, the proponent learned that the respondent had scanned paper documents into electronic form to create a searchable database for the litigation, and it requested copies of the scanned documents. The court directed production, with the proponent required to pay the cost of copying the electronic files. Because the respondent would have created the electronic files for its own use, the court did not require the proponent to pay any of the cost of scanning. 205 F.R.D. at 442-43.

The responding party in Bristol-Meyers Squibb did not contend that the format of the electronic compilation it created for the litigation would reveal attorney work product or privileged information.

E-DISCOVERY
A Guide for Corporate Counsel

If a party maintains electronic data for the purpose of utilizing it in connection with current activities, it may be expected to respond to discovery requests at its own expense. Under such circumstances, the guiding principle is that information which is stored, used or transmitted in new forms should be available in discovery with the same openness as traditional forms. A party that expects to be able to access information for business purposes will be obligated to produce that same information in discovery.[22]

In many instances, production of application files, such as e-mails, word processing documents or spreadsheets in electronic form, will be cheaper and more convenient than printing them out as paper documents:

> Electronic evidence is frequently cheaper and easier to produce than paper evidence because it can be searched automatically, key words can be run for privilege checks, and the production can be made in electronic form, obviating the need for mass photocopying.[23]

This is not always the case. The cost of retrieving electronic data varies considerably, depending on whether it is stored in currently accessible form, archived, or deleted.[24]

---

[22] Rowe, 205 F.R.D. at 430-31.

[23] Zubulake I, 217 F.R.D. at 318. Judge Scheindlin cites to her own article's discussion of the distinctive qualities of electronic evidence. *See* Scheindlin & Rabkin, *supra* note 4, at 335-41. *See also* Bristol-Meyers Squibb, 205 F.R.D. at 444 (expressing preference for electronic production in complex business litigation).

[24] Judge Scheindlin distinguishes five levels of accessibility, from the least to the most expensive: i) active, on-line data accessible in the ordinary course of business; ii) near-line data conveniently stored in removable media such as floppy discs or CD-ROMs, which are fully searchable once inserted in a drive and can be automatically inserted by a mechanical system; iii) removable media that must be manually retrieved and loaded; iv) back-up tapes that must be read in sequence to recover information; and v) deleted data that can be recovered in whole or part only through forensic techniques. Zubulake I, 217 F.R.D. at 318-20. *See also* McPeek II, 212 F.R.D. at 35 (noting that back-up tapes "collect information indiscriminately, regardless of topic," thereby increasing search costs).

In addition, the manner in which the data is stored may be a trade secret or otherwise confidential or privileged.[25]

Accordingly, discovery in electronic form may be denied under Fed. R. Civ. P. 26(b)(2) where the cost of retrieval outweighs the apparent relevance of the information and the probability that relevant information will be found. The cases speak of the "marginal utility" of the requested discovery, *i.e.*, the likelihood that the request will produce additional relevant information, compared to its "marginal cost." Denials on this ground are most likely when the information requested is stored in inaccessible form, particularly back-up e-mail tapes that contain large volumes of irrelevant information in which the potentially relevant files are embedded at random.[26] Some decisions involving back-up media have used a two-phase procedure: in the first phase, a sample of tapes is reviewed for the presence of relevant files to decide whether a more general review would be worthwhile.[27]

Discovery of information in electronic form may also be denied or restricted by protective order under Fed. R. Civ. P. 26(c) to prevent access to privileged, confidential or non-

---

[25] *See, e.g.,* Jones, 2002 WL 1007614 at *12 (finding that arrangement of data in electronic database was the equivalent of a trade secret); Scheindlin & Rabkin, *supra* note 4, at 362-63 (hypothetical customer database as trade secret).

[26] *See, e.g.,* McPeek II, 212 F.R.D. at 35 (directing review only of back-up e-mail tapes where relevant e-mail probably was located); Byers, 2002 WL 1264004 at *10-*12 (denying review of back-up e-mail tapes readable only by obsolete software unless proponent paid cost); McPeek v. Ashcroft, 202 F.R.D. 31, 34 (D.D.C. 2002) ("McPeek I") ("marginal utility" of searching back-up e-mail tapes). *But see* Super Film of Am., Inc., 219 F.R.D. at 657 (no evidence that cost to retrieve archived files unreasonable). The burden of coming forward with evidence of excessive cost to produce is on the party opposing discovery. Super Film of Am., Inc., 219 F.R.D. at 657.

For the related issue of shifting the cost of producing data in electronic form to the proponent in whole or part, see Chapter 7, *infra*.

[27] *See, e.g.,* Rowe, 205 F.R.D. at 433; McPeek I, 202 F.R.D. at 34.

relevant data. That is particularly the case where a proponent has requested direct access to a respondent's system or wholesale copying of electronic files. In electronic discovery, as in paper discovery, the normal model is that the respondent is required to search its files and produce responsive information and is trusted to do so in good faith. Requests for wholesale access to a respondent's electronic data system, as opposed to requests for files containing particular information, are treated with disfavor because of the risk that a general rummaging through the respondent's system or back-up media will allow access to non-discoverable material, including privileged and otherwise confidential matter. It is the proponent's burden to demonstrate that the respondent has withheld relevant information that can be recovered by allowing the proponent to conduct a search of the respondent's electronic records.[28]

C. Evolving Court Rules.

Commentators have recommended that federal and state discovery rules be amended to address electronic discovery

---

[28] *Compare* In re Ford Motor Co., 345 F.3d 1315, 1317 (11th Cir. 2003) (reversing order allowing proponent unrestricted access to respondent's complaint database; no showing respondent had failed to meet discovery obligations); Wright, 320 F.3d at 1205 (denying request for copies of all electronic files produced by five named employees as overbroad and non-relevant); Stallings-Daniel v. N. Trust Co., No. 01 C 2290, 2002 WL 385566, at *1 (N.D. Ill. March 12, 2002) (search of defendant's e-mail system denied; no evidence that defendant had altered or refused to produce relevant e-mail); Jones, 2002 WL 1007614 at *16 (discovery of respondent's database denied where relevance of information outweighed by cost of production and risk of disclosure of confidential information); Nicholas J. Murlas Living Trust v. Mobil Oil Co., 93 C 6956, 1995 WL 124186 at *5 (N.D. Ill. March 20, 1995) (production of nationwide database relating to oil spill cleanups denied; respondent had produced portions relevant to plaintiff's claim) *with* Antioch Co, 210 F.R.D. at 645 (circumstantial evidence of missing documents from respondent's paper files; hard drive mirrored); Tulip Computers Int'l B.V. v. Dell Computer Corp., No. Civ. A. 00-981-RRM, 2002 WL 818061 at *7 (D. Del. Apr.

issues not adequately covered by existing rules.[29] Several states have amended their court rules, and several United States District Courts, including New Jersey, have amended their local rules to address the unique nature of electronic discovery.[30] New Jersey's comprehensive new Local Rule 26.1(d) requires counsel, at the outset of a case, to review client computer and information management systems to gain an understanding of how information is stored and how it can be retrieved. To determine what must be disclosed pursuant to Fed. R. Civ. P. 26(a)(1), the lawyer is further required to review with the client the client's information files, including currently maintained computer files and historical, archival, back-up and legacy computer files, whether in current or historic media formats.[31]

A party seeking discovery of digital or computer-based information is required to notify the opposing party as soon as possible, prior to the Rule 26(f) conference, and to identify as

---

30, 2002) (responding party had pattern of evading paper discovery; hard drive mirrored); Rowe, 205 F.R.D. at 427 (paper discovery showed potential existence of relevant e-mails; court took judicial notice that substantial volume of electronic files was never printed out; back-up tapes searched); and Simon Property Group, L.P., 194 F.R.D. at 641 ("troubling discrepancies with respect to defendant's document production" justified mirroring hard drives on employees' home computers).

[29] See, e.g., Principle 3, Chapter 2, note 47, *supra*.

[30] See Tex. R. Civ. P. § 196.4 (2004) (Requests For Production and Inspection to Parties; Requests and Motions For Entry Upon Property - Electronic or Magnetic Data); U.S. Dist. Ct. Rules, D.N.J., L. Civ. R. 26.1(b)(2) and 26.1(d) (2004) (Discovery of Digital Information Including Computer-Based Information); Mississippi Supreme Court Order 13, amending Rule 26 of the Mississippi Rules of Civil Procedure and its Comment (May 29, 2003); U.S. Dist. Ct. Rules, E.D. Ark. and W.D. Ark., LR 26.1 (2004); and WYO. Fed. Practice L. Civ. Rule 26.1(d)(3)(a) (2004). In addition, other United States District Courts have adopted guidelines addressing electronic discovery. See U.S. District Courts for the District of Kansas ("Electronic Discovery Guidelines") and for the District of Delaware ("Default Standards for Discovery of Electronic Documents").

[31] N.J. L. Civ. R. 26(d)(1) (2004).

clearly as possible the categories of information the party anticipates will be sought.[32] The rule imposes a further duty on the parties to confer at the Rule 26(f) conference and try to agree on discovery matters relating to presentation and production of digital and computer-based information; inadvertent production of privileged information; the necessity for restoration of deleted material; whether back-up data is within the scope of discovery; and who will bear the costs of preservation, production, and necessary restoration of electronic documents.[33]

D.   Proposed Changes to the Federal Rules of Civil Procedure.

After years of study, the U.S. Judicial Conference Advisory Committee on Civil Rules, which is the United States Supreme Court committee responsible for recommending changes to the Federal Rules of Civil Procedure, has recommended changes to the federal discovery rules to address issues relating to electronic discovery. *See* Appendix A, *infra*. The Advisory Committee has decided to address six principal areas, discussed below. An awareness of these areas will enable counsel to stay abreast of the rule change developments and to decide whether to make public comments to assist the Advisory Committee in its work.

1.   Definition of Electronically Stored Information.

In light of experience with the development of computers since 1970, the Advisory Committee decided to separate "electronically stored information" from "documents" as a category of data producible under Fed. R. Civ. P. 34. The definition of "electronically stored information" is intended to be broad enough to include all present and future forms of

---

[32] *Id.* at (d)(2).
[33] *Id.* at (d)(3).

computer-based information.[34] In addition, the Advisory Committee notes make clear that the term "data compilations," already within the language of the rule, is intended to include electronic databases. This definition appears throughout the proposed amendments to the discovery rules. One consequence is that a request for production under amended Rule 34 should specifically call for the production of "electronically stored information" in addition to documents. The amended rule would allow a proponent to request access to electronically stored information for the purpose of testing and sampling.

2. Electronic Discovery as Part of Early Discovery Planning.

Following the approach of some federal courts that have adopted local rules on this subject, the Federal Rules would be altered to require electronic discovery issues to be discussed by the parties in the initial discovery pre-trial conference under Rule 16, following their obligation to meet and confer for discovery planning under Rule 26(f). The amended Rule 26(f) mandates that the parties' initial conference consider all issues relating to electronic discovery, including particularly the preservation of discoverable information,[35] the form in which information is to be produced, and a possible agreement governing inadvertent waiver of privilege. The amended Rule 16(b) would specifically require that the scheduling order include provisions governing electronic discovery and incorporating any agreement with respect to the waiver of privilege.

---

[34] Proposed Fed. R. Civ. P. 34(a), Advisory Committee Note.
[35] The routine operation of electronic systems may overwrite information stored in electronic form, either destroying it or reducing it to inaccessible form that can be recovered only through forensic means. See Chapter 1, *supra*.

3. Form of Production.

Rule 34(b) would be amended to permit but not require a requesting party to specify the form in which electronically stored information is to be produced. If no form is specified, amended Rule 34(b)(ii) would require electronically stored information to be produced either "in the form in which it is ordinarily maintained" or in electronically searchable form. The responding party may object to the form of production, and the parties may agree as to form.

Rule 33(d), which permits a party to respond to interrogatories by producing business records, would be amended to allow their production in the form of electronically stored information. As under the existing rule, this option is available only if the burden of extracting the answer from the records is equal for both proponent and respondent.[36]

4. Privilege Waiver.

The inadvertent production of privileged information is not limited to electronically stored information, but problems in this area intensify with the production of large volumes of electronic information.[37] The federal courts differ on the legal standard for determining when inadvertent production of privileged material waives the privilege.[38] The statute authorizing the promulgation of the Federal Rules of Civil Procedure limits use of the Rules to change the substantive law of privilege;[39] however, the proposed amendments

---

[36] Proposed Fed. R. Civ. P. 33(d), Advisory Committee Note.
[37] *See generally* Chapter 6.
[38] *See* Chapter 6, nn. 11 through 13.
[39] 28 U.S.C. § 2074(b).

provide a procedure under which issues relating to inadvertent production of privileged matter can be managed and, if necessary, litigated.

Amended Rule 26(f)(4) would require the parties to confer about a possible agreement governing the inadvertent production of privileged information. If the parties agree, their agreement would be incorporated in the Rule 16(b) scheduling order. The parties are not required to agree, and the court is not authorized to impose a procedure in the scheduling order.

In the absence of an agreement, amended Rule 26(b)(5)(B) provides the procedure to resolve waiver claims arising from inadvertent production. The party asserting that privileged information was inadvertently produced would have to notify the recipient within a "reasonable time." At that point, the recipient would be required to "promptly return, sequester or destroy" the information, pending litigation on the merits of any waiver claim, and the producing party would be required to preserve the information for production if the court ultimately rules that the privilege has been waived. As pointed out in the Advisory Committee Note, the reasonableness of the interval between inadvertent production and notice depends on when the party claiming the privilege learned of the inadvertent production, the use the recipient has made of the information in the meantime, the difficulty of discerning whether the information was privileged, and the overall volume of information produced.[40]

---

[40] Proposed Amendment to Fed. R. Civ. P. 26(b)(5)(B), Advisory Committee Note.

5. Two-Tiered Discovery – Discovery of Data that Is Not Reasonably Accessible.

Case law on the duty to provide discovery from back-up media and the allocation of the cost of such discovery has brought out the difference between electronically stored information that is routinely available to a party in the ordinary course of its operations, and information that is not routinely available and must be retrieved by extraordinary efforts. Such information may include back-up data, which is stored off-site in a form not easily searchable, legacy data, which is retrievable only by the use of now obsolete software or equipment, or deleted data, which is retrievable only by forensic techniques.[41]

The Advisory Committee has incorporated the distinction in a proposed amendment to Rule 26(b)(2), which provides that a party need not provide discovery of information that it identifies as "not reasonably accessible." On a motion to compel by the proponent of discovery, the responding party has the burden of demonstrating that the information is not reasonably accessible. For good cause shown, the court may order discovery of the inaccessible data on appropriate terms and conditions. In determining what conditions to impose, if any, a court may consider whether cost-shifting is appropriate. This structure establishes a two-tiered system for the discovery of electronically stored information. A responding party is required to produce in the first instance only information that is reasonably accessible. A requesting party must show good cause to require production of information not reasonably accessible, such as that stored on indexed back-up tapes.

---

[41] Proposed Amendment to Fed. R. Civ. P. 26(b)(2), Advisory Committee Note.

6. Safe Harbor from Sanctions.

As discussed in Chapters 1 and 5, the nature of electronic data systems may lead to the overwriting and possible destruction of electronically stored data. The alteration of routine data overwrite or destruction practices to preserve relevant evidence is a critical issue in planning electronic discovery, and failure to take the proper measures may expose a party to discovery sanctions for spoliation. The proposed amendment to Rule 37, which governs motions to compel and sanctions, would add a new subsection (f), providing a limited safe harbor from sanctions based on the routine destruction of electronically stored data.

Where information is not produced because of "loss of the information because of the routine operation of the party's electronic information system," proposed Rule 37(f) would bar discovery sanctions unless (i) the party violated an order requiring preservation, or (ii) the party did not take "reasonable steps" to preserve the information "after it knew or should have known the information was discoverable."

Under proposed Rule 37(f), it will be in the interest of a party who expects to propound requests for electronic discovery to identify what documents it will ask to be produced by giving notice, as early and with as much detail as feasible. Absent such notice, the potential responding party should still take the initiative in ascertaining what information should be preserved and assuring that the proper measures are taken.

The Advisory Committee is still exploring the degree of culpability or fault that will preclude a party from qualifying for the safe harbor from sanctions. Some believe that a greater level of culpability than mere negligence should be required before sanctions may be imposed when electronically stored information is lost or destroyed as a result of the routine operation of a party's computer system. An alternative version of the safe harbor would preclude the imposition of sanctions unless a party either acted intentionally or recklessly in failing to preserve the information or violated a specific court order.[42]

E. August 2004 Changes to the ABA Civil Discovery Standards on Electronic Discovery.

At about the same time the Advisory Committee on Civil Rules published its proposed changes to the rules regarding electronic discovery, the ABA House of Delegates adopted changes to its Civil Discovery Standards to address electronic discovery issues. Although the standards do not have the force of law, they contain a thorough treatment of electronic discovery issues and are widely consulted. The work of the ABA Section of Litigation, the originator of the Standards, is respected by the courts.[43] The Standards address, among other things, preservation of documents; identification of the types of electronic data that parties may be called upon to preserve or produce; places where electronic information may be located; considerations in resolving motions to compel or to allocate the cost of electronic discovery; early planning for electronic discovery; and attorney client/privilege and attorney work product issues attending the production of electronic data. In short, the Standards address most of the issues addressed by the proposed changes to the Federal

---

[42] *Id.*

[43] *See, e.g.*, Zubulake V, 2004 WL 1620866 at *15 ("professional groups such as the American Bar Association .... have provided very useful guidance on thorny issues relating to the discovery of electronically stored information") (footnote omitted).

DISCOVERY OF ELECTRONIC DATA UNDER THE FEDERAL RULES OF CIVIL PROCEDURE — 3

Rules. The purpose of the foregoing subsection is not to describe each of the Standards but simply to alert counsel of the Standards' existence, the subjects addressed, and the fact that they will be increasingly cited for their attention to the subject area.

NON-PARTY ELECTRONIC DISCOVERY

A. Introduction.

Though electronic discovery between litigating parties has garnered significant attention from courts and commentators, and judges have gained a degree of expertise in resolving electronic discovery issues,[1] electronic discovery involving non-parties has largely been ignored by both litigants and commentators.[2]

The lack of attention paid to electronic discovery from non-parties cannot be attributed to an absence of relevant electronic data in their hands. To the contrary, current methods of communication and data retention suggest that litigants should routinely seek electronic discovery from non-parties. By one estimate, the average American worker sends or receives between 60 and 200 e-mail messages per day.[3] In a company of one hundred employees, that could amount to several million e-mails per year. Such files also may contain hidden data that reveals such things as the existence and content of prior drafts, when a message was received, if the recipient opened the message, and to whom the message was forwarded.[4] This type of information is no less valuable in the hands of a non-party.

---

[1] Hon. Shira A. Scheindlin & Jeffrey Rabkin, *Electronic Discovery in Federal Civil Litigation: Is Rule 34 Up To The Task?* 41 B.C. L. Rev. 327, 341 (2000).

[2] Michael Traynor & Lori Ploeger, *Hot Topics In Electronic Discovery*, 712 PLI/Pat 51, 61 (2002).

[3] *See* Market Statistics at http://www.krollontrack.com/eEvidence/eDiscovery/MarketStatistics/, *citing* Kevin Craine, *Here Come the Lawyers. Is Your IT Department Ready?*; *compare* Jacob P. Hart & Anna Marie Plum, *Litigating the Production of Electronic Media: "Disk-Covery" Issues for the 21st Century*, SG007 ALI-ABA 169, 173 (2001).

[4] Traynor & Ploeger, *supra* note 2, at 53; *see* Chapter I, *supra.*

Nevertheless, courts are considerably more protective of non-parties than parties.[5] Electronic discovery requests that may be entirely proper if served on a party may well be quashed or limited if served on a non-party.

The potential expense of conducting electronic discovery is well-known. Because litigants are sometimes less certain that a non-party possesses important information, they are understandably hesitant to incur the expense of time-consuming electronic discovery that may yield little in return.

These concerns are not insurmountable and should not deter litigants from seeking electronic discovery from non-parties. Litigants and their counsel need to be versed in how to obtain electronic discovery from non-parties and, conversely, non-parties need to be aware of their rights and responsibilities if served with an electronic discovery request.

B.   Tasks in Obtaining Electronic Discovery from Non-Parties.

Obtaining electronic discovery from non-parties can be divided into three broad tasks: (1) identifying non-parties who may possess relevant information in electronic format; (2) harvesting the data; and (3) analyzing the data. The Federal Rules of Civil Procedure and their state court equivalents supply the litigating attorney with tools for performing these tasks.

---

[5] Fed. R. Civ. P. 45(c)(2)(B) (2004) ("an order to compel production shall protect any person who is not a party from significant expense. . . ."); U.S. v. Columbia Broadcasting Sys., Inc., 666 F.2d 364, 371-72 (9th Cir. 1982); Concord Boat Corp. v. Brunswick Corp., 169 F.R.D. 44, 49 (S.D.N.Y. 1996); Traynor & Ploeger, *supra* note 2, at 61.

NON-PARTY ELECTRONIC DISCOVERY

4

1. Identify non-parties possessing relevant information.

Establishing a solid factual basis for believing the non-party has relevant electronic information is important for two reasons. The first is cost. Identifying, harvesting, and analyzing electronic data are costly and time-consuming tasks, especially if the assistance of an expert is required. Litigants and counsel concerned about expense should require a higher degree of confidence that the non-party possesses relevant information in electronic format before requesting information beyond paper documents.

The process of identifying non-parties who may possess relevant electronic information is no different from the process of identifying non-parties who may possess relevant paper documents. Familiar sources include client interviews, informal witness interviews, and discovery obtained from the adverse party.

Whether a court will quash a subpoena calling for a non-party to produce electronic discovery could well turn on the requesting party's ability to show that the request is not overbroad and that the information sought is relevant to an important issue in the case, not merely of marginal relevance.[6]

---

[6] *Compare* Dow Chem. Corp. v. Allen, 672 F.2d 1262, 1269 (7th Cir. 1982) (refusing to enforce an administrative subpoena served on a research facility working for plaintiff, finding that plaintiff's need for the data did not outweigh the burden in producing raw research data where the data would not resolve the issue in question in the administrative proceeding) *with* Centurion Indus., Inc. v. Warren Steurer and Assocs., 665 F.2d 323 (10th Cir. 1981) (enforcing subpoena served on third-party over objection that disclosure of computer software could compromise trade secrets where proponent of subpoena made particularized showing of software's relevance to a central issue in the case). *See also* Concord Boat Corp., 169 F.R.D. at 49 (witness's status as a non-party entitles it to extra protection from expense and inconvenience).

2. Harvest the information.

Once a non-party who may have relevant electronic information is identified, the attorney must secure the information. The Federal Rules of Civil Procedure provide an attorney two tools for obtaining information in the hands of non-parties – a subpoena *duces tecum* issued pursuant to Federal Rule of Civil Procedure 45 and a testimonial subpoena issued pursuant to Federal Rule of Civil Procedure 30.

A subpoena issued pursuant to Fed. R. Civ. P. 45 requires the production and/or inspection of documents and things in the possession of others. A Rule 45(a)(1)(C) subpoena can require the person to whom it is directed to:

> ... give testimony or to produce and permit inspection and copying of designated books, documents or tangible things in the possession, custody or control of that person, or to permit inspection of premises, at a time and place therein specified.[7]

Although Rule 45 does not yet mention electronic discovery, data stored on a computer is a "document" as that term is used in the Rule.[8] Little judicial guidance exists as to how Rule 45 applies to electronic discovery because few cases directly address how a non-party receiving a Rule 45

---

[7] Fed. R. Civ. P. 45(a)(1)(c).
[8] In re Trost, 164 B.R. 740, 745 n.5 (W.D. Mich. 1994) (file stored on a laptop computer is a document subject to production pursuant to a Rule 45(a)(1)(C) subpoena); see also Strasser v. Yalamanchi, 669 So. 2d 1142, 1143 (Fla. Dist. Ct. App. 1996) (not only is information contained on a computer a "document" subject to production, but the drive on which it is stored is property that can be searched under a Florida discovery rule permitting "entry upon designated land or other property"). Although it is now settled that the term "documents," as used in the Federal Rules of Civil Procedure, includes electronically stored data, the Federal Rules do not explicitly speak to electronic discovery. If proposed amendments are adopted, they will. *See* Chapter 3, *supra*.

NON-PARTY ELECTRONIC DISCOVERY

subpoena seeking electronic discovery should respond.[9] Accordingly, the plain language of the Rule and court decisions concerning traditional discovery from non-parties must be consulted for direction.

A non-party is not required to undertake Herculean efforts to respond to a Rule 45 subpoena. Unlike Fed. R. Civ. P. 34, which is limited to parties, Rule 45 does not require that a non-party translate computer-based data, if necessary, into "reasonably usable form."[10] Instead, the recipient of a Rule 45 subpoena is entitled to produce documents and other things "as they are kept in the usual course of business or it may label them to correspond with the categories in the demand."[11] Therefore, the task of organizing the information produced as electronic discovery falls primarily on the party issuing the subpoena rather than the non-party.

The process of harvesting electronically stored information is complicated by the dizzying variety of files. A data file may exist on a computer network, a hard drive, a removable disk, or a CD. Well-known data files include word processing files, spreadsheet files, e-mail files, PDA files, other text files, image files and audio files. Lesser known

---

[9] *See* Traynor & Ploeger, *supra* note 2, at 61.
[10] Fed. R. Civ. P. 34(a) – which applies only to parties – authorizes a party to serve on another party a request "to produce and permit the party making the request . . . to inspect and copy, any designated documents (including writings, drawings, graphs, charts, photographs, phonorecords, and other data compilations from which information can be obtained, through translations, if necessary, by the respondent through detection devices into reasonably usable form)." The Advisory Committee Note to the 1970 amendment to Rule 34 expressly acknowledges the exchange of electronic discovery between parties and its potentially burdensome nature, stating that "[i]n many instances, this means that respondent will have to supply a print-out of computer data. The burden thus placed on respondent will vary from case to case, and the courts have ample power under Rule 26(c) to protect respondent from undue burden."
[11] Fed. R. Civ. P. 45(d)(1) (2004).

temporary files include "cookies," other data files relating to the electronic monitoring of employees, intranet webpage files, cache files, embedded files and back-up files.[12] A data file that has been deleted may also remain in a hard drive until it is overwritten, constituting valuable "residual" data. This type of information often can be obtained only by inspecting hard drives, tape drives, and other sources where data files are stored.[13] In the context of discovery among parties to a litigation, courts have required that adverse parties facilitate the discovery process by, among other things, permitting the inspection of hard drives to recover lost data files and lending an adverse party the software necessary to read stored data.[14]

It is unlikely that a court would require a non-party to go the same lengths as parties in facilitating electronic discovery. Although Rule 45 expressly permits a party to request permission to inspect a non-party's premises, in practice such inspections are rare, and courts may be reluctant to enforce a subpoena calling for an on-site inspection of a non-party's property.[15] The traditional judicial reluctance to require that a non-party submit to an intrusive inspection of its property

---

[12] Traynor & Ploeger, *supra* note 2, at 55-56.
[13] Richard. L. Marcus, 64 Law & Contemp. Prob. 253, 269 (Spring/Summer 2001).
[14] *See, e.g.,* Sattar v. Motorola, Inc., 138 F.3d 1164, 1171 (7th Cir. 1998) (defendant given choice of methods to make its electronic data accessible to plaintiff, one of which was lending plaintiff software needed to read the data); Playboy Enterprises, Inc. v. Welles, 60 F. Supp. 2d 1050, 1054 (S.D. Cal. 1999) (holding that plaintiff was entitled to copy defendant's hard drive, subject to protocols designed to protect defendant's privacy and attorney-client communications, for the purpose of recovering deleted e-mails).
[15] *Id.; see also* Belcher v. Bassett Furniture Indus., 588 F.2d 904, 908 (4th Cir. 1978) ("Since entry upon a party's premises may entail greater burdens and risks than mere production of documents, a greater inquiry into the necessity for the inspections would seem warranted").

may carry over to demands to inspect a non-party's computer equipment and files.[16]

Several concerns support the protections afforded to non-parties. First, in performing a hardware inspection, a party may inadvertently destroy or damage the hardware or the corresponding data files. Second, searching for particular data may enable a party to review and/or obtain data files that are privileged or confidential or simply irrelevant to the action. Third, copying hard drives can require shutting down a computer system. Finally, the manner in which computers record, store, and organize data makes it extremely difficult to protect privileged or trade secret information during an on-site inspection.[17] Unless counsel seeking to inspect a non-party's hardware is prepared to offer concrete solutions to these problems, a subpoena directing a non-party to permit the inspection of its computer hardware may not survive a motion to quash.

In the context of electronic discovery among parties, various solutions to these problems have been offered by commentators, courts and litigants. Those solutions include (i) the designation of a neutral party or special master to undertake the inspection; (ii) the creation of a "mirror image" of the hardware data for inspection purposes; and (iii) inspection agreements detailing the methods of inspection, liability, and appropriate remedies for breach.[18] Whether courts will find these solutions adequate in the context of non-party discovery remains to be seen.

---

[16] Traynor & Ploeger, *supra* note 2, at 61 ("It is probably safe to assume that the courts generally will be more protective of non-parties than they are of parties.").

[17] Kenneth J. Withers, *Computer-Based Discovery In Federal Civil Litigation*, 2000 Fed. Cts. L. Rev. 2, § II.G.1 (2000).

[18] *Id.*

Assuming that a party succeeds in persuading a court to require a non-party to submit to an inspection of its computer equipment, the data may be misinterpreted or impossible to read without the non-party's assistance. Although a party can use a Rule 45 subpoena to compel a nonparty's attendance at a hearing, deposition or trial, the party issuing the subpoena may be unable to identify individuals having relevant knowledge and an ability to interpret information in a database.[19] Fed. R. Civ. P. 30 – depositions – provides a useful tool for obtaining the non-party's cooperation in identifying, collecting, and analyzing electronically stored information.[20] That Rule provides authority to subpoena a corporate representative.[21]

Fed. R. Civ. P. 30(b)(6) provides that a party may serve on a non-party corporation a subpoena that instructs the corporation to designate one or more officers or managers to testify on matters "known or reasonably available" to the corporation.[22] The utility of Rule 30(b)(6) lies in its definition of "known or reasonably available," which is not limited to a representative's "personal knowledge." A company's representative has a duty to become familiar with relevant information, even if a review of such information is somewhat burdensome.[23]

Further, even though the corporate representative who was most knowledgeable about a subject may no longer be employed by a company, the company must still produce a

---

[19] Fed. R. Civ. P. 45(c)(2)(A).
[20] Fed. R. Civ. P. 30.
[21] See Fed. R. Civ. P. 30(b)(1), (2); Fed. R. Civ. P. 30(b)(6).
[22] Fed. R. Civ. P. 30(b)(6).
[23] Reed v. Bennett, 193 F.R.D. 689, 692 (D. Kan. 2000); Calzaturficio S.C.A.R.P.A. s.p.a. v. Fabiano Shoe Co., 201 F.R.D. 33, 37 (D. Mass. 2001).

NON-PARTY ELECTRONIC DISCOVERY 4

corporate representative to testify with respect to the subject if relevant documentation and other information exists.[24] As a consequence of this broad definition, the recipient of a Rule 30(b)(6) subpoena must produce a representative well-versed in the subject matter covered by the subpoena. Most often, an information technology officer or an administrator will be designated to testify on matters pertaining to the existence and gathering of electronic information, the reasoning being that an IT officer or administrator is likely to have created or modified the company's IT system and will probably be most familiar with the company's electronic files, software and hardware.

C. Non-Parties' Rights and Duties when Served with a Discovery Demand.

A failure to comply with a properly issued subpoena is punishable as contempt of court.[25] Compliance with a subpoena entails more than making data files available for inspection and producing a corporate designee at a deposition. One issue that frequently arises is the extent of a non-party's obligation to preserve evidence. Traditionally, courts have found no duty to preserve possible evidence to aid others in a future lawsuit against a third party unless there is "some special relationship or duty rising by reason of agreement, contract, statute, or other special circumstance... ."[26] However, several states recognize claims for third-party spoliation of evidence. (*See* Chapter V, *infra*).

---

[24] United States v. Taylor, 166 F.R.D. 356, 362 (M.D.N.C. 1996), *aff'd* 166 F.R.D. 367 (M.D.N.C. 1996).
[25] Fed. R. Civ. P. 45(e) (2004). *See also* Food Lion, Inc. v. United Food and Comm'l Workers Int'l Union, 103 F.3d 1007, 1016 (D.C. Cir. 1997); In re Shur, 184 B.R. 640, 641 (Bankr. E.D.N.Y. 1995).
[26] Koplin v. Rosel Well Perforators, Inc., 734 P.2d 1177, 1179 (Kan. 1987); *see also* Kevin D. Smith & Laura J. Becker, *Recent Developments Affecting Self-Insurers and Risk Managers*, 36 Tort & Ins. L.J. 593, 596 (2001).

Although the point at which a non-party must begin to preserve the electronic data and for how long the data must be preserved are not entirely clear, at a minimum the recipient of a subpoena should takes steps to ensure that data is not destroyed pending compliance or a decision by a court on a motion to quash.

A subpoena demanding the production of electronically-stored data is potentially very intrusive. An inspection of hardware and data files may disrupt business operations and can pry into confidential and privileged information. Consequently, Fed. R. Civ. P. 45 provides a mechanism for a non-party to contest a subpoena on those and other grounds.[27] Pursuant to Fed. R. Civ. P. 45(c)(2)(B):

> [A] person commanded to produce and permit inspection and copying may, within 14 days after service of the subpoena or before the time specified for compliance if such time is less than 14 days after service, serve upon the party or attorney designated in the subpoena written objection to inspection or copying of any or all of the designated materials or of the premises.[28]

The objection may cite grounds beyond undue hardship or expense.[29] If an objection is made, the party serving the subpoena will be allowed to inspect and/or copy the requested materials only pursuant to a court order.[30] A failure to timely

---

[27] Of course, a non-party is also entitled to object to a subpoena issued pursuant to Fed. R. Civ. P. 30.
[28] Fed. R. Civ. P. 45(c)(2)(B).
[29] See Brush v. Harkins, 9 F.R.D. 681 (W.D. Mo. 1950) (privilege); F.T.C. v. Texaco, Inc., 517 F.2d 137, 148 (D.C. Cir. 1975), cert. denied 431 U.S. 974 (1977) (relevance); Syposs v. United States, 181 F.R.D. 224, 228 (W.D.N.Y. 1998) (confidentiality/trade secrets).
[30] Fed. R. Civ. P. 45(c)(2)(B).

NON-PARTY ELECTRONIC DISCOVERY

4

serve the written objection or to provide proper detail in the written objection waives grounds for objection.[31]

Objections to a subpoena usually fall into three broad categories. First, the subpoena may violate the express provisions of Fed. R. Civ. P. 45. For example, it may subject a person to an undue burden in producing the documents.[32] Second, the subpoena may command the production or inspection of confidential information, such as trade secrets, confidential research, development or commercial information, or attorney-client or other privileged material.[33] Third, the subpoena may be otherwise improper, such as failing to allow reasonable time for compliance.[34]

Ordinarily, to assert privilege defenses successfully, a non-party must make the claim expressly and provide a list describing the contents and nature of the documents or other things claimed to be privileged so the demanding party can evaluate the privilege claim.[35] The party issuing the subpoena may then move to compel production of the information if it does not believe the material to be privileged.[36]

Unlike paper documents, which the non-party can readily review for privileged items that can then be listed on a privilege log, a computer hard drive cannot be reviewed in similar manner, and privileged files cannot be segregated from discoverable files.[37] A court may require that the

---

[31] *See, e.g.*, United States ex rel. Schwartz v. TRW, Inc., No. Cv 96-3065-RSWL, 2002 WL 31688812, at *3 (C.D. Cal. Nov. 13, 2002); *but see* Concord Boat Corp., 169 F.R.D. at 49 (no waiver where non-party witness actively communicated with plaintiff in procuring time extension on the basis of undue burden, among other reasons).

[32] Fed. R. Civ. P. 45(c)(3)(A)-(B) (2004).

[33] *Id.*

[34] *Id.*

[35] Fed. R. Civ. P. 45(d)(2) (2004).

[36] Fed. R. Civ. P. 45(c)(2)(B) (2004).

[37] *See* Playboy Enterprises, Inc. v. Welles, 60 F. Supp. 2d at 1054-55.

proponent of the subpoena, at its own expense, implement a procedure to protect the non-party's privileged files from disclosure.[38] For example, a court could require that the proponent of the discovery pay for a computer specialist to act as a special master to create a mirror image of the hard drive and print out hard copies of all deleted files for review by the non-party prior to production.[39] Obviously, a litigant would be ill-advised to go to such an expense without substantial likelihood that the hard drive contained critical deleted files.

D.   Cost Issues.

The party responsible for the issuance and service of a subpoena on a non-party pursuant to Fed. R. Civ. P. 45 is under an affirmative duty to "take reasonable steps to avoid imposing undue burden or expense on a person subject to that subpoena."[40] Breach of this duty is punishable by appropriate sanctions, which include, but are not limited to, an award of lost earnings and reasonable attorneys' fees.[41]

A subpoena may impose undue burden or expense on a non-party if the request is overbroad in subject matter or time frame, if the requests are not appropriately detailed, or if the period provided for a response to be prepared is too short.[42] Sometimes, the party issuing the subpoena may be required to

---

[38]   *Id.*
[39]   *Id.* at 1055.
[40]   *Id.* Fed. R. Civ. P. 45(c)(1); *see also* United States v. Columbia Broadcasting Sys., Inc., 666 F.2d 364, 371-72 (9th Cir.) (ruling that non-party status is important factor for determining whether discovery costs should be borne by demanding or producing party), *cert. denied* 457 U.S. 1118 (1982).
[41]   *Id.*
[42]   *See* Mann v. Univ. of Cincinnati, 824 F. Supp. 1190, 1201-1203 (S.D. Ohio), *aff'd* 152 F.R.D. 119 (S.D. Ohio 1993), *aff'd by unpublished opinion* 114 F.3d 1188 (6th Cir. 1997); Concord Boat Corp., 169 F.R.D. at 44.

reimburse the non-party for the cost of compliance.[43] A court may also require that a party issuing a Rule 45 subpoena advance reasonable production costs to a non-party.[44] Where a non-party has an interest in the outcome of the case, counsel may be able to persuade the court to order that the non-party share the cost of compliance commensurate with the degree of the non-party's interest in the case.[45]

E. Conclusion.

Non-party electronic discovery is a complex process involving competing interests. Counsel for litigants seeking non-party electronic discovery will wish to identify, harvest,

---

[43] *See* Standard Chlorine of Del., Inc. v. Sinibaldi, 821 F. Supp. 232, 265 (D. Del. 1992) (holding that a party issuing a subpoena was required to reimburse the non-party recipient for the cost of making 2,500 photocopies). Although Standard Chlorine of Del., Inc. concerned the cost of photocopying paper documents, the rationale that non-parties should be protected from undue expense applies with equal force to electronic discovery. *See also* Cantaline v. Raymark Indus., Inc., 103 F.R.D. 447, 450 (S.D. Fla. 1984)(ordering that plaintiff propounding subpoena on non-party advance the cost of compliance to the non-party).

[44] *See* Cantaline, 103 F.R.D. at 450 *But see* McCabe v. Ernst & Young, LLP, 221 F.R.D. 423 (D.N.J. 2004)(non-parties would not be awarded attorney fees and other production expenses incurred in complying with discovery subpoenas where they did not object to subpoenas within 14 days of their service, did not condition compliance on reimbursement of expenses and had earlier agreed in settlement agreement that removed them from action to comply with discovery requests in ongoing action).

[45] *See* In re Exxon Valdez, 142 F.R.D. 380, 384 (D.D.C. 1992) (non-party trade organization must pay twenty-nine percent of cost of producing documents where it received twenty-nine percent of its income from dues paid by defendants); *see also* F.T.C. v. U.S. Grant Resources, No. Civ.A. 04-596, 2004 WL 1396315 at *4 (E.D.La. June 18, 2004)(magistrate judge denies non-party's request to quash subpoena served on Attorney General's office for copies of defendants' own documents seized in a related, active criminal matter involving the same deceptive scheme alleged by the FTC; court applies three-part Exxon

and analyze relevant electronically-stored information at a reasonable cost. The non-party recipient of an electronic discovery demand often has no interest in the outcome of the litigation and hence has little incentive to cooperate. It is likely interested only in protecting the integrity of its data and minimizing the cost and inconvenience to itself of complying with the subpoena. Ultimately, the courts must balance these competing interests.

Valdez analysis in determining whether non-party should bear all or part of cost of production: (1) whether non-party has an interest in the outcome of the case; (2) whether the non-party can more readily bear the cost; and (3) whether the litigation is of public importance).

SPOLIATION OF EVIDENCE

Parties to emerging disputes and, by extension, their counsel must take affirmative steps to ensure the preservation of potentially relevant paper documents and electronic data that: (1) the party knows or should know are relevant; (2) could lead to the discovery of admissible evidence; (3) are reasonably likely to be requested during discovery; or (4) are the subject of a pending discovery request. Immediate action may be required to prevent spoliation – the negligent or intentional loss or destruction of relevant evidence. Preserving information is particularly urgent where a routine document destruction policy is in place, and relevant documents – paper or electronic – would otherwise be destroyed in the normal course.

Preserving electronic documents presents difficult and evolving challenges. In smaller offices, employees are sometimes responsible for storing and maintaining electronic documents on their own hard drives rather than in a central records area. E-mail communications can easily be deleted, either by employees manually or by the computer system automatically in the normal course of a business day. One of the greatest difficulties is ensuring that all the individuals who create or have access to potentially relevant documents are aware of the obligation to maintain such evidence and are informed of the methods by which to maintain it.

It is not necessary to keep all electronic documents. Only relevant evidence must be preserved. This chapter discusses the duty to preserve, ways to preserve, and penalties associated with spoliation.

A. The Duty To Preserve Evidence.

All litigants have a duty to preserve evidence that they know or should know is relevant to an imminent or ongoing litigation.[1] As one federal court noted, "fundamental to the duty of production of information is the threshold duty to preserve documents and other information that may be relevant in a case."[2] The availability of evidence relevant to the parties' claims is essential for effective dispute resolution and necessary to maintain the integrity of the judicial system.[3] The duty to preserve is imposed by the courts upon all parties to a dispute to ensure that relevant evidence will be available for production in litigation.[4] The need for relevant evidence is so crucial to the litigation process that imposing and enforcing the duty falls squarely within the court's inherent power to control the litigation before it.[5]

B. When the Duty To Preserve Arises.

The duty to preserve evidence is triggered when a party receives notice of its relevance to a pending or future

---

[1] See U.S. ex rel Koch v. Koch Indus., 197 F.R.D. 463, 482 (N.D. Okla. 1998)(a litigation is imminent if it is "likely to be commenced"); Turner v. Hudson Transit Lines, Inc., 142 F.R.D. 68, 73 (S.D.N.Y. 1991).

[2] Danis v. USN Communications, Inc., No. 98 C 7482, 2000 WL 1694325, at *1 (N.D. Ill. Oct. 23, 2000).

[3] See Cabinetware Inc. v. Sullivan, No. Civ. S. 90-313 LKK, 1991 WL 327959, at *3 (E.D. Cal. July 15, 1991).

[4] Danis, 2000 WL 1694325 at *33.

[5] See Stevenson v. Union Pac. R.R. Co., 354 F.3d 739, 747-748 (8th Cir. 2004)(adverse inference against defendant for pre-litigation destruction of tape recordings of communications between train crew and dispatchers on day of collision); Residential Funding Corp. v. DeFeorge Fin. Corp., 306 F.3d 99, 106-07 (2d Cir. 2002); Barnhill v. United States, 11 F.3d 1360, 1367 (7th Cir. 1993); Trigon Ins. Co. v. United States, 204 F.R.D. 277, 285 (E.D. Va. 2001); Pennar Software Corp. v. Fortune 500 Sys., No. 01-01734 EDL, 2001 WL 1319162, at *5 (N.D. Cal. Oct. 25, 2001); Computer Assocs. Int'l, Inc. v. Am. Fundware, Inc., 133 F.R.D. 166, 168 (D. Colo. 1990).

SPOLIATION OF EVIDENCE

litigation.[6] Notice can be supplied in several ways, ranging from pre-litigation correspondence or the filing of a complaint to discovery requests or court orders requiring preservation of specific documents. Once a party is put on notice that evidence is relevant, failure to preserve it could result in a finding of spoliation, making the party vulnerable to a host of sanctions discussed below. Most often, service of a complaint triggers the duty to preserve, but the duty could arise even before that.

A complaint can trigger the duty to preserve if the allegations are sufficiently specific to put the defendant on notice that certain documents or classes of documents would be discoverable.[7] A vague complaint, though permitted by the Federal Rules of Civil Procedure,[8] will not trigger the duty to preserve information that cannot be determined to be relevant from a fair reading of the complaint.[9] If the complaint does not effectively provide notice of the relevance of documents, notice can be provided by a discovery request. Service of a discovery request calling for relevant evidence triggers the

---

[6] Sheila J. Carpenter and Shaunda A. Patterson, *Discovery of Electronic Documents*, 29-SUM Brief 64, 67 (2000); Kronisch v. United States, 150 F.3d 112, 126 (2d Cir. 1998); Telecom Int'l Am., Ltd. v. AT&T Corp., 189 F.R.D. 76, 81 (S.D.N.Y. 1999)(notice gives rise to the duty to preserve); Koch, 197 F.R.D. at 466.

[7] Danis, 2000 WL 1694325 at *36 (finding the complaint specific enough to provide notice that certain types of documents were relevant); Turner, 142 F.R.D. at 73 (complaint explicitly charged that the bus lacked "good and sufficient brakes," so that defendant was on notice that maintenance records should be preserved).

[8] *See* Fed. R. Civ. P. 8(a) (2004) (requiring only a "short and plain statement"). Rule 8(a) is commonly referred to as requiring only "notice pleading."

[9] Danis, 2000 WL 1694325 at *36 (one must preserve only "discoverable information that a party knows or reasonably should know may be relevant to a pending or impending litigation").

E-DISCOVERY
A Guide for Corporate Counsel

5

duty to preserve the types and categories of information called for in the request.[10]

If a party is made aware that litigation is imminent or likely, the duty to preserve can arise even before the complaint is filed. For example, pre-litigation correspondence has been held to trigger the duty to preserve documents[11] that parties know or should know would be relevant to a potential future litigation.[12] A corporation can be charged with notice when an officer or director learns of allegations against the company, as from attendance at a deposition in a separate action.[13]

On occasion, courts will issue orders requiring the preservation of documents. To obtain a preservation order, a party must show a likelihood that documents will be destroyed and that irreparable harm will result in the absence of an order.[14] Because parties are obligated to preserve relevant documents even in the absence of a court order,

---

[10]   Telecom, 189 F.R.D. at 81; Cohn v. Taco Bell Corp., No. 92 C 5852, 1995 WL 519968, at *5 (N.D. Ill. Aug. 30, 1995); Turner, 142 F.R.D. at 73.

[11]   Kronisch, 150 F.3d at 126; Telecom, 189 F.R.D. at 82 (finding adequate notice was provided by letter nearly two years before the complaint was filed); ABC Home Health Servs. v. IBM Corp., 158 F.R.D. 180, 182 (S.D. Ga. 1994) ("destruction of documents is sanctionable even if it takes place prior to the filing of an action"); William T. Thompson Co. v. Gen. Nutrition Corp., 593 F. Supp. 1443, 1446 (C.D. Cal. 1984) (finding that "[n]otice was provided by the pre-litigation correspondence between counsel for the parties").

[12]   Telecom, 189 F.R.D. at 81-82 (pre-complaint correspondence provided notice of a future litigation because it "clearly and specifically" requested relevant documents); William T. Thompson Co., 593 F. Supp. at 1446 (finding that pre-complaint correspondence triggered duty to preserve as to several categories of documents).

[13]   Koch, 197 F.R.D. at 466 (company was deemed to have received notice when in-house counsel heard deposition testimony in a different lawsuit a year and a half before a complaint was filed).

[14]   Peter Sloan, *infra* note 40, at 8 (*citing* In re Potash Antitrust Litig., No. 3-93-197, MDL No. 981, 1994 WL 1108312, at *8 (D. Minn. Dec. 5, 1994) and Abdallah v. Coca-Cola Co., No. Civ.A. 1:98 CV 3679-RW, 1999 WL 527835, at *2 (N.D. Ga. July 16, 1999)).

SPOLIATION OF EVIDENCE

5

orders preserving documents tend to address specific concerns or discrete subsets of relevant documents.[15] Such orders are narrower in scope than the common-law preservation duty and are carefully tailored to accomplish the purpose of preserving discovery in a particular case.[16] Courts consider the costs of preservation and balance them against the potential benefit to avoid imposing undue burden or expense on the producing party.[17]

Under certain circumstances, documents must be retained even in the absence of foreseeable litigation. Some regulated entities and individuals are subject to statutes and regulations requiring certain documents to be preserved in the ordinary course.[18] Although this duty arises independently of litigation or claim, the failure to maintain documents in violation of a law can amount to spoliation of evidence, leaving the regulated party vulnerable to the same consequences as if the duty arose at the beginning of a litigation.[19]

C. Who Has the Duty To Preserve.

Parties and their attorneys share responsibility for complying with the duty to preserve relevant evidence. Both attorneys

---

[15] See William T. Thompson Co., 593 F. Supp. at 1447 (party was ordered to preserve "all purchase, sale and inventory records maintained…in the ordinary course of business at its headquarters").

[16] See Wright v. AmSouth Cancorp., 320 F.3d 1198, 1205 (11th Cir. 2003); S. Diagnostic Ass'n v. Bencosme, 833 So. 2d 801, 803 (Fla. Dist. Ct. App. 2002).

[17] See McPeek v. Ashcroft, 202 F.R.D. 31, 34 (D.D.C. 2001) ("McPeek I") (including "economic considerations" in its analysis and explaining that spending hundreds of thousands of dollars to produce one e-mail cannot be justified).

[18] Statutes such as the Sarbanes-Oxley Act of 2002 and the Securities Exchange Act of 1934 impose record-keeping obligations independent of litigation. See Chapter 2, *supra*, Section A2.

[19] See Byrnie v. Town of Cromwell, 243 F.3d 93, 109 (2d Cir. 2000).

and parties can be sanctioned for breaching the duty and for violating procedural rules relating to discovery.[20]

Attorneys have a "heightened responsibility" to inform their clients of their preservation obligations as soon as such obligations arise.[21] Attorneys should advise their clients in writing of the type of information that is potentially relevant and should assist in implementing an effective preservation plan.[22] Though counsel need not supervise every aspect of their client's document retention, counsel should instruct clients about their discovery obligations generally, including what constitutes a "document."[23] Clients have been sanctioned for their attorneys' failures in overseeing document management and production. For example, sanctions have been issued where responsibility for document retention was delegated to a layperson who lacked an understanding of the client's discovery obligations.[24] Attorneys are also obliged to follow up with their clients to ensure that the clients comply with their preservation duties.[25]

Notwithstanding the obligations placed on counsel, the senior management of a corporate party bears the ultimate responsibility for developing and implementing procedures to ensure the preservation of relevant evidence. Federal case

---

[20] See Metro. Opera Assoc., Inc. v. Local 100, 212 F.R.D. 178, 231 (S.D.N.Y. 2003) (ordering sanctions against attorneys and parties for spoliation of evidence and other discovery abuses); Danis, 2000 WL 1694325 at *49 ("At some point, a party and/or its attorneys must be held responsible for knowing what documents are discoverable and where to find them."); Nat'l Ass'n of Radiation Survivors v. Turnage, 115 F.R.D. 543, 551, 558 (N.D. Cal. 1987) (imposing sanctions on both the party and the attorneys responsible for the spoliation of relevant evidence).

[21] Kenneth J. Withers, *Computer-Based Discovery in Federal Civil Litigation*, 2000 Fed. Cts. L. Rev. 2, II. A.2 (2000).

[22] Id.; Turner v. Hudson Transit Lines, Inc., 142 F.R.D. 68, 73 (S.D.N.Y. 1991).

[23] Metro. Opera Assoc., 212 F.R.D. at 222.

[24] Id. (finding that layperson was unaware that client was required to retain such documents as drafts and e-mail communications).

[25] Id.

SPOLIATION OF EVIDENCE

5

law notes that "[t]he obligation to preserve documents that are potentially discoverable materials is an affirmative one that rests squarely on the shoulders of senior corporate officers."[26] A party can be sanctioned if its senior management fails to implement proper policies or delegates the retention function to personnel who are unqualified to fulfill the responsibility.[27] Like the company's attorneys, senior management is obliged to exercise ongoing oversight to ensure proper document retention.[28]

D. What Must Be Preserved.

The duty to preserve covers any relevant evidence in a party's custody or control that the party knew or reasonably should have known would be relevant to a potential litigation.[29] Litigants are not required to keep everything, only discoverable information, *i.e.,* material reasonably calculated to lead to the discovery of admissible evidence.[30] Discoverable information includes both paper records and electronically stored data of all types. Preserving paper records in anticipation of litigation can be burdensome and even overwhelming, and preservation of electronic data presents a myriad of additional challenges.

---

[26] Danis, 2000 WL 1694325 at *32 (issuing sanctions against senior manager for failing to implement an appropriate document preservation policy) (*quoting* In re Prudential Ins. Co. of Am. Sales Practices Litig., 169 F.R.D. 598, 615 (D.N.J. 1997)), *rev'd on other grounds* 133 F.3d 225 (3rd Cir. 1998).

[27] *See* Danis, 2000 WL 1694325 at *38.

[28] *Id.* at *38-39 (sanctioning a senior manager who delegated the entirety of the company's preservation obligations to an in-house attorney with neither litigation experience nor experience developing or implementing a retention policy).

[29] Danis, 2000 WL 1694325 at *32 (*quoting* China Ocean Shipping Group, Inc. v. Simone Metals, Inc., No. 97 C 2694, 1999 WL 966443, *3 (N.D. Ill. Sept. 30, 1999)).

[30] *See* Danis, 2000 WL 1694325 at *32; Wm. T. Thompson Co., 593 F. Supp. at 1446.

E-DISCOVERY
A Guide for Corporate Counsel

5

In response to increasing confusion surrounding discovery of electronic documents, the American Bar Association Section of Litigation (ABA) has drafted proposed guidelines. The ABA draft advises that categories of discoverable data are broad, and the ABA standards recommend retention of data on, among other things, networks, servers, back-up systems and even hand-held personal devices.[31]

Electronic data can easily disappear. Hard drives of former employees are frequently erased to be reused; e-mail communications are routinely deleted. Even when the data is stored, it can be hard to find, as on back-up tapes. All forms of electronic data must be retained. Findings of spoliation have resulted from actions such as defragmenting a computer to hide prior deletions from the hard drive,[32] downloading music onto a hard drive, resulting in destruction of other files,[33] purging computer databases,[34] failing to preserve information contained in a Palm Pilot,[35] and destroying back-up tapes and files.[36]

---

[31] The ABA's complete list of data sources that may contain relevant evidence is: "(a) databases; (b) networks; (c) computer systems, including legacy systems; (d) servers; (e) archives; (f) back up or disaster recovery systems; (g) tapes, discs, drives, cartridges and other storage media; (h) laptops; (i) personal computers; (j) internet data; and (k) personal digital assistants." Draft Amendments to ABA Civil Discovery Standards, Standard 29 (Nov. 2003).

[32] See RKI, Inc. v. Grimes, 177 F. Supp. 2d 859, 869 (N.D. Ill. 2001).

[33] See Minn. Mining & Mfg. v. Pribyl, 259 F.3d 587, 606 (7th Cir. 2001).

[34] See Danis, 2000 WL 1694325 at *18-*19; Long Island Diagnostic Imaging v. Sony Brook Diagnostic Assocs., 728 N.Y.S.2d 781, 782 (2d Dep't 2001).

[35] See Mathias v. Jacobs, 197 F.R.D. 29, 36 (S.D.N.Y. 2000), *vacated on other grounds* 2001 WL 1149017 (S.D.N.Y. 2001).

[36] Koch, 197 F.R.D. at 463.

SPOLIATION OF EVIDENCE 5

Most discovery requests define the term "document" so broadly[37] that it fairly includes data on each of these types of electronic storage and can even include more, such as databases, internet usage records, metadata and embedded data.[38] Preservation orders can include extremely broad definitions of types of data and media that must be preserved, including data compilations, e-mail communications and back-up tapes.[39]

E. How Preservation Can Be Accomplished.

Preservation of evidence is not a passive, static obligation. Ongoing, affirmative acts are required to ensure that relevant documents are being retained.[40] As discussed at greater length in Chapter 2, the first step is to draft and implement a

---

[37] See Linnen v. A.H. Robins Co., No. 97-2307, 1999 WL 462015, at *9 (Mass. Super. June 16, 1999) (document request defined "document" to include "internal memoranda, correspondence, reports, statements, charts, graphs, lists, drafts, outlines, applications, summaries, and compilations, and also includes any record or compilations of information of any kind or description however made, produced or reproduced, or stored whether by hand or by any electronic, photographic, magnetic, optical, mechanical, computer or other process or technology. Documents can take the form of any medium on which information can be stored including, without limitation, computer memory, computer disk, film, paper, photographs, tape recordings, video tapes and video disks.").

[38] Metadata is unseen information concerning electronic data. Peter Sloan, infra note 40, at 1; "embedded data," also unseen, is user-crafted rather than machine-created; see Chapter 1, supra.

[39] Linnen, 1999 WL 462015 at *8 (defining documents to be preserved as "computer memory, computer disks, data compilations, e-mail messages sent and received and all back-up computer files or devices, including but not limited to electronic, optical or magnetic storage media"); In re Prudential, 169 F.R.D. at 600 (requiring parties to "preserve all documents and other records containing information potentially relevant to the subject matter of this litigation").

[40] See Danis, 2000 WL 1694325 at *32 (requiring management to play active role in establishing and distributing comprehensive document retention policy); Peter Sloan, Retention, Preservation, and Spoliation of Electronic Data, Ontrack Datatrail (2002) at 6 (acknowledging that the duty to preserve is elastic; it changes and expands to include new claims).

comprehensive document retention policy that includes specific provisions addressing retention of documents for potential litigation and the criteria for finding and securing such evidence.[41] The plan should be disseminated to all employees. Each employee should be informed of the need to preserve documents and the consequences of not doing so.[42]

The most effective document retention policies ensure that needed material is retained, and unneeded data purged. But automatic destruction policies must be re-assessed when notice of an imminent litigation is received. At that point, automatic destruction of data should be suspended to the extent necessary to preserve relevant evidence.[43] Litigants should also coordinate data retention directives with all outside vendors and consultants who assist in document management or computer maintenance.[44]

Some types of electronic data are particularly vulnerable to spoliation and require special attention. E-mail communications, for example, generally are drafted and retained on the hard drive of an individual employee's computer and on a server.[45] Under the protocols followed in many corporations, e-mails or back-up tapes are periodically

---

[41] Danis, 2000 WL 1694325 at *37.
[42] Id.; Sheila J. Carpenter and Shaunda A. Patterson, Discovery of Electronic Documents, 29-SUM Brief 64, 67 (2000).
[43] Pillsbury Winthrop, Electronic Data Discovery: Duty to Preserve Evidence, Bulletin No. 03-13, Nov. 26, 2003 at 3; see also Computer Assocs. Int'l, Inc. v. Am. Fundware, Inc., 133 F.R.D. 166, 170 (D. Colo. 1990) (finding that continued destruction pursuant to a pre-existing business practice is intentional and willful destruction).
[44] See id.; see also Keir v. Unumprovident Corp., No. 02 Civ. 8781 (DLC), 2003 WL 21997747, *13 (S.D.N.Y. Aug. 22, 2003) (finding party's actions responsible for vendor's inadvertent overwriting of back-up tapes).
[45] Kenneth J. Withers, supra note 21, at II. C. 1.

SPOLIATION OF EVIDENCE 5

deleted. If an employee is unaware of the corporation's obligation to retain these communications, an e-mail can be deleted from the system. Even if a back-up exists, the cost may be high to restore e-mail communications from back-up tapes if the tapes are in a format that is not easily searchable.[46]

Even the most comprehensive and perfectly drafted retention plan is not enough by itself to fulfill the duty to preserve relevant evidence. To be effective, retention plans must be disseminated to the appropriate personnel and must be strictly enforced. Simply informing senior management is inadequate.[47] Every employee who may have access to potentially relevant evidence should be informed of pending or foreseeable litigation.[48] Every employee should be trained to implement the document retention protocols that are in place. Both senior management and their attorneys must provide ongoing supervision over the retention process throughout the litigation.[49]

F.   Spoliation of Evidence.

Spoliation of evidence is "the destruction or significant alteration of evidence, or the failure to preserve property for another's use as evidence in pending or reasonably foreseeable litigation."[50] Failure to preserve evidence in the face of a duty to do so results in spoliation of evidence, which

---

[46] Id.
[47] See U.S. ex rel Koch, 197 F.R.D. at 463.
[48] Id. (memo notifying approximately twenty employees of pending litigation is insufficient to discharge duty to preserve documents because the employees that actually handled the relevant evidence were not informed).
[49] See Metro. Opera Assoc., 212 F.R.D. at 222; Danis, 2000 WL 1694325 at *5; see also Pillsbury Winthrop, *supra* note 43, at 3.
[50] Byrnie, 243 F.3d at 107 (*quoting* West v. Goodyear Tire & Rubber Co., 167 F.3d 776, 779 (2d Cir. 1999)).

may be punished by the courts.[51] Because spoliation is judicially enforced in the context of a particular litigation, the accusing party bears the burden of proving that spoliation occurred before the court will impose sanctions.[52]

Spoliation may be sanctioned even if negligent. Courts view the availability of relevant evidence as essential and fundamental to the fact-finding process because disputes cannot be effectively resolved without access to all relevant evidence.[53] As such, sanctions are imposed against spoliators to protect the integrity of the process and the justice system as a whole.[54]

Imposing sanctions for spoliation serves three important judicial goals: compensation, punishment and deterrence. Spoliators are sanctioned to prevent their benefiting from their wrongdoing and to minimize the prejudice suffered by the opposing party.[55] Courts also view spoliation as grounds

---

[51] In addition to the judicial prohibition against spoliation by parties to a litigation, Model Rule of Professional Conduct 3.4(a) addresses spoliation by attorneys. Rule 3.4(a) states that a lawyer shall not "unlawfully obstruct another party's access to evidence or unlawfully alter, destroy or conceal a document or other material having potential evidentiary value [and] shall not counsel or assist another to do any such act."

[52] See Byrnie, 243 F.3d at 109.

[53] See Cabinetware Inc. v. Sullivan, No. Civ. S. 90-313 LKK, 1991 WL 327959, *4 (E.D. Cal. July 15, 1991) ("Destruction of evidence cannot be countenanced in a justice system whose goal is to find the truth through honest and orderly production of evidence under established discovery rules.").

[54] See Danis, 2000 WL 1694325 at *2 ("[W]hen a charge is made that relevant information has been destroyed, and especially when a charge is made of intentional destruction, it is a charge that strikes at the core of our civil litigation system.").

[55] See Trigon Ins. Co., 204 F.R.D. at 284 (noting that spoliators should not be permitted to benefit from their wrongdoing); Telectron v. Overhead Door Corp., 116 F.R.D. 107, 132 (S.D. Fla. 1987) (sanctions serve to ameliorate the prejudice caused to an innocent party by a discovery violation).

SPOLIATION OF EVIDENCE

for punishment because an affirmative duty has been violated. Finally, sanctions discourage other parties from committing similar violations.[56]

G. The Elements of Spoliation.

To prove spoliation and receive the benefit of a sanctions award, the accusing party must demonstrate three elements: (1) the intentional or negligent destruction or failure to preserve relevant evidence; (2) in the face of a duty to preserve;[57] (3) that results in prejudice to the accusing party.[58] Because the duty to preserve frequently attaches very early in the proceedings, most disputes regarding spoliation focus on the intent requirement and the existence of prejudice.

A finding of spoliation may not require a showing of intentional destruction. Some courts have found negligence sufficient as a basis for sanctions against the spoliator.[59] Inadvertent failure to preserve evidence, such as continued destruction pursuant to a pre-existing business practice, can amount to spoliation.[60] Similarly, the failure of a party to establish a systematic process to comply with discovery requests can also amount to spoliation.[61]

---

[56] Telectron, 116 F.R.D. at 135.
[57] Discussed *supra* at Part B.
[58] Byrnie, 243 F.3d at 109.
[59] *Id.*; Danis, 2000 WL 1694325 at *38; United States ex rel Koch, 197 F.R.D. at 463; Residential Funding Corp. v. DeGeorge Fin. Corp., 306 F.3d 99, 108 (2d Cir. 2002); *but see* Morris v. Union Pac. R.R., 373 F.3d 896, 901 (8th Cir. 2004) ("there must be a finding of intentional destruction indicating a desire to suppress the truth" before an adverse inference instruction is justified).
[60] *See* Computer Assocs. Int'l, Inc., 133 F.R.D. at 170.
[61] *See* Nat'l Ass'n of Radiation Survivors, 115 F.R.D. at 551, 553.

There can be no spoliation without prejudice to the opposing party. Destruction of documents is insignificant unless it is relevant to a pending or imminent litigation and results in prejudice. The accusing party must therefore show that the destroyed records were relevant to a contested issue and are not available from another source.[62] Being denied access to relevant information can prejudice a party in several ways. It can impair the party's ability to obtain expert advice, delay the proceedings, deprive the party of the best evidence, deprive the party of information that is unavailable from other sources, and generate costs in vain attempts to obtain evidence that did not exist.[63] In the absence of prejudice, no sanction will be imposed.[64]

H.   The Consequences of Spoliation.

Breach of the duty to preserve relevant evidence exposes the spoliator to court-imposed sanctions that can be significant enough to determine the outcome of the litigation. The sanctions range from a small fine to entry of an adverse judgment, with a host of options in between. Judges have broad discretion to fashion discovery sanctions within certain limitations.[65] The determination of sanctions is a fact-intensive inquiry, and the sanction must be proportionate to the circumstances.[66] Accordingly, the severity of the sanction

---

[62]   Byrnie, 243 F.3d at 109; Kronisch, 150 F.3d at 127; Danis, 2000 WL 1694325 at *48.
[63]   See William T. Thompson Co., 593 F. Supp. at 1451 .
[64]   See Danis, 2000 WL 1694325 at *48 (finding no substantial prejudice if the destroyed evidence is available from an alternative source).
[65]   Trigon, 204 F.R.D at 285.
[66]   See Crown Life Ins. Co. v. Craig, 995 F.2d 1376, 1382 (7th Cir. 1993) (explaining that proportionality guides a judge in all judicial applications of sanctions); see also United States v. Philip Morris USA Inc., 327 F. Supp. 2d 21 (D.D.C. 2004)(sanctions for defendant's continued destruction of 60-day old e-mails despite a court order requiring preservation of all potentially relevant documents include preclusion of defendant's calling any employee who failed to

SPOLIATION OF EVIDENCE

will be in direct proportion to the intent exhibited and the prejudice suffered.

Entry of an adverse judgment is the most severe sanction. This final disposition is reserved for the most egregious cases and will be employed only as a last resort.[67] The issuance of a dismissal or default judgment against the spoliator requires a showing that the destruction was done willfully or in bad faith, that serious prejudice resulted to the requesting party, and that alternative sanctions are not adequate to punish the wrongdoer and deter future violations.[68] The entry of an adverse judgment is rarely imposed; far more often, courts look for a lesser punishment.

The most frequently imposed sanction is a jury instruction containing an adverse inference that the content of the missing data would be harmful to the spoliator and favorable to the innocent party.[69] The bad faith destruction of evidence relevant to prove an issue at trial gives rise to an inference that production of the document would have been unfavorable

---

follow the retention policy as a fact or expert witness at trial, costs relating to the spoliation, and monetary sanctions of $2.75 million; request for adverse inference denied as disproportional to offense committed).

[67] See Computer Assocs. Int'l, Inc., 133 F.R.D. at 169-70.

[68] Id. (ordering default judgment for continued destruction pursuant to business practice); see also Danis, 2000 WL 1694325 at *33 (noting that default judgment is appropriate "where there is evidence of willfulness, bad faith, or fault by the noncomplying party"), and QZO, Inc. v. Moyer, 594 S.E.2d 541, 547-48 (S.C. Ct. App. 2004)(default judgment is a sanction within trial court's discretion where defendant reformatted computer, erasing all evidence, the day before turning it over pursuant to court order); but see Cabinetware Inc., 1991 WL 327959 at *3 (noting that prejudice is an "optional consideration" for a court determining a sanction).

[69] Todd Thompson, *The Paper Trail Has Gone Digital: Discovery in the Age of Electronic Information*, 71 J. Kan. B.A. 16, 19 (March 2002) ("The typical punishment is that all things are presumed against a despoiler or wrongdoer.") (citation omitted).

to the party responsible for its destruction.[70] The rationale is that if the evidence were not damaging, but favorable, the spoliator would have taken precautions to protect it for use in the litigation. As one district court noted, "Most probably [the spoliator] would have been meticulously careful to preserve evidence that could have demonstrated lack of merit in [the opposition]'s case."[71] Because the information was destroyed by the spoliator, a court may grant an inference against the spoliator.[72] Courts find this sanction appealing because it achieves all three goals, *i.e.*, compensation, punishment and deterrence.

Because an adverse inference can be a formidable hurdle, some courts will not impose such an inference for the negligent loss or destruction of evidence.[73] They require a showing of intentional destruction. Some courts require a spoliator to have formed a specific intent to avoid discovery.[74] These courts reason that absent a specific intent to evade production, there is no reason to believe the destroyed document was harmful to the spoliator or even that the spoliator knew the content.[75] For these courts, destruction in the absence of bad faith will not support an adverse inference.

---

[70] Kronisch, 150 F.3d at 126; Procter & Gamble Co. v. Haugen, 179 F.R.D. 622, 631 (D. Utah 1998) (*quoting* Arambura v. Boeing Co., 112 F.3d 1398, 1407 (10th Cir. 1997)).

[71] Computer Assocs. Int'l, Inc., 133 F.R.D. at 170 ("*A fortiori*, where a party destroys evidence after being put on notice that it is important to a lawsuit, and being placed under a legal obligation to preserve and produce it, the compelling inference is that the evidence would have supported the opposing party's case.") (citations omitted).

[72] Thompson, *supra* note 73, at 19 (*quoting* Black's Law Dictionary, 1086 (6th ed. 1990)).

[73] Pillsbury Winthrop, *supra* note 46, at 4; Trigon, 204 F.R.D. at 287; Pennar Software Corp. v. Fortune 500 Sys., No. 01-01734 EDL, 2001 WL 1319162, at *5 (N.D. Cal. Oct. 25, 2001).

[74] The Seventh and Tenth Circuits are among those that require specific intent to hamper discovery in the litigation.

[75] *See* Danis, 2000 WL 1694325 at *5; Koch, 197 F.R.D. at 486 (an adverse inference requires a "consciousness of a weak case").

SPOLIATION OF EVIDENCE

5

Conversely, some courts, including the Second Circuit, hold that "intentional destruction" does not necessarily require an affirmative action. It may include the failure to take steps to preserve evidence that the party knew or should have known would be relevant.[76] For such courts, the failure to discharge a known duty is sufficient to support a finding of intentional destruction.[77] In other words, a flagrant disregard or dereliction of preservation obligations amounts to bad faith even in the absence of a deliberate act.[78] The requirement in these jurisdictions is framed as an intent to destroy as distinguished from an intent to obstruct the opposing party's case.[79] Only the former is needed to support an adverse inference. Thus, continued destruction pursuant to pre-existing business practice has been deemed to be intentional and willful destruction.[80] Failure to maintain such electronic data as back-up tapes, hard drives and archived e-mails in the face of a duty to preserve such material could also result in an adverse inference.

---

[76] See Trigon, 204 F.R.D. at 289 (finding destruction pursuant to a document retention policy to be willful and intentional spoliation).

[77] Id.

[78] See Lauren Corp. v. Century Geophysical Corp., 953 P.2d 200, 205 (Colo. Ct. App. 1998).

[79] The Second Circuit has imposed adverse inferences based on as little as negligence. See Residential Funding Corp. v. DeFeorge Fin. Corp., 306 F.3d 99, 108 (2d Cir. 2002) (negligence is a sufficiently culpable state of mind because "each party should bear the risk of its own negligence"); see also Byrnie, 243 F.3d at 108 (urging a case-by-case approach to determine the appropriate state of mind needed). In Residential Funding, the court approvingly quoted Turner v. Hudson Transit Lines, Inc., 142 F.R.D. 68, 75 (S.D.N.Y. 1991): "It makes little difference to the party victimized by the destruction of evidence whether that act was done willfully or negligently." In Byrnie, the Second Circuit found sufficient grounds for sanctions from intentional destruction without intent to obstruct discovery. The intent considered by the court was the intent to destroy, not the intent to avoid production. Because the destruction was pursuant to a policy and thus not accidental, it was intentional and warranted sanctions. 243 F.3d at 109.

[80] See Computer Assocs. Int'l, Inc., 133 F.R.D. at 170.

E-DISCOVERY
A Guide for Corporate Counsel

A range of other sanctions is available to deal with spoliation. Courts may, for example, issue jury instructions stating that any gaps in the evidence are a result of the spoliator's failure to produce the relevant documents.[81] Sanction orders can exclude evidence proffered by the spoliator, strike sections of a spoliator's pleading relating to the missing evidence, or issue findings of fact supporting the opponent's claims or defenses.[82] Monetary sanctions are available in the form of fines, attorneys' fees and/or costs. Fines can be paid either to the opposing party or to the court and can be for any appropriate amount determined by the trial judge.[83] Fees and costs may be awarded as a sanction in a reasonable amount that the innocent party demonstrably incurred as a result of both the defendants' failure to produce the requested documents and the motion practice and discovery that ensued.[84] This includes time dedicated to depositions on the spoliation issue, costs associated with experts used to determine spoliation, and any costs associated with obtaining evidence from other sources.[85]

---

[81] See Danis, 2000 WL 1694325 at *51; Koch, 197 F.R.D. at 486.

[82] See Trigon, 204 F.R.D. at 291; Peter Sloan, *supra* note 40, at 14; *see also* Arista Records, Inc. v. Sakfield Holding Co. S.L., 314 F. Supp. 2d 27, 35 (D.D.C. 2004)(court infers that destroyed electronic records include transactions with District of Columbia residents sufficient to support finding of continuous and systematic contacts with D.C.).

[83] See Danis, 2000 WL 1694325 at *51 (finding fine is appropriate sanction even without prejudice because wrongdoing still must be punished); Nat'l Ass'n of Radiation Survivors, 115 F.R.D. at 559 (fine ordered to compensate for "the unnecessary consumption of the court's time and resources").

[84] See Illinois Tool Works, Inc. v. Metro Mark Prods., 43 F. Supp. 2d 951, 962 (N.D. Ill. 1999).

[85] Id.; William T. Thompson Co., 593 F. Supp. at 1456; Linnen, 1999 WL 462015 at *13; Lauren Corp., 953 P.2d at 204 (awarding fees and costs even in the absence of a discovery order).

SPOLIATION OF EVIDENCE

5

The Honorable Shira A. Scheindlin of the United States District Court for the Southern District of New York recently imposed sanctions for the knowing destruction of relevant e-mails notwithstanding a litigation hold. In *Zubulake v. UBS Warburg* – the court's fifth reported opinion on discovery issues – the court outlined the scope of counsel's obligation to preserve documents for litigation.[86] The court emphasized that a party's discovery obligations do not end with the implementation of a litigation hold. "[T]o the contrary, that's only the beginning. Counsel must oversee compliance with the litigation hold, monitoring the party's efforts to retain and produce the relevant documents."[87]

The court cautioned that to ensure that all sources of potentially relevant information are identified and preserved, counsel must take the following affirmative steps, among others:

- Become fully familiar with the client's document retention policies and data retention architecture;
- Communicate with key players in the litigation to understand how they stored information; and, in the alternative,
- Run a system-wide keyword search, preserving a copy of each "hit."[88]

On an ongoing basis, counsel should:

- Supply additional responsive information as it is located;
- Update answers to interrogatories or supply additional documents if counsel has knowledge that a prior response is incorrect or incomplete;

---

[86] No. 02 Civ. 1242 (SAS), 2004 WL 1620866 (S.D.N.Y. July 20, 2004) ("Zubulake V").
[87] *Id.* at *7.
[88] *Id.* at *8.

- Reissue the litigation hold so that new employees are aware of it and so it is fresh in the minds of all employees;
- Periodically remind the key players of their preservation duties;
- Continue to segregate relevant back-up media; and
- Instruct all employees to produce electronic copies of their relevant active files.[89]

Because UBS personnel destroyed e-mails after being told not to do so, they were found to have done so willfully, which meant that the lost information was automatically deemed relevant, satisfying the third element of the three-part spoliation test: (1) duty to preserve; (2) culpable state of mind (negligence suffices; willfulness obviates the need to show relevance); and (3) relevance of the lost information.[90]

The court imposed the following sanctions:

- The jury would be given an adverse inference instruction with respect to e-mails deleted after the litigation hold was issued in August 2001 and with respect to e-mails irretrievably lost when UBS's back-up tapes were recycled;[91]
- UBS must pay the costs of any depositions or re-depositions required by the late production;

---

[89] *Id.* at *8-*10.
[90] *Id.* at *12.
[91] The adverse inference instruction to the jury would read as follows:
You have heard that UBS failed to produce some of the e-mails sent or received by UBS personnel in August and September 2001. Plaintiff has argued that this evidence was in defendants' control and would have proven facts material to the matter in controversy.
If you find that UBS could have produced this evidence, and that the evidence was within its control, and that the evidence would have been material in deciding facts in dispute in this case, you are permitted, but not required, to infer that the evidence would have been unfavorable to UBS.

SPOLIATION OF EVIDENCE 5

- UBS must pay to restore an August 2001 back-up tape and must pay for any re-deposition of two individuals whose e-mails would be found on that tape; and
- UBS must pay the costs of the motion for sanctions.[92]

The court also noted a "self-executing sanction" in the fact that some of UBS's witnesses, not having seen the lost or delayed e-mails, had already given deposition testimony contradictory of the newly discovered e-mails.[93]

I. Conclusion.

Spoliation of evidence carries serious penalties. One way to avoid sanctions for failure to preserve documents is to implement and enforce an effective document retention policy detailing the procedures for isolating and preserving documents related to potential litigations as they arise. In some instances, the policy may require suspending the company's usual retention and destruction policy, under which e-mails and other documents could be inadvertently destroyed. It is also important to remember that the duty to preserve relevant evidence is not static. Both counsel and senior management should take affirmative steps throughout a litigation to ensure that the policies and procedures relating to document preservation are being followed.

In deciding whether to draw this inference, you should consider whether the evidence not produced would merely have duplicated other evidence already before you. You may also consider whether you are satisfied that UBS's failure to produce this information was reasonable. Again, any inference you decide to draw should be based on all of the facts and circumstances in this case. *Id.* at *15.

[92] *Id.* at *12-*15.
[93] *Id.* at *13.

6

MATTERS OF PRIVILEGE AND CONFIDENTIALITY

A recurrent problem in discovery is the responding party's need to guard against the disclosure of information that is legally exempt from scrutiny but loses its legal protection if voluntarily disclosed. Privileged communications lose their protection if deliberately disclosed, and in some jurisdictions they may lose protection even through inadvertent disclosure.[1] Trade secrets and other confidential commercial data also lose their legal protection – against misappropriation – if they are voluntarily disclosed to the public.[2]

---

[1] *See, e.g.,* United States v. Rigas, 281 F. Supp. 2d 733, 737-38 (S.D.N.Y. 2003) (setting out differing judicial views on the consequences of inadvertent disclosure of privileged communications in discovery); *see* United States v. Stewart, 294 F. Supp. 2d 490 (S.D.N.Y. 2004) (Martha Stewart waives attorney-client privilege for e-mail sent to her lawyer and copied to her daughter).

[2] *See* Kewanee Oil Co. v. Bicron Corp., 416 U.S. 470, 474-76 (1974):
The subject of a trade secret must be secret, and must not be of public knowledge or of a general knowledge in the trade or business. . . . The protection of disclosure is against the disclosure or unauthorized use of the trade secret by those to whom the secret has been confided under the express or implied restriction of nondisclosure or nonuse. The law also protects the holder of a trade secret against disclosure or use when the knowledge is gained, not by the owner's volition, but by some 'improper means' . . . . A trade secret law, however, does not offer protection against discovery by fair and honest means, such as by independent invention, *accidental disclosure,* or by so-called reverse engineering. [Emphasis added].

Id., citing Restatement, Torts § 757.

Section 757(d) of the Restatement provides that a person who uses what he or she knows to be an accidentally disclosed trade secret has misappropriated it. Consistently with the Restatement, the Uniform Trade Secrets Act, promulgated after Kewanee and enacted in forty-three states, also prohibits a person from using an accidentally disclosed trade secret if the person learns that the disclosure was accidental before he or she makes use of the secret. Uniform Trade Secrets Act § 1(2)(ii)(C) (definition of "misappropriation"); *see, e.g.,* Fireworks Spectacular, Inc. v. Premier Pyrotechnics, Inc., 107 F. Supp. 2d 1307, 1308-09 (D. Kan. 2000) (enjoining use of plaintiff's secret customer list, which defendant knew had accidentally been disclosed).

The scope of discoverable material is generally defined to include "matter not privileged."[3] Relevant trade secrets are within the scope of discoverable material, but the responding party may obtain a protective order prohibiting their disclosure or limiting it to certain persons to prevent the deliberate or inadvertent disclosure of the trade secret.[4] With respect to both privileged matter and trade secrets, the responding party has the initial burden of identifying confidential material and taking the necessary steps to protect it from disclosure.[5]

Electronic files can be produced in discovery in two contexts. In the first, as in traditional paper discovery, the responding party has full control of the production, including the power to screen and identify privileged or confidential material before producing it. The second context typically arises where the propounding party demonstrates that a responding party has failed to produce responsive electronic documents or has attempted to delete or destroy them. Courts may then allow a search by the propounding party or a special master of a mirror image of all the raw electronic data stored

---

[3] *See, e.g.,* Fed. R. Civ. P. 26(b)(1) (2004).
[4] *See* Fed. R. Civ. P. 26(c)(7); *see, e.g.,* Brown Bag Software v. Symantec Corp., 960 F.2d 1465, 1470-72 (9th Cir. 1992) (affirming protective order that barred in-house counsel from access to trade secrets in order to prevent inadvertent disclosure); U. S. Steel Corp. v. United States, 730 F.2d 1465, 1468-69 (Fed. Cir. 1984) (criteria for when in-house counsel should be denied access).
[5] *See* Rowe Entm't, Inc. v. William Morris Agency, Inc., 205 F.R.D. 421, 432 (S.D.N.Y. 2002) (responding party's burden to separate confidential from non-confidential documents filed together); Lois Sportswear, U.S.A., Inc. v. Levi Strauss & Co., 104 F.R.D. 103, 105-06 (S.D.N.Y. 1985) (pre-production review of documents for privilege).

MATTERS OF PRIVILEGE AND CONFIDENTIALITY

on hard drives or back-up media.[6] Such searches pose additional risk of the disclosure of privileged or confidential files, and they require special procedures and safeguards.[7]

A. Production by the Respondent.

A high volume of document discovery always poses a risk of inadvertent disclosure because of misfiling, failure to segregate privileged or confidential documents, attention fatigue, or other error by the individuals who perform the first-line review of the documents. Production of documents in electronic form mitigates some risks of insufficient review while posing others. Electronic searching simplifies but does not replace manual review of the documents' content. The responding party should select search terms broad enough to identify, for manual review, all documents that might contain privileged or other confidential material. In the case of attorney-client or work product privilege, these should include the names of all counsel known to have worked on the matter. They should also include key words characteristic of the subject matter and the terms "attorney-client," "work

---

[6] See, e.g., Antioch Co. v. Scrapbook Borders, Inc., 210 F.R.D. 645, 653 (D. Minn. 2002) (hard drive imaged and searched for deleted files); Simon Property Group, L.P. v. mySimon, Inc., 194 F.R.D. 639, 641-42 (S.D. Ind. 2000) (hard drive imaged to search for deleted files); Playboy Enterprises Inc. v. Welles, 60 F. Supp. 2d 1050, 1052-1054 (S.D. Cal. 1999) (hard drive imaged to search for deleted e-mail). See In re Ford Motor Co., 345 F.3d 1315, 1317 (11th Cir. 2003) (proponent not entitled to search respondent's electronic database directly without showing of respondent's spoliation or non-compliance with discovery rules).

[7] See In re Ford Motor Co., 345 F.3d at 1315 (mandamus vacating discovery order that allowed plaintiff to search defendant's data base; order did not limit search terms to relevant files or contain safeguards to protect privileged or confidential matter).

product," "privileged" and "confidential." If the proper search terms are used, electronic screening can substantially lessen the burden of eventual manual review.[8] It limits the number of documents to be checked, and it captures privileged or confidential documents that might have been misfiled.

But electronic production poses distinctive dangers. The first is that the sheer ease with which documents in electronic form can be copied may result in the responding party producing documents without manual review.[9] The second is that the apparent precision of an electronic search may create false confidence that all the appropriate documents have been identified and segregated for manual review.[10] Care must be taken to select search terms broad enough to include all potentially privileged or confidential documents while minimizing the number of irrelevant or nonresponsive documents selected for manual screening.

Failures will inevitably occur, resulting in the unintended production of privileged or otherwise confidential documents.

---

[8] Linder v. Calero-Portocarrero, 180 F.R.D. 168, 173 (D. C. Cir. 1998), is a good illustration of the interaction between electronic search terms and subsequent manual review. The opinion discusses in detail the burdens on the FBI or CIA of complying with a subpoena for information relating to the Nicaraguan Contras in a wrongful death action, and the mitigation of those burdens by the proper drafting of electronic search terms.

[9] See Nat'l Wildlife Fed'n v. EPA, 286 F.3d 554, 574 (D.C. Cir. 2002), in which a government employee accidentally e-mailed a file of trade secret information to opposing counsel after a motion to compel production had been denied; cf. Richards v. Jain, 168 F. Supp. 2d 1195, 1198-99 (W. D. Wash. 2001), in which plaintiff employee downloaded and provided to his own attorney ten thousand e-mails stored on the hard drive of his work computer, including the defendant employer's privileged documents.

[10] United States v. Triumph Capital Group, Inc., 211 F.R.D. 31, 49-50 (D. Conn. 2002), contains a good description of the limits of keyword searches: they will not detect variations or misspellings; they will not work on documents preserved as scanned images; and they will not work on binary files.

MATTERS OF PRIVILEGE AND CONFIDENTIALITY

6

With respect to privileged documents, the federal courts have taken three distinct approaches. At one extreme, the strict approach holds that any production of privileged matter to an adverse party, even accidentally, waives the privilege.[11] At the other extreme, the lenient approach holds that waiver must be knowing and that accidental disclosure can never constitute a waiver.[12] The most prevalent approach in the federal courts is to decide on a case-by-case basis whether inadvertent disclosure has waived the privilege. Courts using this approach apply four factors:

- The reasonableness of the precautions taken to prevent inadvertent disclosure;
- The volume of discovery compared to the volume of inadvertent disclosure;
- How quickly the responding party discovered and attempted to rectify the error; and
- The interests of justice under the circumstances.[13]

Few and minor accidental disclosures, made after reasonable efforts to prevent them and promptly called to the

---

[11] See, e.g., In re Sealed Case, 877 F.2d 976, 978 (D.C. Cir. 1989) (privileged documents "must be guarded like jewels"); FDIC v. Singh, 140 F.R.D. 252, 253 (D. Me. 1992); see Weinstein's Federal Evidence § 5.03.42 [3].
Even under the strict rule, waiver will not be found if a third party lawfully in possession of privileged information, and not under the control of the party holding the privilege, releases it despite the privilege holder's reasonable efforts to prevent release. See Nat'l Wildlife Fed'n, 286 F.3d at 574-76 (government agency's accidental release of private trade secrets in a regulatory proceeding); SEC v. Lavin, 111 F.3d 921, 929-30 (D.C. Cir. 1997) (no waiver of employer's tapes of marital telephone communications where spouses had made reasonable efforts to assert control over tapes).
[12] See, e.g., United States v. Zolin, 809 F.2d 1411, 1415 (9th Cir. 1987), aff'd in part, vacated in part on other grounds 491 U.S. 554 (1989); see Weinstein's Federal Evidence § 5.03.42 [2].
[13] See Rigas at 281 F. Supp. 2d at 737, citing Lois Sportswear, U.S.A., Inc., 104 F.R.D. at 105; see generally Weinstein's Federal Evidence § 5.03.42 [4]. Weinstein considers the number and extent of inadvertent disclosures to be separate factors.

6

E-DISCOVERY
A Guide for Corporate Counsel

adversary's attention, are less likely to be considered a waiver than would a broad release of privileged documents after cursory review, followed by a failure to challenge the release for a substantial period. "The middle test . . . accounts for the errors that inevitably occur in modern document-intensive litigation but treats carelessness with privileged material as an indication of waiver....It requires a detailed court inquiry into the document practices of the party who inadvertently released the document."[14] It follows that in a case of inadvertent production of privileged electronic documents, the extent of the measures taken by the responding party to search out potentially privileged documents, identify them, and segregate them from disclosure may be critical.

United States v. Rigas,[15] though its facts are unusual, is illustrative. In *Rigas,* the United States Attorney subpoenaed mirror images of twenty-six hard drives in a criminal investigation. These were installed on computers in the U.S. Attorney's office for review. The technical staff who did the installation were instructed that the hard drives were evidence and should be installed in a way that would prevent additions or deletions. By an unforeseen technical error,[16] the files of a paralegal were automatically backed up to one of the hard drives without anyone's knowledge. In response to a defense subpoena, the government allowed the defense to mirror the evidentiary hard drives in its possession, with the result that privileged files on the one hard drive were copied by the

---

[14] Gray v. Bicknell, 86 F.3d 1472, 1483-84 (8th Cir. 1996); *accord* United States v. Gangi, 1 F. Supp. 2d 256, 264 (S.D.N.Y. 1998) (middle-of-the-road test "recognizes that mistakes will be made" but creates "incentive for counsel to guard the privilege closely"); *see* In re Lernout & Hauspie Sec. Litig., 222 F.R.D. 29 (D. Mass. 2004) (claim of inadvertent disclosure of e-mail rejected even though e-mail did not identify recipient as an in-house attorney because document reviewers knew he was an attorney from other e-mails).
[15] 281 F. Supp. 2d 733, 736 (S.D.N.Y. 2003).
[16] Defendants' expert testified that he had never seen such a result before this case; nor had any other witness. Rigas, 281 F. Supp. 2d at 738.

MATTERS OF PRIVILEGE AND CONFIDENTIALITY

6

defense. As soon as defense counsel discovered this, they notified the prosecutor, as was their ethical obligation.[17] The United States immediately sought suppression of the privileged files.

Applying a four-factor test for waiver by inadvertent disclosure, the district court found no waiver and enforced the privilege. It found that the volume of disclosure was small in relation to the case, that the government had acted promptly to cure the disclosure, and that the interests of justice required that the privilege be enforced. Most importantly for our purposes, it reviewed in detail the operation of the United States Attorney's computer system and concluded that reasonable precautions had been taken. In particular, the technical personnel had been properly instructed by the attorneys as to the objective of segregating information; the attorneys had reasonably relied on the work of the technical personnel; the copying of the hard drive by the defense expert had been under the scrutiny of the government's personnel;

---

[17] In many jurisdictions a lawyer receiving materials that appear to be privileged or confidential in circumstances that suggest inadvertent disclosure is required to immediately notify the adversary and to refrain from examining them in the meanwhile. Rigas, 281 F. Supp. 2d at 742, *citing* ABA Formal Ethics Opinion 92-368 (1992); Richards, 168 F. Supp. 2d at 1195.

Failure to abide by this ethical duty may result in disqualification. In Jain, plaintiff's counsel obtained from his own client a CD-ROM containing ten thousand e-mails, which included defendants' attorney-client communications, without defendants' knowledge. Some of the e-mails were marked "Attorney-Client Confidential." Plaintiffs' law firm reviewed the disk and copied relevant e-mails, including privileged ones. Defendant did not learn that plaintiffs' counsel had the disk until eleven months later, at plaintiff's deposition. As a result, plaintiff's counsel was disqualified.

Not all jurisdictions follow Opinion 92-368. Some do not require the receiving lawyer to return the inadvertently produced material but do require prompt notice to the producing lawyer. Others, including Illinois and the District of Columbia, allow counsel who does not know that the material was inadvertently produced to retain and use it. The authorities are collected in Redgrave & Nimsger, *Electronic Discovery and Inadvertent Production of Privileged Documents*, 49 Federal Lawyer 37, 38 nn. 6-8 (July 2002).

and the writing of back-up copies on the evidentiary hard drive was unforeseeable.[18] *Rigas* distinguishes a paper discovery case, *SEC v. Cassano*,[19] in which the government waived the privilege because its attorney had negligently supervised a paralegal who released a privileged document.

In line with general principles of waiver through inadvertent disclosure, *Rigas* teaches that counsel is ultimately responsible for the precautions taken to screen, identify and segregate privileged electronic documents before production. Though it may be reasonable to rely on non-lawyers and technical personnel to carry out the screening in the first instance, it is clearly counsel's responsibility to define what is to be done, to make those objectives clear to non-lawyers, and to review the results of their work. As *Rigas* also illustrates, whether counsel exercised due care in this regard depends on whether the type of electronic disclosure is one that should have been foreseeable. As the level of general sophistication about electronic documents increases, the standard of foreseeability, and hence of the technical knowledge a lawyer should have, can be expected to rise. Finally, one commentator has suggested that, where possible, a party should backstop the risk of privileged material leaking out by obtaining in advance either an agreement or a protective order governing the inadvertent disclosure of privileged communications in electronic form.[20]

Similar considerations apply to the protection of trade secrets. A certain amount of leeway is allowed by the Uniform Trade Secrets Act's definition of a trade secret,

---

[18] Rigas, 281 F. Supp. 2d at 737-38.
[19] 189 F.R.D. 83, 84-85 (S.D.N.Y. 1999). In Cassano, opposing counsel had requested a copy of a document that he found in a review of the agency's files; when the paralegal asked for instructions from her superior, the SEC attorney did not review the document before authorizing the paralegal to release it.
[20] Redgrave and Nimsger, *Electronic Discovery and Inadvertent Production of Privileged Documents*, 49 Fed. Law. 37, 39 (July 2002).

MATTERS OF PRIVILEGE AND CONFIDENTIALITY

6

which requires efforts "reasonable under the circumstances to maintain its secrecy."[21] Moreover, one who receives a trade secret with knowledge or reason to know that disclosure was inadvertent may not make use of it.[22] Based on these provisions, it has been held that the disclosure of a trade secret in public court records, without further dissemination, does not destroy trade secret status, at least where the disclosure is brief, and the owner takes prompt steps to restore secrecy.[23] It would follow that where a protective order has identified the nature of trade secret information in a particular case, an adversary receiving information within that description through discovery, electronic or otherwise, would have reason to know that the disclosure was inadvertent, and the information would retain its status as a trade secret.[24] Nevertheless, the requirement of "reasonable" efforts to preserve secrecy requires counsel responding to discovery to take adequate steps to screen, review, identify and segregate trade secret information in accordance with the provisions of any protective order.

---

[21] Uniform Trade Secrets Act, § 1(4)(ii).

[22] Id. at § 1(2)(ii)(C).

[23] See Hoechst Diafoil Co. v. Nan Ya Plastics Corp., 174 F.3d 411, 417-19 (4th Cir. 1999) (presence in public court file does not destroy trade secret); Gates Rubber Co. v. Bando Chem. Indus., Ltd., 9 F.3d 823, 848-49 (10th Cir. 1993) (introduction of trade secret in evidence does not destroy status as trade secret where owner moves promptly to seal transcript); see also Fireworks Spectacular, Inc., 107 F. Supp. 2d at 1309-11 (plaintiff took immediate steps to retrieve confidential customer lists accidentally sent to eleven customers).

[24] See Nat'l Wildlife Fed'n, 286 F.3d at 573-76 ("confidential business information" in possession of EPA retained status after file was inadvertently e-mailed to opposing counsel). It should be noted that the information was the trade secret of third parties who had submitted it to the EPA. After the court had denied opposing counsel's motion to compel production, the EPA accidentally released it in an e-mail. See In re Kagan, 351 F.3d 1157, 1157-58 (D.C. Cir. 2003).

B. Production by Intervention of an Expert Not Under Respondent's Direct Control.

Fed. R. Civ. P. 34 requires the production of data in electronic form "which is in the possession, custody or control" of the responding party. This may include data that the respondent believes it has deleted from the computer, either in the ordinary course of business or to avoid discovery. Such data is recoverable by standard forensic techniques for searching computer hard drives and other storage media. In cases where a proponent has demonstrated that the responding party has withheld or attempted to destroy information stored in electronic form, some courts have authorized the copying and searching of hard drives, back-up tapes and other electronic storage media by or on behalf of the proponent. Such searches require special precautions to protect privileged or other confidential information from disclosure. Beginning with the cases of *Playboy Enterprises, Inc. v. Welles*[25] and *Simon Property Group, L.P. v. mySimon, Inc.*,[26] the federal courts have developed a standard protocol for the conduct of such forensic searches, including the protection of privileged and confidential matter.

To the general computer user,[27] the files on a computer are those that can be retrieved through various application programs (word processing, spreadsheet, e-mail, and so on), or through the file manager program such as Windows

---

[25] 60 F. Supp. 2d 1050, 1054-55 (S.D. Cal. 1999)("Welles").
[26] 194 F.R.D. 639, 641-643 (S.D. Ind. 2000).
[27] It is assumed that the ordinary individual who uses a computer for business or personal word processing, data processing, storage and retrieval or communication, including the ordinary attorney, knows as little of how the computer works as of how his or her automobile works. Common applications and popular operating systems are designed to be "user friendly," *i.e.,* to allow the ordinary user to perform the desired function without technical knowledge.

MATTERS OF PRIVILEGE AND CONFIDENTIALITY

6

Explorer. These data files can conveniently be called "active data."[28] The same information is preserved elsewhere on the computer's hard drive or the office network in several forms. First, operating systems may create duplicate files ("replicant data") on the user's hard drive as back-ups in the event of malfunction or in the course of printing a paper copy. Second, business computer networks periodically copy information to removable media, such as tapes, as a precaution ("back-up data"). Back-up data provides a historical snapshot of the system at the time of copying. Third, some or all of a file remains at various locations on a hard drive after the user has "deleted" it ("residual data").[29]

Residual data may be particularly important because many everyday computer users believe, incorrectly, that a deleted file or e-mail no longer exists. Deletion does not eradicate the contents of a file; it merely removes that file from the "file allocation table" and allows the operating system to write new data to the space formerly occupied by the file.[30] Until overwritten in the normal course or "wiped"

---

[28] The typology of "active data," "back-up data," "replicant data" (a form of back-up data) and "residual data" is taken from Feldman, *The Basics of Computer Forensics*, 12 Practical Litigator 17, 18-20 (March 2001). *See also* Chapter 1, Section C, *supra*.

[29] *See* Feldman, *supra*, 12 Practical Litigator at 18-21; Hon. Shira A. Scheindlin & Jeffrey Rabkin, *Electronic Discovery in Federal Civil Litigation: Is Rule 34 Up to the Task?* 41 B.C. L. Rev. 327, 336-38 (2001).

[30] *See* Triumph Capital Group, Inc., 211 F.R.D. at 45-46 n. 7; Feldman, *supra*, at 18-21; Scheindlin & Rabkin, *supra*.

Any further activity on the computer, including the process of turning it on and booting it up, may overwrite data on the hard drive and destroy data that could have been retrieved. Forensic software allows a mirror image of a hard drive to be downloaded and copied to a "write protected," *i.e.,* non-changeable, storage medium. Copying of files on a hard drive without using such software may be sanctionable destruction of evidence. *See* Gates Rubber Co. v. Bando Chem. Indus. Ltd., 167 F.R.D. 90, 112-13 (D. Colo.) (party copying hard drive in discovery responsible to use "best technology available" to prevent overwriting of files).

by special software,[31] the contents of the deleted file can be recovered in whole or part, either by the use of commands in the operating system or by forensic software. In addition, portions of deleted files may remain in what is known as "slack" space or "swap files," where they are recoverable by forensic software.[32] Such recoveries can be of great value in litigation. An unsuccessful deletion may allow an inference of guilty knowledge. Moreover, the apparent ease of deletion often leads individuals to be much more colloquial, expansive, or outright imprudent in committing their thoughts to e-mail than they would in a paper document.

To ensure that recovery of residual data from a hard drive or other storage medium does not destroy data in the process, it is necessary to take what is known as a "mirror image" of the medium, which contains its entire contents, and to conduct searches of the mirror image.[33] Wholesale inspection of the mirror image of a hard drive, or of back-up media, is not routinely granted. Creating and searching a mirror image is expensive, and it exposes the responding party to the disclosure of non-discoverable information. Accordingly, the

---

[31] Utility programs are used routinely to wipe unneeded data to consolidate active files and speed up their retrieval from a hard drive. Products such as Evidence Eliminator™ software claim to wipe data sufficiently to prevent forensic recovery. Evidence that such a program has been used, and the number of files it has wiped, may remain on the computer and be recovered by forensic examination. Use of such a program during litigation may be grounds for discovery sanctions or liability for spoliation. See Kucala Enterprises Ltd. v. Auto Wax Co., Inc., No. 02 C 1403, 2003 WL 21230605, at *3 (N. D. Ill. May 27, 2003) (plaintiff deleted more than 14,000 files using Evidence Eliminator™ before defendant's forensic examination of hard drive; complaint dismissed as sanction); Gates Rubber Co. v. Bando Chem. Indus. Ltd., 167 F.R.D. 90, 120 (D. Colo. 1996) (proper forensic examination can detect use of Wash Disk™ software to overwrite files).

[32] A hard drive stores files in "sectors," which are grouped in "clusters." "Slack" is the excess portion of a sector or cluster that is not needed to hold the file; it is not overwritten and may contain portions of previously deleted files. See Triumph Capital Group, Inc., 211 F.R.D. at 45-46 n. 7.

[33] See Gates Rubber Co., 167 F.R.D. at 111-13; Feldman, *supra* note 28, at 25.

MATTERS OF PRIVILEGE AND CONFIDENTIALITY

6

party propounding discovery must demonstrate that relevant, discoverable information can be recovered from the hard drive or back-up medium.[34] Evidence that the respondent routinely deletes e-mails or other files in the ordinary course,[35] that prior discovery has shown the possible withholding of relevant electronic files,[36] or that the respondent is about to delete relevant files,[37] has been held sufficient grounds to mirror a hard drive where the deleted files may remain as residual or back-up data.

---

[34] In Fennell v. First Step Designs, Ltd., 83 F.3d 526, 532-34 (1st Cir. 1996), the Court of Appeals affirmed the District Court's denial of plaintiff's request to mirror a hard drive of defendant's that contained privileged information and trade secrets. Plaintiff was unable to demonstrate to the courts' satisfaction that the hard drive contained relevant information, and her proposed search terms were so indefinite as to lead the courts to characterize the search as the proverbial "fishing expedition." See also In re Ford Motor Co., 345 F.3d 1315, 1317 (11th Cir. 2003) (District Court had abused its discretion in ordering that plaintiff have unlimited direct access to defendant's customer and dealer complaint databases without a showing that defendant had violated its discovery obligations, and without designation of search terms to limit the scope of the search); Positive Software Solutions, Inc. v. New Century Mortgage Co., 259 F. Supp. 2d 561, 562 (N.D. Tex. 2003) (request for forensic image of respondent's servers overbroad).

[35] See Welles, 60 F. Supp. 2d at 1050 (defendant's "custom and practice of deleting electronic mail soon after sending or receiving"); In re Triton Energy Sec. Litig., No. 5:98CV256, 2002 WL 32114464, at *3 (E.D. Tex. March 7, 2002) (defendant did not instruct outside directors to preserve relevant files on their personal computers during litigation).

[36] See, e.g., Antioch Co., 210 F.R.D. at 645 (circumstantial evidence of missing documents from respondent's paper files); Tulip Computers Int'l B.V. v. Dell Computer Corp., No. Civ. A. 00-981-RRM, 2002 WL 818061, at *6 (D. Del. Apr. 30, 2002) (responding party's pattern of evading paper discovery); Rowe, 205 F.R.D. at 427 (paper discovery showed potential existence of relevant e-mails; court took judicial notice that substantial volume of electronic files was never printed out); Simon Property Group, L.P., 194 F.R.D. at 641 ("troubling discrepancies with respect to defendant's document production" justified mirroring hard drives on employees' home computers).

[37] Antioch Co., 210 F.R.D. at 645 (copyright infringement; defendant said it would be going out of business and refused to consent to mirroring of hard drive).

6

E-DISCOVERY
A Guide for Corporate Counsel

Two U.S. District Court decisions mentioned earlier, *Playboy Enterprises, Inc. v. Welles*[38] and *Simon Property Group, L.P. v. mySimon, Inc.*,[39] set out what has become a standard protocol for protecting privileged and other confidential information during the forensic examination of a hard drive or back-up media.[40] The essential elements of the *Welles-Simon* protocol are as follows:

- A third-party expert is appointed as an officer of the court to create the forensic image. The expert is proposed by the proponent of discovery, and the respondent has the right to object to the proponent's choice.
- The expert and any assistants sign and adhere to all existing protective orders.
- Access for forensic imaging takes place at a time agreed to by the parties or ordered by the court.
- The forensic image is held in the custody of either the expert or respondent's counsel. If held by the expert, it is destroyed at the end of the litigation.
- The permissible scope of the forensic image is defined.[41]

---

[38] 60 F. Supp. 2d at 1050.
[39] 194 F.R.D. at 639.
[40] Decisions employing the Welles-Simon protocol or a variant include First USA Bank N.A. v. PayPal, Inc., No. 03-1558, 2003 WL 22071558, at **1 (Fed. Cir. Aug. 21, 2003) (dismissing appeal of order searching non-party's hard drive); Computer Assocs. Int'l, Inc. v. Quest Software, Inc., No. 02 C 4721, 2003 WL 21277129, at *1 (N.D. Ill. June 3, 2003); Medtronic Sofamor Danek, Inc. v. Michelson, No. 01-2373-MIV 2003 WL 21468573, at *10-*12 (W.D. Tenn. May 13, 2003); Antioch Co., 210 F.R.D. at 645; Tulip, 2002 WL 818061 at *7; In re Triton, 2002 WL 32114464 at *6; Rowe, 205 F.R.D. at 421.
[41] In Welles, the entire hard disk was mirrored. 60 F. Supp. 2d at 1054. In Simon, the forensic image excluded operating system files and high level program files; it was confined to "all available word processing documents, electronic mail messages, powerpoint or similar presentations, spreadsheets and similar files." 194 F.R.D. at 641. Where extensive back-up media are to be

MATTERS OF PRIVILEGE AND CONFIDENTIALITY

6

- The expert provides the respondent with copies of (i) all recovered files; (ii) information as to when any recovered deleted file was deleted; and (iii) available information about the deletion and content of deleted files whose content cannot be fully recovered.
- Disclosure to the expert of privileged or confidential matter on the forensic image does not constitute a waiver.
- The expert is to report to the court on the scope of work performed, including a chain of custody and a general description of the recovered data.
- Respondent's counsel will review the forensic image and produce non-privileged files responsive to discovery requests.[42]
- Respondent will review the forensic image for privileged and other confidential material and create the appropriate log identifying allegedly privileged or confidential material for further proceedings.
- The forensic image will be destroyed at the conclusion of the case.[43]

Under the *Welles-Simon* protocol, the examination of the forensic image, the production of material responsive to the proponent's discovery requests, and the identification and protection of privileged or confidential matter remain under the control of respondent's counsel. There have been both less intrusive variations, in which the forensic image is prepared and examined by the respondent in the first instance,

---

searched, the protocol may provide for a preliminary sampling to determine the likelihood of recovering discoverable material. *See* Rowe, 205 F.R.D. at 433 (proponent's option to sample copies of e-mail back-up tapes).

[42] *Cf.* In re Triton, 2002 WL 32114464 at *6-*7, in which the expert was to report to the court and the parties whether or to what extent the respondent or its employees had destroyed data.

[43] Welles, 60 F. Supp. 2d at 1054-55; Simon, 194 F.R.D. at 641-42; Antioch Co., 210 F.R.D. at 653-54.

and more intrusive variations, in which the proponent has conducted the examination. The cases appear to differ based on the trial judge's view of the proper allocation of costs between the parties and the likelihood of abuse based on the good or bad faith demonstrated in the discovery process up to that point.

In *Rowe Entm't, Inc. v. William Morris Agency*, the District Court ordered that back-up media containing respondents' e-mails be reviewed by proponent's counsel on an attorneys' eyes only basis. The court would determine the permissible search expressions after respondents had a chance to object to proponent's proposed search terms. Proponents would screen the back-up media in accordance with the approved search terms, identify all e-mails they considered material, and provide them to respondents' counsel to be reviewed for privilege. Proponents' scrutiny of privileged documents during the initial screening would not be deemed a waiver. This variation seems to provide less protection to privileged material than the *Welles-Simon* protocol. The *Rowe* court apparently adopted it to allocate among the parties the cost of reviewing a very large volume of back-up media.[44]

---

[44] Rowe, 205 F.R.D. at 432-33.
Rowe set out eight factors to determine what portion of the cost of search should be shifted from the respondent to the proponent: (1) The specificity of proponent's requests, (2) the likelihood of a successful search, (3) the availability of the material from other sources, (4) whether the respondent would access the searched files in the ordinary course of business, (5) whether both parties benefit from the search, (6) the total cost, (7) the relative ability to control search and review costs, and (8) the parties' overall resources. Rowe, 205 F.R.D. at 430-31. However, the cost of review to protect privileged or confidential material is not shifted from the respondent. *Id.* at 432. *Accord* Medtronic Sofamor Danek, Inc., 2003 WL 21468573 at *11 (search costs allocated 60:40 to respondent; respondent bears full cost of privilege review).

MATTERS OF PRIVILEGE AND CONFIDENTIALITY

6

In contrast, the court in *Medtronic Sofamor Danek, Inc. v. Michelson* ordered that the respondent prepare the forensic images, conduct the searches in accordance with court-ordered search terms, review the material for privilege, and identify responsive non-privileged files to the proponent. The process was conducted under the oversight of a neutral computer expert appointed as special master.[45]

The law governing the forensic examination of hard drives or other storage media in civil litigation, including the protection of privileged and confidential material in such examination, is still developing. The *Welles-Simon* protocol is not the last word, but its procedures are the starting point for any respondent faced with a request for mirroring of a hard drive or wholesale review of back-up material.

---

[45] 2003 WL 21468573 at *9-*12.
In evaluating the particular allocation of costs in Rowe, it should be noted that, while respondents in that case opposed the search of their backed up e-mails as burdensome and unnecessary, there had been no finding of intentional concealment or bad faith.

COST-SHIFTING

7

COST-SHIFTING

Fed. R. Civ. P. 26(c) permits a court to shift some or all of the cost of discovery to the requesting party to protect the responding party from "undue burden and expense."[1] Over the past 20 years, a considerable body of case law has developed on the issues of when and to what extent a party asked to produce data in electronic form may shift the cost to the proponent. As computers have become commonplace in business operations and in litigation, the law has rapidly become more sophisticated. The day is long past when a call for the production of data in electronic form was considered extraordinary. Current cases analyze in great detail the type of data sought, the medium in which it is stored, the ease with which the responding party can retrieve it in the ordinary course of business, the costs the responding party can be expected to incur in retrieving the data for its own use in the litigation, and the incremental cost of responding to the proponent's request to produce. As a result, more recent authority should be viewed as having greater weight.

A. The General Rule Regarding Cost-Shifting.

Early in the development of electronic discovery, the United States Supreme Court laid down the fundamental principle that under the discovery rules, "the presumption is that the responding party must bear the expense of complying with discovery requests," but that the trial court had discretion to spare the responding party "undue burden and expense" by shifting all or part of the cost to the proponent.[2] This

---

[1] Fed. R. Civ. P. 26(c)(2004); Oppenheimer Fund, Inc. v. Sanders, 437 U.S. 340, 358 (1978).
[2] Oppenheimer Fund, Inc., 437 U.S. at 358. Oppenheimer involved the question whether the plaintiff in a putative class action should bear some or all of the cost of recovering and compiling a list of potential class action plaintiffs from the defendants' electronic files.

presumption remains the starting point in any discussion of shifting the cost of electronic discovery.[3] Notwithstanding the potentially formidable cost of electronic discovery, the norm is that the respondent bears the burden of searching out and retrieving the information, copying it, reviewing it for privileged and confidential matter, and producing it to the proponent. It is not uncommon for parties in commercial litigation to spend substantial sums, sometimes millions of dollars, to comply with discovery requests.[4] Ironically, where electronic data is retrievable in the ordinary course of business, it may actually be less expensive to retrieve and produce in electronic form than to convert to paper records.[5]

Notwithstanding the potential for the production of electronic records to magnify the burden on the producing party, courts have recognized that cost-shifting may change the tactical balance in litigation and may sometimes defeat the financially weaker party:

> [C]ost-shifting may effectively end discovery, especially when private parties are engaged in litigation with large corporations. As large companies move increasingly to paper-free environments, the frequent use of cost-shifting will have the effect of crippling discovery in discrimination and retaliation cases. This will both undermine the "strong public policy favor[ing] the resolution of disputes on their merits," and may ultimately deter the filing of potentially meritorious claims.[6]

---

[3] See, e.g., Zubulake v. UBS Warburg, LLC, 217 F.R.D. 309, 317 (S.D.N.Y. 2003) ("Zubulake I"); Rowe Entm't, Inc. v. William Morris Agency, Inc., 205 F.R.D. 421, 429-32 (S.D.N.Y. 2002).

[4] See Rosenberg, *Electronic Discovery Proves Effective Legal Weapon*, Oklahoma City Journal Press (April 21, 1997), 1997 WL 14390671.

[5] See Zubulake I, 217 F.R.D. at 317 (electronic data can be retrieved and searched by keyword, and duplication of electronic file is cheaper than mass photocopying); In re Bristol-Meyers Squibb Sec. Litig., 205 F.R.D. 437, 442-44 (D.N.J. 2002) ("Bristol-Meyers Squibb") (preference for electronic production in complex securities litigation).

[6] Zubulake I, 217 F.R.D. at 317-18 (citation omitted).

COST-SHIFTING

7

It follows that a responding party that moves for a protective order shifting the cost of electronic discovery must show not merely burden and expense but "undue" burden and expense in light of the ordinary costs of discovery, the form in which the electronic data is stored, and the merits of the case.

Nevertheless, discovery of electronic data poses distinct problems that may justify cost-shifting. The sheer volume of electronic data that must be searched is always a concern.[7] As one court has pointed out, e-mail is not merely a substitute for paper correspondence. Its ease and informality has led people to transmit and record in permanent form "many informal messages that were previously relayed by telephone or at the water cooler."[8] In addition to the increased ease with which electronic files are deliberately created, ordinary application software automatically creates duplicate files of which the common user may not be fully aware. Examples are the history files and web page snapshots created by internet

---

[7] Hon. Shira A. Scheindlin & Jeffrey Rabkin, *Electronic Discovery in Federal Civil Litigation: Is Rule 34 Up to the Task?* 41 B.C. L. Rev. 327, 338-39, 366-67 (2000).

[8] Byers v. Illinois State Police, No. 99C8105, 2002 WL 1264004, at *10 (N.D. Ill. June 3, 2002). Those "informal messages" may include jokes or disparaging comments that would never previously have been committed to paper, as well as business related topics discussed with oral candor rather than written circumspection. *See, e.g.,* Sattar v. Motorola, Inc., 138 F.3d 1164, 1167 (7th Cir. 1998) (supervisor e-mailed employee "literally hundreds of e-mail messages . . . with citations to the Koran and dire warnings of the divine punishments that awaited those who turned their back on Islam"); Caldera, Inc. v. Microsoft, Inc., 72 F. Supp. 2d 1295, 1332 (D. Utah 1999) (summary judgment denied on antitrust claim; defendant e-mail stating, "If you're going to kill someone there isn't much reason to get all worked up about it and angry-- you just pull the trigger. . . . We need to smile . . . while we pull the trigger."); Owens v. Morgan Stanley & Co., Inc., No. 96 CIV. 9747 (DLC), 1997 WL 793004, at *1 (S.D.N.Y. Dec. 24, 1997) (African-American employees sued investment banking firm whose white employees allegedly circulated racist e-mails).

7
E-DISCOVERY
A Guide for Corporate Counsel

browsers; back-up files created by word processing and spreadsheet programs; and the temporary files created whenever an electronic document is printed. E-mail programs create multiple copies in the computers of sender and recipients, and these copies can in turn be multiplied when the messages are forwarded. All these copies may survive in undeleted form and be retrievable by ordinary search methods.

Electronic data also persists in forms that are not accessible in the ordinary course and which the user may believe have been destroyed. Large users routinely back up e-mail and other system data on tapes or optical storage media. Because information on back-up tapes is typically stored in the sequence in which it was recorded, without organization, searching such tapes is time-consuming and costly.[9] In some instances, e-mails and other backed up files will have been created by software that is now obsolete and perhaps unavailable, requiring the respondent to reacquire or recreate it.[10] In addition, files deleted by a user may still be recovered from a hard drive or similar storage media if they have not been overwritten by new files.[11] Their recovery requires the creation of a mirror image of the hard drive or other medium and its examination by specialized forensic software, with extraordinary inconvenience and cost.

---

[9] *See, e.g.*, McPeek v. Ashcroft, 202 F.R.D. 31, 32-33 (D.D.C. 2001) ("McPeek I"); Rowe, 205 F.R.D. at 429-30.
 More modern back-up media, such as optical discs, may allow non-sequential access and therefore be less expensive to search. In Zubulake I, 217 F.R.D. at 313-15, the defendant investment banking house backed up e-mails from outside sources onto optical disks for easy retrieval, while internal e-mails were backed up on tape.
[10] *See, e.g.*, Byers, 2002 WL 1264004 at *34 - *35 (to search back-up tapes, defendant would have to license former e-mail program at a cost of $8000 per month).
[11] Antioch Co. v. Scrapbook Borders, Inc., 210 F.R.D. 645, 652 (D. Minn. 2002) ("well accepted proposition that deleted computer files, whether they be e-mails or otherwise, are discoverable"); Simon Property Group L.P. v. MySimon,

COST-SHIFTING

In sum, the mere request that a business entity search, copy and produce relevant electronic records is generally not grounds for cost-shifting. Such requests are, for the most part, deemed a "foreseeable risk" of the modern age in the absence of a showing of particular hardship.[12] As discussed in Part B, a hardship analysis balances the nature of the information requested, the manner in which it can be recovered and the cost of doing so, the relative hardship to the parties and the significance of the issues involved.

B. The Factors Governing Cost-Shifting.

The starting point for the analysis of cost-shifting is that only "undue" expense may be imposed on the proponent. Fed. R. Civ. P. 26(b)(2) enumerates several factors according to which a trial court may determine that the burden or expense of requested discovery is undue:[13] whether the requested discovery is unreasonably cumulative, duplicative, or more easily obtainable from another source; whether the proponent has already had "ample" opportunity to obtain the information sought, and whether the burden outweighs the probable benefit, considering the needs of the case, the relative

---

Inc., 194 F.R.D. 639, 640 (S.D. Ind. 2000) ("computer records . . . that have been 'deleted,' are documents discoverable under Fed. R. Civ. P. 34"); Playboy Enterprises Inc. v. Welles, 60 F. Supp. 2d 1050, 1053-55 (N.D. Cal. 1999) (defendant's hard drive mirrored to recover deleted e-mail).

[12] In re Brand Name Prescription Drugs Antitrust Litig., Nos. 94 C 897, MDL 997, 1995 WL 360526, at *2 (N.D. Ill. June 15, 1995), citing Daewoo Elect. Co. v. United States, 650 F. Supp. 1003, 1006 (Ct. of Intl. Trade 1986).

[13] Fed. R. Civ. P. 26(b)(2) provides in pertinent part:
The frequency or extent of use of the discovery methods otherwise permitted under these rules and by any local rule shall be limited by the court if it determines that: (i) the discovery sought is unreasonably cumulative or duplicative, or is obtainable from some other source that is more convenient, less burdensome, or less expensive; (ii) the party seeking discovery has had ample opportunity by discovery in the action to obtain the information sought; or (iii) the burden or expense of the proposed

resources of the parties, the amount in controversy, the importance of the issues and the importance of the information sought to resolve them. Two recent decisions of the United States District Court for the Southern District of New York, *Rowe Entm't, Inc. v. William Morris Agency, Inc.*[14] and *Zubulake v. UBS Warburg, LLC* (discussed in other Chapters as well),[15] provide the most comprehensive discussion of how the Rule 26(b)(2) criteria have most recently been applied to shift the cost of electronic discovery to the proponent. *Rowe* was the decision of a Magistrate Judge and has been widely cited.[16] *Zubulake* was decided by Judge Shira Scheindlin, a prominent figure in the developing law of electronic discovery.[17] The *Zubulake* opinions refine the *Rowe* cost-shifting analysis in light of experience and

---

discovery outweighs its likely benefit, taking into account the needs of the case, the amount in controversy, the parties' resources, the importance of the issues at stake in the litigation, and the importance of the proposed discovery in resolving the issues. The court may act upon its own initiative after reasonable notice or pursuant to a motion under Rule 26(c).

[14] 205 F.R.D. 421 (S.D.N.Y. 2002).

[15] 217 F.R.D. 309 (S.D.N.Y. 2003).

[16] *See, e.g.*, United States v. Jasper, No. 00 CR. 0825 (PKL), 2003 U.S. Dist. LEXIS 12619, at *14 (S.D.N.Y. July 22, 2003); Chao v. 3RE.com, Inc., No. 01-2350-MIV, 2003 WL 21946597, at *2 (W.D. Tenn. July 28, 2003); Builders Ass'n of Greater Chicago v. City of Chicago, 215 F.R.D. 550, 554 (N.D. Ill. 2003); Bristol-Myers Squibb, 205 F.R.D. at 437; In re Livent, Inc. Noteholders Sec. Litig., No. 98 CIV. 7161 VMDFE, 2003 WL 23254, at *3 (S.D.N.Y. Jan. 2, 2003); Antioch Co., 210 F.R.D. at 645.

The Magistrate Judge's decision in Rowe was affirmed by the District Court. 2002 WL 975713 (S.D.N.Y. 2002). Zubulake describes Rowe as having become the "gold standard" on this issue. 217 F.R.D. at 320.

[17] Judge Scheindlin is the co-author of the widely cited Scheindlin & Rabkin, *Electronic Discovery in Federal Civil Litigation: Is Rule 34 Up to the Task?* 41 B.C. L. Rev. 327 (2000). She sits on the Advisory Committee on the Federal Rules of Civil Procedure of the Judicial Conference of the United States.

COST-SHIFTING 7

academic commentary.[18] Although *Zubulake* and *Rowe* will doubtless not be the last word, they appear to be the current state of the art. The discussion below follows the *Zubulake-Rowe* analysis, supplemented by other decisions.

1. The Accessibility Threshold.

Beginning with the premise that respondents normally bear the cost of discovery and that only "undue" cost can be shifted, *Zubulake* held that the issue of cost-shifting did not arise unless the electronic data sought was stored in "inaccessible" form. The decision identifies five different levels of accessibility:

- active, on-line data accessible in the ordinary course of business;
- near-line data conveniently stored in removable media such as floppy discs or CD-ROMs, which are fully searchable once inserted in a drive and can be automatically accessed by a mechanical system;
- removable media that must be manually retrieved and loaded;
- back-up tapes that must be read in sequence to recover information; and
- erased or fragmented data that can be recovered in whole or part only through forensic techniques.[19]

The first three classes of data are "accessible," that is, they are intended to be retrievable for ordinary business use and

---

[18] Zubulake I, 217 F.R.D. at 320-21; Zubulake v. UBS Warburg, LLC, 216 F.R.D. 280, 283 (S.D.N.Y. 2003) ("Zubulake III"); Zubulake v. UBS Warburg, LLC, No. 02 CIV. 1243 (SAS), 2003 WL 22410619, at *1 (S.D.N.Y. Oct. 22, 2003) ("Zubulake IV"); Zubulake v. UBS Warburg, LLC, 2004 WL 1620866 (S.D.N.Y. July 20, 2004) ("Zubulake V").
[19] Zubulake I, 217 F.R.D. at 318-20.

can be retrieved, once loaded, by using standard search tools. "In the world of electronic data, thanks to search engines, any data that is retained in a machine readable format is typically accessible."[20]

The last two classes are "inaccessible" because they require extraordinary measures. Unlike a hard drive, floppy disk or optical disk, back-up tapes do not allow the searcher to go directly to the information sought by using a search program. Information is loaded on the back-up tapes in chronological order, and it can be searched only after first retrieving the tape and then uploading it onto a hard drive.[21] Deleted, erased or otherwise damaged data can be recovered only by the use of forensic software after making a mirror image of the hard drive or other media to be searched. The technique requires the use of experts, and it is generally performed under judicial supervision to avoid the disclosure of irrelevant or privileged material turned up by the search.[22] Neither the uploading of back-up tapes nor forensic examination would be performed by a respondent as part of its ordinary use of its electronic data, and the cost and inconvenience of doing so crosses the threshold at which cost sharing must be considered.

Although the terminology of "accessible" and "inaccessible" data to define the threshold of potential cost sharing is original to *Zubulake*, the concept is not. The essence of the distinction is that it "corresponds closely to the cost of production."[23] Extraordinary cost, compared to the

---

[20] *Id.* at 318.
[21] *See, e.g.*, Xpedior Creditor Trust v. Credit Suisse First Boston (USA), Inc., No. 02 CIV. 9149 (SAS), 2003 WL 22283535, at *5 (S.D.N.Y. Oct. 2, 2003) (data on optical disk system decommissioned in ordinary course of business inaccessible because system would have to be reconstructed); Zubulake I, 217 F.R.D. at 314; Rowe, 205 F.R.D. at 430; McPeek I, 202 F.R.D. at 33.
[22] *See* Chapter 6, *supra*, at nn. 25-43.
[23] OpenTV v. Liberate Tech., 219 F.R.D. 474, 476 (N.D. Cal. 2003); Zubulake, 217 F.R.D. at 318.

COST-SHIFTING 7

retrieval of the same data for the respondent's own use in the ordinary course of business, may justify the shifting of part of that cost to the proponent.[24]

2. Cost Allocation Factors.

For data in inaccessible form, *Zubulake* sets out seven factors to be considered in determining whether, and if so to what extent, the cost of search, retrieval and production is to be shifted to the proponent. These are:

1. The extent to which the request is specifically tailored to develop relevant information;
2. The availability of such information from other sources;[25]
3. The total cost of production, compared to the amount in controversy;
4. The total cost of production, compared to the resources of each party;
5. The relative ability of each party to control costs and its incentive to do so;
6. The importance of the issues at stake in the litigation;[26] and

---

[24] Because the cost of producing accessible data is borne by the respondent, one court has concluded that even though the cost of restoring inaccessible data to accessible form should be split, the cost of searching the data once restored should be borne by the responding party alone. OpenTV, 219 F.R.D. at 479.

[25] This includes the same information previously produced in paper form. See, e.g., Bristol-Meyers Squibb, 205 F.R.D. at 441-444.

[26] This factor, according to Judge Scheindlin, is "a critical consideration" but "one that will rarely be invoked." It comes into play when a case has "a potential for broad public impact," such as toxic tort, environmental, institutional reform litigation, or other cases raising significant legal or constitutional issues. Zubulake I, 217 F.R.D. at 322. Unstated is the assumption that plaintiffs in such cases will often lack the financial resources to accept cost-shifting.

E-DISCOVERY
A Guide for Corporate Counsel

7. The relative benefits to the parties of obtaining the information.[27]

These factors are not of equal weight. The first two are the most important. Whether the request is specifically tailored to develop relevant information that is not available from other sources is another way to describe the "marginal utility" of the request, *i.e.*, the likelihood that it will produce relevant information:

> The more likely it is that the back-up tape contains information that is relevant to a claim or defense, the fairer it is that the [responding party] search at its own expense. The less likely it is, the more unjust it would be to make the [responding party] search at its own expense. The difference is "at the margin."[28]

It is therefore of critical importance that a proponent seeking to avoid cost-shifting use the most precise search terms that it can and present to the court an explanation of

---

[27] Zubulake I, 217 F.R.D. at 324. Zubulake modified the eight factors enumerated in Rowe in several respects. It added consideration of the amount in controversy and the importance of the issues involved in the litigation, as required by Fed. R. Civ. P. 26(b)(2). It also measured the parties' relative wealth not in the abstract but in comparison to the cost of production. The object of these changes was to approach "undue" burden by balancing the absolute cost of production against the both the available resources and the issues in controversy. "A response to a discovery request costing $100,000 sounds (and is) costly, but in a case potentially worth millions of dollars, the cost of responding may not be *unduly* burdensome." *Id.* at 321 (emphasis added).

Rowe also considered the "specificity" of the discovery request. 205 F.R.D. at 429-430. Vague and unfocused requests require a broader and more expensive search than narrowly focused ones. *See* Rowe, 205 F.R.D. at 429; Byers, 2002 WL 1264004 at *12 (multi-year search of back-up tapes). Zubulake therefore folds this factor into the overall relevance of the material requested and into the relative ability of the parties to control costs. 217 F.R.D. at 321.

Rowe had also taken into account the purpose for which the information was retained, holding that it was unduly burdensome to require a search of back-up media that the respondent did not intend to use in the ordinary course of business. 205 F.R.D. at 431. Zubulake eliminates this factor because, in Judge Scheindlin's view, it is simply another way of stating the accessibility threshold. 217 F.R.D. at 321-22.

[28] Zubulake I, 217 F.R.D. at 323, *quoting* McPeek I, 202 F.R.D. at 34.

COST-SHIFTING 7

In *Medtronic Sofamor Danek, Inc. v. Michelson*,[35] a trade secret violation suit, defendant sought to compel discovery of information on computer network back-up tapes, and the court ordered that a portion of the discovery costs be shifted. Several factors influenced the court's decision. First, the court found that defendant's request was overly broad and that defendant had made no effort to narrow it.[36] Second, defendant did not offer evidence that the electronic materials he sought contained relevant information.[37] Third, the court estimated the potential cost of responding to the request to be between $597,600 and $1,109,046 and found it unnecessarily high because it was the result of the defendant's refusal to limit the scope of its request.[38] Based on these factors, the court held that cost-shifting was appropriate.[39]

Similarly, in *Byers v. Illinois State Police*,[40] an employment discrimination case, the court held that the plaintiff employees were entitled to discover the e-mails referencing them, which were saved on a legacy e-mail system, but the court ordered them to pay the $8,000 monthly cost to license the old program that was needed to view the e-mails on the back-up tapes.[41]

---

[35] No. 01-2373-MIV, 2003 WL 21468573, at *1 (W.D.Tenn. 2003).
[36] *Id.* at *11-*13.
[37] *Id.* at *15-*16.
[38] *Id.* at *28.
[39] *Id.* at *31.
[40] No. 99 C 8105, 2002 WL 1264004, at *2 (N.D.Ill. June 3, 2003).
[41] *Id.* at *35 -*38. The total cost of producing all the e-mails requested by plaintiffs was estimated to be between $20,000 and $30,000.

C. Review for Privileged or Confidential Material.

The foregoing discussion relates to the shifting the cost of searching material that is ultimately produced to the proponent, presumably for the proponent's benefit. The responding party will, for its own protection, review the search results for privileged communications or other non-discoverable confidential material. Because that review is entirely for the benefit of the responding party and results in the withholding rather than the production of information, courts have usually determined that the cost of such review should be borne by the responding party.[42]

---

[42] Rowe, 205 F.R.D. at 432; Medtronic Sofamor Danek, Inc. v. Michelson, No. 01-2373-MIV, 2003 WL 21468573, at *11 (W.D. Tenn. May 13, 2003).

THE ROLE OF EXPERTS IN ELECTRONIC DISCOVERY

In all but the simplest cases, a litigant should seriously consider enlisting the help of a computer forensics expert. Internal MIS departments can address some electronic discovery issues, but they generally lack access to the powerful forensic tools regularly used by government agencies and available to computer forensics experts. The danger of loss or alteration of electronic data resulting from bungled efforts to deal with it may outweigh the cost of retaining the expert.[1]

Computer forensics is the preservation, collection, analysis and presentation in court of electronic evidence.[2] Unlike paper documents, which remain static, electronic evidence is inherently dynamic – some electronic information will change automatically every time a file is accessed or even when a PC is turned on – making preservation and restoration of the information a challenge. Using specialized software, forensics experts can not only preserve the status quo, but they can collect and reconstruct deleted, temporary or fragmented information.[3] They can even analyze whether

---

[1] *See* Kenneth J. Withers, *Computer-Based Discovery In Federal Civil Litigation*, 2000 Fed. Cts. L. Rev. 2, III. f.2 (2000)("Computer based discovery has the potential to reduce costs and shorten the length of civil litigation, although it is widely viewed by the legal profession as costly, time-consuming, and more complicated than conventional discovery.").

[2] Computer forensics has been defined as "the science of obtaining, preserving, and documenting evidence from digital electronic storage devices, such as computers, pagers, PDAs, digital cameras, cell phones, and various memory storage devices." Steven M. Abrams & Philip C. Weis, *Knowledge Of Computer Forensics Is Becoming Essential For Attorneys In The Information Age*, 75 N.J. St. B.J. 8, 12 (Feb. 2003).

[3] Joan E. Feldman, *The Expert's Role In Computer-Based Discovery*, Association of Trial Lawyers of America, Winter 2003 Convention Reference Materials (Feb. 2003), *available on* WESTLAW at Winter 2003 ATLA-CLE 157 ("The expert's review of computer-based data may include a number of

8

E-DISCOVERY
A Guide for Corporate Counsel

a user wiped, cleaned-up or defragmented the hard drive. They can also help ensure that while they do their work, no evidence is damaged, no viruses are introduced, extracted data is protected, and a proper chain of custody is maintained and presented to the court for authentication purposes.[4]

In sum, the computer forensics expert's skills in preserving, collecting, analyzing, and authenticating both active and archival or legacy data from a wide range of commonly-used electronic storage devices can be essential in analyzing the merits of potential or threatened litigation as well as in preparing for, initiating and responding to electronic discovery in pending litigation. Moreover, their ability to explain the unique and often technically complex issues attendant to electronic discovery to a judge or magistrate can be critical to resolving discovery disputes that could paralyze litigants' businesses. This chapter explores the roles of experts from pre-litigation through preparing for and conducting electronic discovery and, ultimately, trial. The areas where forensics experts can help litigants will undoubtedly evolve as litigants and their counsel become increasingly savvy, as the problems change, and as new technological solutions emerge in this developing field.

---

processes, such as the forensic capture and restoration of data; parsing out privileged data; re-creating database environments; re-creating electronic mail system environments; text-searching and sorting data for review.").

[4] Devin Murphy, *The Discovery Of Electronic Data In Litigation: What Practitioners And Their Clients Need to Know*, 27 Wm. Mitchell L. Rev. 1825, 1843 (2001).

THE ROLE OF EXPERTS IN ELECTRONIC DISCOVERY   8

A. Why You Need an Expert.

1. Offensive Reasons.

a. Discovering a Basis for Suit.

Computer forensics experts can help determine whether a reasonable basis exists for bringing an action and can protect a party against sanctions for having brought an action. In *The Carlton Group, Ltd. v. Tobin*,[5] the plaintiffs alleged that former employees deleted computer files, conspired to steal confidential and proprietary information in electronic form, and used that information to compete unlawfully with plaintiffs. The plaintiffs also sued PDP Capital, whose only connection with the other parties was that it maintained an office in the same building and shared a switch and data transmission line that connected the computers of all the tenants by way of the internet.[6] The plaintiffs alleged that PDP Capital conspired with the former employees to steal proprietary information by means of an electronic shortcut that linked plaintiffs' computer system to the computer used by a PDP Capital employee.[7] Essentially, the plaintiffs claimed that proprietary information was transferred from plaintiffs' computer system to the PDP Capital employee's computer and from there to the computer system of the former employees' new company.[8]

PDP Capital moved successfully to dismiss and sought sanctions, arguing that the allegations were factually unsupported and insufficient to establish a theory of

---

[5] No. 02 Civ. 5065 SAS, 2003 WL 21782650, at *1 (S.D.N.Y. July 31, 2003).
[6] *Id.*
[7] *Id.*
[8] *Id.*

conspiracy.⁹ In analyzing whether sanctions were appropriate, the court examined the evidentiary support for the plaintiffs' claims.¹⁰ The court noted that the plaintiffs' information technology administrator had discovered the electronic link while investigating the former employees and had determined that no reason existed for such a link to have been created.¹¹ Following that discovery, the plaintiffs retained a computer forensics expert to review and confirm the information gathered by the information technology administrator.¹² After the expert determined that the electronic link could not have been created without the knowledge and permission of the operator of the PDP Capital computer and that the link would permit someone on the plaintiffs' computer system to move data back and forth between the plaintiffs' computer network and the PDP Capital computer, the plaintiffs retained yet another computer forensics expert to review the complaint before it was filed.¹³ These efforts by the plaintiffs, together with the facts discovered by the experts in their investigation, led the court to conclude that plaintiffs had a reasonable basis for believing that a conspiracy existed, and the court denied the request for sanctions.¹⁴

Tobin stands for the proposition that retaining a qualified computer forensics expert can protect a complaining party from sanctions even if the allegations in the complaint are ultimately found to be incorrect or not worth pursuing. Retention of the expert shows that the company took

---

⁹ *Id.* at *2. Although the plaintiffs voluntarily dismissed their claims against PDP Capital, PDP Capital nevertheless refused to withdraw its request for Rule 11 sanctions.
¹⁰ *Id.* at *3 -*5.
¹¹ *Id.* at *4.
¹² *Id.*
¹³ *Id.*
¹⁴ *Id.* at *4 -*5.

THE ROLE OF EXPERTS IN ELECTRONIC DISCOVERY

reasonable steps to investigate the basis for allegations before making them in a complaint.

b.   Shaping Discovery Requests.

As discussed at greater length in Chapter 3, *supra*, the Federal Rules of Civil Procedure and their state law equivalents generally require that the parties and the court evaluate the technological feasibility and the cost of preserving, retrieving, reviewing and producing electronic data in view of the nature of the underlying litigation and the amount in controversy.[15] Electronic discovery implicates unique factors that make this balancing especially problematic: (a) vast quantities of data; (b) multiple repositories; (c) complex internal structures of data collections and relationships of one document to another; (d) differing formats and coding schemes requiring that data be converted into text to be understood; and (e) constant changes in information technology.[16] Accordingly, courts often refuse to enforce or, alternatively, narrow the scope of poorly drafted discovery requests that identify thousands upon thousands of pages of

---

[15]   The court has inherent power under Fed. R. Civ. P. 26(b)(2) to limit discovery:

> The frequency or extent of use of the discovery methods otherwise permitted under these rules and by any local rule should be limited by the court if it determines that: (*i*) *the discovery sought is unreasonably cumulative or duplicative, or is obtainable from some other source that is more convenient, less burdensome, or less expensive*; (*ii*) the party seeking discovery has had ample opportunity by discovery in the action to obtain the information sought; or (*iii*) *the burden or expense of the proposed discovery outweighs its likely benefit, taking into account the needs of the case, the amount in controversy, the parties' resources, the importance of the issues at stake in the litigation, and the importance of the proposed discovery in resolving the issues*. [Emphasis added].

[16]   *The Sedona Principles: Best Practices Recommendations & Principles for Addressing Electronic Document Production*, Comment 2.b. (Sedona Conference Working Group Series 2004) *available at* http://www.sedonaconference.org.

potentially responsive, but probably unhelpful, electronic documents.[17] Experts can help craft narrowly tailored discovery requests that will survive court challenges, based on their expertise in how electronic data is created, stored and destroyed.[18] For the same reason, the expert can also be instrumental in the requesting party's effort to convince the court that it should issue an order requiring the responding party to take affirmative measures to preserve electronic materials.[19]

The expert can assist in formulating discovery aimed at learning the "topography" of the adversary's computer system, which helps identify how, where and why information is stored.[20] Experts can help draft requests for electronic evidence from sources such as (1) wireless telephones that contain stored telephone numbers and the text

---

[17] See, e.g., S. Diagnostic Assoc. v. Bencosme, 833 So.2d 801, 802-03 (Fla. Dist. Ct. App. 2002) (quashing order compelling discovery of documents contained in company's computer system because order was overly broad, in that it did not set limitations on inspection of the computer system and failed to take into account company's confidentiality and privilege concerns); Ex parte Wal-Mart, Inc., 809 So.2d 818, 822-23 (Ala. 2001) (narrowing electronic discovery request to specific incidents regarding alleged negligence). See also In re Brand Name Prescription Drugs Antitrust Litig., Nos. 94 C 897, MDL 997, 1995 WL 360526, at *1 -*3 (N.D. Ill. June 15, 1995) (because plaintiffs' discovery request for computer-stored e-mail would require defendant to search through thirty million pages of e-mail data and incur estimated costs of $50,000 to $70,000, the court ordered the parties to consult and agree upon meaningful limitations on the scope of any e-mail search).

[18] See Elizabeth Bacon Ehlers, et al., *E-Discovery*, in BUSINESS, LAW, AND THE INTERNET (Illinois Institute for Continuing Legal Education, March 2002), *available on* WESTLAW at BLI IL-CLE 2-1, 2.35.

[19] Andrew Johnson-Laird, *Smoking Guns And Spinning Disks*, 11 No. 8 Computer Law 1, 3 (Aug. 1994). See also Lisa M. Arent, Robert D. Brownstone & William A. Fenwick, *E-Discovery: Preserving, Requesting & Producing Electronic Information*, 19 Santa Clara Computer & High Tech. L.J. 131, 176 (Dec. 2002)("The lack of an expert may preclude court enforcement of what might otherwise qualify as a valid discovery request.").

[20] See Shira A. Scheindlin & Jeffrey Rabkin, *Retaining, Destroying And Producing E-Data: Part 2*, N.Y.L.J., May 9, 2002, at Col. 1.

THE ROLE OF EXPERTS IN ELECTRONIC DISCOVERY

of e-mail messages; (2) pagers; (3) facsimile machines containing stored faxes and transmission logs; and (4) smart cards, which store monetary amounts, vendor information and transactions.[21] Armed with an understanding of the entire topography, an expert can help formulate requests to preserve and produce that limit the universe of data to key individuals, particular date ranges and media that likely contain the information sought.[22] In addition, because multiple copies of identical data may reside in active storage, back-up, or archives because of the dynamic nature of computer system management, experts can help frame preservation requirements and discovery requests that are limited to what is reasonably necessary to preserve and secure the evidence needed for a fair resolution of the underlying dispute.[23]

This economy can be critical for a variety of reasons. Perhaps the most obvious reason is the risk of payback. "A party that propounds discovery requests that require its adversary to unearth large quantities of electronic information at great expense may well be hard-pressed to resist similar discovery efforts by that adversary."[24] Limiting the body of electronic data to be reviewed also minimizes secondary costs, such as the burden on technical personnel and lawyers who have to review the data retrieved.[25] Furthermore, where an expert can demonstrate that the inclusiveness of the discovery requests is unavoidable, the court may be persuaded to allocate the cost of compliance to the producing party, whose conduct created the need.

---

[21] *See Digital Forensics: Tales From The Computer Hard Drive*, NJ Lawyer: The Weekly Newspaper, June 23, 2003, at A4.
[22] *See* Arent, Brownstone & Fenwick, *supra* note 19.
[23] It stands to reason that, having relied on the expert to identify the raw data that should be requested, the expert is the one who will know what to do with it once it is obtained.
[24] *See* Scheindlin & Rabkin, *supra* note 20.
[25] *See* Withers, *supra* note 1.

E-DISCOVERY
A Guide for Corporate Counsel

8

In *Zubulake v. UBS Warburg*,[26] a gender discrimination case, Judge Shira Scheindlin, who sits on the Discovery Subcommittee of the Advisory Committee on Civil Rules, articulated a seven-factor test for shifting the cost of electronic discovery based on whether it is inaccessible and, if so, why.[27] Applying the test, the court ordered UBS Warburg to produce all responsive e-mails on its optical disks or its active servers (both accessible formats) at its own expense.[28] The court also ordered UBS Warburg to produce, at its own expense, responsive e-mails from sample back-up tapes (inaccessible format) selected for review to determine the types of information contained thereon and the costs involved in restoring them.[29] After the sample tapes were produced, the plaintiff moved for production of the remaining back-up tapes. In *Zubulake III*,[30] the court engaged in the cost-shifting analysis outlined in *Zubulake I*. It ordered UBS Warburg to restore the remaining tapes and to pay seventy-

---

[26] 217 F.R.D. 309, 322 (S.D.N.Y. 2003) ("Zubulake I"); *see* Zubulake discussions in Chapters 5 and 7, *supra*.

[27] Judge Scheindlin grouped electronic discovery into five categories: (1) active, online data; (2) near-line data; (3) offline storage/archives; (4) back-up tapes; and (5) erased, fragmented or damaged data. Only the last two categories are deemed inaccessible materials. The court determined that cost-shifting should be considered only in those cases in which the electronic data to be searched is maintained in an "inaccessible format," such as on back-up tapes. In cases where the data to be searched is contained in a relatively "accessible" format, such as offline archived data on optical disks, courts should not even entertain requests to shift costs to the requesting party. *See* Chapter 7, *supra*, for a discussion of the Zubulake cost-shifting factors. The Zubulake test was reiterated and applied by Judge Scheindlin in Xpedior Creditor Trust v. Credit Suisse First Boston, No. 02 Civ. 9149 (SAS), 2003 WL 22283835, at *5- *6 (S.D.N.Y Oct. 2, 2003).

[28] Zubulake I, 217 F.R.D. at 324.

[29] *Id.*

[30] Zubulake v. UBS Warburg, 216 F.R.D. 280, 284-290 (S.D.N.Y. 2003) ("Zubulake III").

THE ROLE OF EXPERTS IN ELECTRONIC DISCOVERY

8

five percent of the costs, as well as all the costs incurred in reviewing the restored documents for privileged information.[31] The plaintiff was ordered to pay twenty-five percent of the cost of back-up tape restoration.

c.   Recovering Electronic Data.

Not only can experts help shape document preservation demands and discovery requests, but they can participate in the actual recovery of electronic information by analyzing a computer system and creating a non-invasive, sector-by-sector "mirror-image" of a computer's hard drive, network storage space, e-mail accounts, back-up tapes and archived e-mails without disrupting the original evidence.[32] In the simplest cases, this involves nothing more than connecting a cable from the original hard drive to a replica hard drive and making a copy so the original computer drive is not contaminated by the investigation.[33] This type of analysis freezes time by taking a complete snapshot of the subject drive at the time it is imaged, mounts it as a read-only drive, and permits an expert to search computer storage devices using defined criteria such as keywords, dates or authors.[34]

---

[31]   *Id.* at 291.

[32]   United States v. Triumph Capital Group Inc., 11 F.R.D. 31, 48 (D. Conn. 2002) ("Making a mirror image of the hard drive is central to the examination process. It is done to maintain the integrity and security of the original evidence. A mirror image is an exact duplicate of the entire hard drive, and includes all the scattered clusters of the active and deleted files and the slack and free space. Having such a mirror image of the hard drive also allows the examiner to reconstruct the steps of his examination at a later time.").

[33]   *See* Ohio v. Cook, 777 N.E.2d 882, 886-87 (Ohio App. 2002) (finding that the mirror image of the defendant's hard drive, which resulted in a "report hundreds of pages long, containing a complete history of everything on the computer's hard drive," was an authentic copy of the original and therefore admissible in court).

[34]   *See, e.g.,* United States v. Scott, 83 F. Supp. 2d 187, 197 (D. Mass. 2000)(after making a mirror image of suspect's hard drive, law enforcement computer specialist was able to search for "hits" based on specific names). *See also* Tulip Computer Int'l v. Dell Computer Corp., No. Civ. A. 00-981-RRM,

E-DISCOVERY
A Guide for Corporate Counsel

New technology even allows concept searching, which identifies word patterns and occurrences in documents and translates those patterns into concepts.[35] For instance, search programs such as dtSearch allow a forensics expert to index every word in active files, on a hard drive, or on an associated network to facilitate searches.[36] The concept search engine then compares the concepts across the document set.[37] Combined with traditional Boolean searching, concept searching allows for quicker and more accurate document identification.[38] It may also discover smoking guns that would otherwise not have been located[39] and eliminate superfluous junk documents, such as jokes and other unrelated, informal communications. Moreover, with keyword and concept searching, the expert can conduct a quick and efficient search through many gigabytes of electronic data.[40] In short, computer forensics experts can be invaluable in locating responsive data.[41]

Forensics consultants can recover active data (data that was accessible to the particular user working with the computer), recovered data (files and directories recovered after being deleted from the active data) and unused data ("free space" or unallocated portions of the hard drive that

---

2002 WL 818061, at *4 (D. Del. Apr. 30, 2002) (ordering plaintiff to turn over several hard disks so that plaintiff's expert could perform key word search).

[35] See Abrams, *supra* note 2, at 13.

[36] Beryl A. Howell & Eric M. Friedberg, *21st Century Forensics: Searching For The" Smoking Gun" In Computer Hard Drives*, The Prosecutor, Nov./Dec. 2003, at 23.

[37] See Abrams, *supra* note 2, at 13.

[38] See Dale M. Cendali, Susan Rodihan & Emily Dorsett, *Electronic Discovery*, Seventh Annual Internet Law Institute, 615, 626 (Practicing Law Institute ed. 2003), *available on* WESTLAW at 755 PLI/Pat 615 ("A Boolean search is similar to the type of search one would do on Westlaw, Lexis or the World Wide Web.").

[39] See Johnson-Laird, *supra* note 19.

[40] Howell & Friedberg, *supra* note 36, at 23.

[41] Feldman, *supra* note 3.

THE ROLE OF EXPERTS IN ELECTRONIC DISCOVERY

8

contain file space that is free because it was never used or because information previously contained there was deleted).[42] In other words, forensics experts are often able to identify and recover deleted documents in whole or in fragments.[43]

In addition to preserving and retrieving files, forensics consultants can often determine whether computer evidence was altered, damaged or removed.[44] They can examine hidden information associated with recovered files (including deleted data or data from inactive or unused storage areas) and provide a historical ledger of the content of the files.[45] They can examine invisible or embedded information, such as hidden columns on spreadsheets that show up electronically but not on printed versions, and such as a "bcc" field on an e-mail.[46]

Computer files also contain metadata,[47] which reveals, among other things, when files were created, modified or

---

[42] See Kristin M. Nimsger Esq., et al., *Electronic Discovery In Technology Litigation*, 23rd Annual Institute on Computer Law 297, 372-373 (Practicing Law Institute ed. 2003), *available on* WESTLAW at PLI/Pat 297.

[43] See *supra* note 21 ("Even if the suspect has deleted all files, formatted the hard drive and installed a new version of Windows, a data forensics specialist can typically recover most data pertinent to the case."). *See also* Howell & Friedberg, *supra* note 36, at 23, 26.

[44] See, e.g., Four Seasons v. Consorcio Barr, 267 F. Supp. 2d 1268, 1281 (S.D. Fla. 2003). *See also* Lesley Friedman Rosenthal, *Electronic Discovery Can Unearth Treasure Trove Of Information Or Potential Land Mines*, 75 N.Y. St. B.J. 32, 34 (Sept. 2003); Mary Kay Brown & Paul D. Weiner, *Digital Dangers: A Primer On Electronic Evidence In The Wake of Enron*, 74 PA Bar Assn. Quarterly 1, 3 (Jan. 2003) ("It is metadata that provides the blueprint of a backdated document, or reveals a party's improper attempts to delete relevant information immediately after receiving notification of a lawsuit.").

[45] *See also* James A. Snyder & Angela Morelock, *Electronic Data Discovery: Litigation Gold Mine Or Nightmare?* 58 J. Mo. B. 18, 19 (Jan/Feb. 2002).

[46] *See* Brown & Weiner, *supra* note 44.

[47] *See* Snyder & Morelock, *supra* note 45. *See also* John L. Carroll, *Discovery Disputes and Electronic Media*, America, ALI-ABA Course of Study, 421, 424 (2001), *available on* WESTLAW at SG405 ALI-ABA 421.

deleted and what user name was associated with each of those operations.[48] Metadata provides the blueprint of a backdated document or reveals improper attempts to delete relevant information.[49] It is also of critical importance in detecting faking of electronic evidence. Using specialized software, forensics experts can reveal metadata and use it to document destructive actions as well as unauthorized access, copying, downloading, printing or e-mailing, which are of particular interest where theft of trade secrets is at issue.[50]

The use of these tools has had dramatic results. For example, in *Kucala Enterprises, Ltd. v. Auto Wax Co.*,[51] a patent suit, a computer forensics expert using an image of plaintiff's hard drive discovered that the night before the hard drive was produced in compliance with an inspection order, the plaintiff had used "Evidence Eliminator," a wiping software utility, to delete and overwrite more than 12,000 files.[52] The expert was also able to determine that approximately 3,000 additional files had been deleted and overwritten three days earlier.[53] Plaintiff's conduct was held to be "egregious," warranting, in part, the Magistrate's recommended sanctions.[54] In addition to sanctions, the requesting party was allowed to present evidence of Kucala's destruction of requested documents to the jury to establish damages.[55]

---

[48] *See* Brown & Weiner, *supra* note 44.
[49] *See id.*
[50] *See, e.g.,* Consorcio, 267 F. Supp. 2d at 1294-98; *see also* Abrams & Weis, *supra* note 2, at 12.
[51] No. 02 C 1403, 2003 WL 21230605, at *1 (N.D. Ill. May 27, 2003).
[52] *Id.* at *5.
[53] *Id.*
[54] *Id.* at *4 -*5.
[55] *Id.*

THE ROLE OF EXPERTS IN ELECTRONIC DISCOVERY

8

Impressive discoveries were made by the computer forensics experts in *Four Seasons Hotels and Resorts v. Consorcio Barr*,[56] where the plaintiff's expert used forensic software to detect tampering and forgery and to establish that much of defendant's evidence, which was provided on floppy discs, was fabricated.[57] In that case, the Four Seasons Hotel chain brought charges against one of its licensees for breach of a license agreement and for violation of the Computer Fraud and Abuse Act, the Electronic Communications Privacy Act, the Lanham Act for trademark infringement, and Florida's Uniform Trade Secrets Act.[58] Using Vogon, a computer forensics program commonly used in Europe, and Encase, one of the major forensic programs available in the United States, plaintiff's expert was able to determine that defendant had deleted numerous e-mails and was able to recover many of them, including several business-related e-mails.[59] During his examination of the computers, the expert also discovered that someone had installed "undeletion software."[60] The court viewed the presence of this software suspiciously and interpreted it as showing that the user of the computer was trying to find out how well deleted documents could be retrieved through these programs.[61] Furthermore, the expert uncovered several Trojan horses[62] and other questionable programs commonly used by hackers.[63] Even more damaging to defendant, Consorcio's own forensics expert admitted that it had "deleted 350 files and wrote over

---

[56] 267 F. Supp. 2d 1268, 1281 (S.D. Fla. 2003).
[57] *Id.* at 1300.
[58] *Id.*
[59] *Id.* at 1296.
[60] *Id.* The expert was not only able to determine that e-mail had been deleted, but he could also provide details on when and from where they had been deleted.
[61] *Id.* at 1295.
[62] "Trojan horse is a method widely used by hackers to gain access to networks." *Id.*
[63] *Id.* at 1296-97.

half a gigabyte of data prior to his computer being turned over for inspection to Four Seasons."[64] The experts' evidence weighed heavily in the court's decision to award substantial damages to Four Seasons.[65] *Kucala* and *Consorcio* show just how much information an expert can uncover by using powerful forensic software programs and how pivotal that information can be in the outcome of a case.

d.   Authenticating Discovery.

To be admissible, electronic evidence must be authenticated and must clear hearsay hurdles.[66] Generally, computer evidence may be admitted under the business records exception to the hearsay rule, but that requires that the proponent prove that it was created "at or near the time" of the transaction, act or event recorded.[67] By customizing reports about the data, providing information during the course of the litigation and providing expert testimony at hearings on motions and at trial, computer forensics experts support the process of authentication by explaining the process and the product of their examination.[68]

With regard to documenting the chain of custody of electronic evidence for authentication purposes, computer

---

[64] *Id.* at 1299.
[65] *Id.* at 1332-33.
[66] *See* Fed. R. Evid. 901(a); *see also* Monotype Corp. v. Int'l Typeface Corp., 43 F.3d 443, 449-50 (9th Cir. 1994); United States v. Bowers, 920 F.2d 220, 223 (4th Cir. 1990); United States v. Catabran, 836 F.2d 453, 458 (9th Cir. 1988); United States v. Vela, 673 F.2d 86, 90 (5th Cir. 1982); *see also, e.g.*, Uncle Henry's Inc. v. Plaut Consulting Inc., 240 F. Supp. 2d 63 (D.Me. 2003) (*citing* United States v. Siddiqui, 235 F.3d 1318 (11th Cir. 2000) and holding that "e-mails (like letters and other documents) must be properly authenticated or shown to be self-authenticating").
[67] Fed. R. Evid. 803(6); *see* United States v. Hutson, 821 F.2d 1015, 1019-20 (5th Cir. 1987).
[68] *See* Nimsger, et al., *supra* note 42, at 376.

THE ROLE OF EXPERTS IN ELECTRONIC DISCOVERY

experts can be crucial in ensuring admissibility in court.[69] Experts may be called upon to testify to the methods used to retrieve the electronic data and to dispel the possibility of tampering or forgery.[70] When investigating, the experienced examiner maintains a log with a step-by-step narrative of what has been done to gather information, beginning with when the media arrived and by whom it was delivered and continuing through all operations and results.[71] After the examination is complete, a report is generally prepared, documenting the examination and the data found. The failure to follow these or similar procedures to verify that electronic information was not altered while being copied or analyzed can lead to serious challenges.[72]

---

[69] See Catabran, 836 F.2d 453, 458; Cook, 773 N.E.2d 882, 887 (mirror image of hard drive properly authenticated and admitted where law enforcement forensics technician testified on chain of custody and authentication and detailed process by which mirror images were generated and data downloaded). *See also* Abrams & Weis, *supra* note 2, at 9 ("The work must be done in a way that preserves the value and admissibility of the evidence collected. This requires the investigator to always maintain a well-documented chain of custody, and to follow industry-established procedures for the collection, preservation, and documentation of the data."). Maintaining a proper chain of custody involves the following steps: (1) no data is added or changed; (2) a complete copy is made, meaning a mirror image copy; (3) the expert uses a reliable copying process; and (4) all media is secured. Joan E. Feldman, *Cyber-Sleuthing: Obtaining Facts From Electronic Copies Of Defendants' Documents, Recovering Deleted Files, And The Like,* ATLA Annual Convention Reference Materials (July 2003), *available on* WESTLAW at 2 Ann. 2003 ATLA-CLE 1811.

[70] See also Ellen Byron, *Computer Forensics Sleuths Help Find Fraud*, The Wall Street Journal, March 18, 2003, at B1; Synder & Morelock, *supra* note 45, at 23.

[71] The log should detail how the medium was handled, how it was protected from alteration, and what process was used for making a forensic copy. The log should also contain the condition under which the medium was examined (machine time, operating system, software tool set, etc.). As each tool is used to process the medium, a description of the tool, the results from using the tool, and any printable output from the tool should be contained in the log. The concept is that anyone who could follow the steps in the log should be able to duplicate the results of the examination.

[72] See Joan E. Feldman & Rodger I. Kohn, *The Essentials Of Computer Discovery*, Seventh Annual Internet Law Institute (PLI Patents, Copyrights, Trademarks, & Literary Property Course Handbook Series No. GO-018F, 2003), *available on* WESTLAW at 755 PLI/Pat 649.

Authentication also requires an explanation of the product, *i.e.,* the nature of the electronic documents themselves. For example, the introduction of documentary evidence is governed in part by the Best Evidence Rule, which was developed to assure trustworthiness, accuracy and evidential value and to prevent the admission of fraudulent, fabricated or incomplete copies of records.[73] Though precise and identical duplicates of paper documents can be made with microfilm copiers and facsimile machines, reproducing a complete copy of a complex e-transaction document is considerably more challenging.

Paper documents generally merge content (*i.e.,* what is said) and context (*i.e.,* what a document is and why it came into existence), letting the reader know from the face of the document what it is and why it came into existence. Because e-records were created to promote information functionality, not trustworthiness, accuracy, or evidential significance, their structure is different. They are usually comprised of a group of distinct electronic files often stored in diverse physical locations.[74] For example, in a typical form-based e-transaction or on-line filing, the questions (*e.g.,* boxes to be filled out) are not physically retained with the answers (*i.e.,* the data).[75] Therefore, the content is not connected to the structure or form of the e-record unless a system is implemented to capture both. The testifying expert witness

---

[73] JOHN STRONG ET AL., MCCORMICK ON EVIDENCE, Vol. II, 62-64 (5th ed. 1999).

[74] *See* Martin H. Redish, *Electronic Discovery & The Litigation Matrix,* 51 Duke L. J. 561, 588 (Nov. 2001) ("Electronic documents are likely to be stored in more locations, to be distributed to a wider audience, and to have more prior drafts retained than would paper documents.").

[75] *See, e.g.,* Public Citizen v. Carlin, 2 F. Supp. 2d 1, 5 (D.D.C. 1997), *rev'd on other grounds* 184 F.3d 900 (1999).

THE ROLE OF EXPERTS IN ELECTRONIC DISCOVERY

not only provides the techniques for retrieving the e-document itself, but the expert can uncover and explain the metadata that links the content and context, providing the completeness required for admissibility.[76]

2. Defensive Reasons.

a. Creating Document Retention Programs.

Even with the tremendous storage capabilities of modern computers, a company cannot save everything forever, and it would not want to. On the other hand, some obligation to have retained electronic as well as paper records is sure to be imposed if litigation ensues. *See* Chapter 5, *supra.* A computer forensics expert can help strike the proper balance by assisting in the development of a document retention program.[77] Experts can identify what data is accessible and can be retrieved, and they can estimate the cost of retrieval in the event of litigation.[78] They can also preserve potentially relevant electronic evidence by making mirror images of computer hard drives and by recommending policies that provide for creating such mirror images whenever the computers of employees who leave the company are reassigned. Businesses that are adequately prepared to exchange electronic discovery before litigation arises may avoid costly and time-consuming mistakes and disputes over

---

[76] *See, e.g.*, Armstrong v. Executive Office of the President, 1 F.3d 1274, 1284 (D.C. Cir. 1993) (recognizing that metadata is an essential part of an e-mail and expanding record retention requirements of the Federal Records Act (FRA), 44 U.S.C. §§2101-2118, 2901-2910, 3101-3107, 3301-3324 (1994), to include the complete electronic record of e-mail communications), *rev'd on other grounds* 90 F.3d 553 (1996).

[77] *See* Scheindlin & Rabkin, *supra* note 20 (The authors explain that "[t]he cost and complexity of storing and retrieving electronic data increases with the volume and variety of data stored. For practical reasons, businesses must have some way of deciding what they can discard, and what they must keep. A well-crafted electronic document retention policy is an important first step.").

[78] *See id.*

the retrieval of such information. Having an efficient document retention program will facilitate compliance with court rules mandating that litigants review their information management systems in preparation for discovery.[79] See Chapter 2, *supra*.

Experts can also help companies recognize and adjust to changing requirements for the preservation of electronic data. For instance, securities investigators analyzing the practices of licensed brokers and dealers on Wall Street have recently focused on a new type of evidence: instant messaging records.[80] Unlike e-mail, instant messages are direct person-to-person communications that bypass a company's computer server unless special filtering software has been installed to capture them.[81] In the securities industry, and in a growing number of other industries throughout the country, instant messages need to be archived and retained in the same manner as written correspondence and e-mail.[82] Companies that fail to retain computer forensics experts to provide advice

---

[79] For example, the recently enacted local rule for the United States District Court for the District of New Jersey mandates that "counsel shall review with the client the client's information management systems including computer-based and other digital systems, in order to understand how information is stored and how it can be retrieved." The rule further provides that counsel shall "review with the client the client's information files, including currently maintained computer files as well as historical, archival, backup, and legacy computer files, whether in current or historical media or formats, such as digital evidence which may be used to support claims or defenses [and] identify . . . persons with knowledge about the client's information management systems . . . with the ability to facilitate, through counsel, reasonably anticipated discovery." D.N.J. Loc. Civ. R. 26.1(d). Arkansas, California, Illinois, Maryland, Texas and Wyoming have also enacted rules to codify electronic discovery. See E.D. Ark. Loc. Civ. R. 26.1; W.D. Ark. Loc. Civ. R. 26.1; Cal. Code Civ. P. § 2017; Ill. Sup. Ct. R. 201(b) and 214; Md. R. Civ. P. 2-504.3; Tex. R. Civ. P. 196.4; D. Wy. Loc. Civ. R. 26.1(d).
[80] *See* Elliot Blair Smith, *Wall St. Bloodhounds Track IMs For Clues*, USA Today, Sept. 18, 2003, at B1.
[81] *See id.*
[82] *See id.*

regarding document retention policies in view of new and changing forms of electronic communication, such as instant messages, risk liability for failing to preserve electronic evidence.[83] As discussed in greater detail in Chapter 5, *supra,* courts have imposed sanctions not only for intentional spoliation, but also for negligent retention programs. Sanctions can include adverse inferences to the jury, rulings that evidence is inadmissible, monetary fines, dismissal of case or claim, or default judgment.[84]

In *Danis v. USN Communications, Inc,*[85] for example, the United States District Court for the Northern District of Illinois fined a corporate officer $10,000 and allowed the jury to draw a negative inference after several important documents and e-mails were unintentionally destroyed under the USN Communications, Inc. document retention program. *Danis* involved a suit by investors against USN Communications, Inc. for misrepresentation and securities fraud under § 10(b).[86] The court reprimanded and then fined the corporate officer because he ordered an inexperienced in-house counsel to create the company's retention policy.[87] The ineffective program ultimately led to the destruction of relevant materials.[88] Though the court recognized that the spoliation was unintentional, the court also took note that the officer failed to enlist outside counsel in developing and implementing a comprehensive document retention plan.[89]

---

[83] Rosenthal, *supra* note 44.
[84] Christopher D. Wall & Michele C.S. Lange, *Recent Developments In Electronic Discovery*, Washington Lawyer, March 2003, at pg 3.
[85] No. 98 C 7482, 2000 WL 1694325, at *118 (N.D. Ill. Oct. 23, 2000).
[86] *Id.*
[87] Danis, 2000 WL 1694325 at *120-*21, *158.
[88] *Id.*
[89] *Id.* at *119 - *20.

b. Responding to Discovery Requests.

In the event of litigation, retained experts can anticipate problems in responding to discovery requests, assist counsel in locating and preserving documents and, by highlighting duplicative files and information, can reduce the number of hours that counsel must spend reviewing documents.[90] Using the methods discussed above, they can also restore and authenticate data for production when necessary.

Computer forensics experts can also help counsel prepare a privilege log or develop appropriate search tools to identify non-responsive or privileged data.[91] Doing so can help prevent the inadvertent disclosure of privileged or confidential information, which becomes more likely as the volume of electronic data increases.[92] The costs associated with protecting confidential information cannot generally be shifted to the requesting party. For example, in *Computer Assoc. Int'l, Inc. v. Quest Software, Inc.*,[93] a copyright infringement and trade secret misappropriation suit arising from the allegedly improper use of the plaintiff's source code, plaintiff requested access to a number of the defendants' employees' work and home computer hard drives for electronic imaging so they could be searched for deleted files.[94] Quest argued that, because the drives contained privileged information relating to the litigation, they had to hire a computer consultant to remove it from the images and indicate where the redacted information had been located.[95]

---

[90] Scheindlin & Rabkin, *supra* note 20.
[91] *See* Joan E. Feldman, *The Expert's Role In Computer-Based Discovery*, 14 No. 1 Pract. Litigator 37 (Jan. 2003).
[92] *See* Michael Traynor & Lori Ploeger, *Hot Topics In Electronic Discovery*, Sixth Annual Internet Law Institute, 51, 72-73 (PLI Patents, Copyrights, Trademarks, and Literary Property Course Handbook Series No. G0-00ZE, 2002). *See also* Feldman, *supra* note 91.
[93] No. 02 C 4721, 2003 WL 21277129, at *2 (N.D. Ill. June 3, 2003).
[94] *Id.*
[95] *Id.* at *2-*3.

THE ROLE OF EXPERTS IN ELECTRONIC DISCOVERY 8

Quest sought to have the plaintiff reimburse it for the associated cost of preparing the drives for disclosure.[96] The court refused on the basis that the review was no different from a normal review for privileged information and was for the benefit of the producing party.[97]

B. Who the Experts Are.

Experts usually have a background in law enforcement or computer technology and, as set forth above, provide an array of services regarding the discovery of electronic evidence.[98] Computer forensics experts either perform the traditional role of an expert, helping to educate parties and the court by reviewing computer evidence and preparing forensics reports and affidavits, or they provide consulting or project management tasks instead of preparing a report of their findings.[99] Some of the more common tasks performed by a computer forensics expert in a consulting role in civil litigation include ensuring that an attorney understands the data available for review, identifying and locating computer-based documents, acquiring data from network servers or computer hard drives, reviewing and restoring data, and assisting in the redaction of privileged or confidential information.[100]

Obviously, the expert must be qualified. Experts who use outdated or inappropriate technology may inadvertently destroy computer-based evidence, causing serious repercussions.[101] For example, in *Gates Rubber v. Bando*

---

[96] *Id.* at *3.
[97] *Id.* at *5.
[98] In Consorcio, plaintiff's expert had eleven years' experience working in law enforcement and three in the private sector. 267 F. Supp. 2d at 1294; *see also* Byron, *supra* note 70.
[99] *See* Feldman, *supra* note 91.
[100] *See id.*
[101] *See* Johnson-Laird, *supra* note 19.

Chem. Indus.,[102] defendants and their attorneys were threatened with sanctions for destroying evidence by continuing to use their computers. Ironically, a mitigating factor was that the plaintiff's expert, who had been hired to preserve evidence on the defendants' computers, had inadvertently destroyed massive amounts of evidence through technical ignorance.[103]

C. Selecting a Testifying Expert.

Three main industry associations establish minimum training standards for computer forensics specialists and promulgate industry accepted procedures for the examination of computer media and other electronic evidence.[104] They are (1) the International Association of Computer Investigative Specialists, whose membership is limited to law enforcement personnel and civilian employees of law enforcement agencies; (2) the High Technology Crime Investigation Association, which limits membership primarily to law enforcement personnel but allows civilian computer forensics specialists to become members if they pass background screening; and (3) the High Tech Computer Network, which certifies computer forensics specialists who can meet the organization's standards for training and computer forensics investigation experience.

In addition to possessing the requisite training and expertise in computer forensics, a testifying expert should have litigation experience because the expert is required not only to understand the technical aspects of electronic data

---

[102] 167 F.R.D. 90, 112-13 (D. Colo. 1996). *See also* Johnson-Laird, *supra* note 19, at 3.
[103] *See* Johnson-Laird, *supra* note 19, at 3.
[104] Abrams & Weis, *supra* note 2, at 9.

THE ROLE OF EXPERTS IN ELECTRONIC DISCOVERY

8

retention and restoration but also to authenticate electronically retrieved documents and information at trial.[105] Perhaps most importantly, the testifying expert must be able to explain electronic evidence to a judge or jury concisely and comprehensibly.[106] Explanations that are too complex or too simplistic may dilute the significance of the evidence.[107]

The flexibility of electronic evidence allows for live interactive computer demonstrations, which can make technical points more understandable. For example, the ability to show a jury how embedded edits in an electronic document can be retrieved with a click of the mouse may be far more effective than a detailed technical explanation. Similarly, an expert's demonstrating with metadata that the recipient of an e-mail was selected from the address book entitled "Personal Contacts" is highly effective in contradicting a claim that the sender had no prior contact with the recipient.

The existence of metadata itself creates problems that the computer forensics expert's unique skills can be effective in solving. Unlike paper documents, which contain no hidden information and which, as a result of physical space limitations, are routinely discarded, electronic documents generate staggering amounts of information that can sit indefinitely in electronic storage. It has been estimated that

---

[105] Michelle Johnson, Esq., *Electronic Evidence At Trial: Authentication, Experts, And Focus*, Digital Discovery & e-Evidence, Vol. 1, No. 8 (Sept. 2001).

[106] *Id.; see also* Michael J. Michalowicz, *Computer Harassment? Tap Data-Forensics Sleuths, Steps To Take When Problems Arise*, N.J. Lawyer: The Weekly Newspaper, April 21, 2003, at A3 (noting that "[f]rom depositions to trial, the worth of the data forensics expert often is judged by his or her presentation").

[107] Johnson, *supra* note 105. *See also* Arent, Brownstone & Fenwick, *supra* note 19, at 177 ("The prevailing party in an electronic discovery dispute may be the one whose expert has better credentials and/or more detailed explanation of his or her client's position.").

the metadata for a typical e-mail contains approximately 1,200 pieces of information. With such a wealth of information available, the challenge at trial is to maintain the jury's focus on what is most important. An experienced expert can keep the jury focused on the critical proofs and not allow it to be distracted by computer system details.

Some commentators have suggested that reliance on outside computer forensics experts to locate and analyze electronic data may diminish as the number of in-house experts in law firms increases.[108] On the other hand, the testimony of in-house computer experts may be perceived as biased and therefore less credible than that of an outside expert.[109] Either way, one thing is almost certain: the use of experts will expand as electronic discovery becomes pervasive.

D.   Cost of Experts.

Most computer forensics experts charge between $250 and $500 per hour, depending on the complexity of the task and the volume of records.[110] Less expensive experts can be found.[111] Flat fees are also negotiated for some projects.[112]

---

[108]   See Richard L. Marcus, *Confronting The Future: Coping With Discovery Of Electronic Material*, Law & Contemporary Problems, 253, 269-70 (Spring/Summer 2001).

[109]   See Byron, *supra* note 70 (noting that because computer forensics experts are often outsiders, "[t]hat may make them more credible in the eyes of a judge or jury").

[110]   See id.

[111]   See Earl Ainsworth, *E-Discovery, Five Steps To Success*, Guide to Internet Service 2003-2004, Supplement to New Jersey Lawyer (stating that experts in electronic discovery range in price from $80 to $150 per hour, and that in unusual cases involving sophisticated forensics, the rate can be as high as $250).

[112]   See Byron, *supra* note 70.

E. Court-Appointed Experts.

Rule 706 of the Federal Rules of Evidence gives federal courts the authority to appoint neutral experts in cases involving computer-based discovery.[113] Similarly, when a case involves especially complex technical matters, Rule 53 of the Federal Rules of Civil Procedure allows federal courts to appoint "special masters" to control certain aspects of electronic discovery.[114] Under this rule, special masters are appointed to handle only particularly difficult discovery matters; however, upon consent of both parties, a magistrate may be appointed as a special master, regardless of the nature or complexity of the case.[115] Many states have analogous provisions to govern the appointment of computer forensics experts.

A judge may appoint a neutral third party expert in contentious situations to resolve an impasse between the parties, to supervise technical aspects of electronic discovery, or to act as a repository for particularly sensitive data or data that is otherwise disputed.[116] Courts may also appoint experts

---

[113] Fed. R. Evid. 706 states, in pertinent part, that "[t]he court may on its own motion or on the motion of any party enter an order to show cause why expert witnesses should not be appointed, and may request the parties to submit nominations. The court may appoint any expert witnesses agreed upon by the parties, and may appoint expert witnesses of its own selection."

[114] Reference to a master is the exception and not the rule. *See* Advisory Committee Notes to Rule 53, 2003 Amendments. Appointment of a special master may be deemed inappropriate or unnecessary by the court. *See, e.g.,* Medtronic, 2003 WL 21468573 at *31 -*32 (denying the requesting party's request for appointment of a special master to oversee electronic records production and to review data files produced because the issues were not unusually complicated, and neither party showed that an exceptional condition applied). *But see* Abrams & Weis, *supra* note 2, at 15 (arguing that "[w]here the court is uncertain of the procedures to follow, or lacks the expertise to properly evaluate electronic evidence, special masters, who themselves are experts in the field of computer forensics, should be appointed to aid the court").

[115] Fed. R. Civ. P. 53(b) (2004).

[116] *See* Withers, *supra* note 1.

to address concerns about protecting confidentiality and avoiding harm to a party's computer operating system.[117] In *Dodge, Warren & Peters Ins. Services, Inc. v. Riley*,[118] the California Court of Appeals affirmed the trial court's issuance of a preliminary injunction requiring "the preservation of electronic evidence by prohibiting [the] defendants from destroying, deleting or secreting from discovery any of their electronic storage media and by requiring them to allow a court-appointed expert to copy all of it, including computer hard drives and discs, to recover lost or deleted files and to perform automated searches of that evidence under guidelines agreed to by the parties or established by the court."[119] The court explained that without such an order, the electronic evidence could be irretrievably lost, and that because the copied material would not be available to anyone except upon agreement of the parties or court order, "the concerns over privacy and privilege were minimized to the point of nonexistence."[120]

In some cases, courts may appoint computer forensics experts to examine the authenticity of critical documents. In *Munshani v. Signal Lake Venture Fund II, LP*,[121] the court appointed a computer forensics expert to determine the authenticity of an e-mail. The plaintiff alleged that he was entitled to some $25 million for services rendered to the defendants in connection with the raising of capital for a venture capital fund.[122] In response to a motion to dismiss a similar suit in federal court on Statute of Frauds grounds, the

---

[117] *See* Ehlers, et al., *supra* note 18, at 2.42.
[118] 105 Cal. App. 4th 1414, 1417, 1420-21 (Cal. Ct. App. 2003).
[119] *Id.* at 1417.
[120] *Id.* at 1421.
[121] No. 005529BLS, 2001 WL 1526954, at *1 (Mass. Super. Oct. 9, 2001).
[122] *Id.*

THE ROLE OF EXPERTS IN ELECTRONIC DISCOVERY

plaintiff produced an e-mail, allegedly sent from the chief executive officer of one of the defendants, that would have resolved the Statute of Frauds issue in the plaintiff's favor.[123] After conducting an investigation, the defendants asserted that the e-mail was fraudulent, and the plaintiff responded by proposing that the court appoint a neutral expert to examine the disputed e-mail's authenticity.[124] The court accepted the plaintiff's proposal and appointed a computer forensics expert, who concluded, in a 147-page report, that the e-mail was clearly not authentic.[125] As a result, the court dismissed the complaint and ordered the plaintiff to reimburse the defendants for their contributions towards the costs and fees of the court-appointed expert and for the fees and expenses reasonably charged by defendants' counsel in all matters relating to the discovery of the fraud.[126] Although most cases are not as dramatic as *Munshani*, that case demonstrates the significant role that court-appointed experts can play in resolving electronic discovery disputes.

Courts may also appoint experts to retrieve electronic evidence that has presumably been destroyed. For example, in *Trigon Ins. Co. v. United States*,[127] in response to a motion by the plaintiff, the court ordered that the defendant retain an independent computer forensics expert to report on the retrievability of documents that were allegedly deleted on various computer systems and ordered that both parties report to the court regarding the results of the expert's investigation. The expert located a significant number of missing documents thought to have been destroyed.[128] Defendant was

---

[123] *Id.* at *2.
[124] *Id.*
[125] *Id.* at *2-*3.
[126] *Id.* The court later awarded defendants $62,035.52 in reimbursement for discovery costs.
[127] 204 F.R.D. 277, 290 (E.D. Va. 2001).
[128] *Id.* at 290.

ordered to pay plaintiff $179,725.70 for fees and expenses for the losses incurred from the spoliation of evidence.[129]

In a case involving computer inspections conducted by a court-appointed computer forensics expert, courts are likely to use the following procedure, with modifications depending on the facts of the particular case:

- The parties agree on a neutral, third-party expert to carry out the inspection on behalf of the court. If they cannot so agree, the court appoints the expert based on suggestions by the parties.
- The parties agree on the scope of the inspection, including, but not limited to, target computers or servers; departments; date ranges; and other scope-defining criteria. They also agree on the form of the eventual production of the electronic evidence.
- The expert creates a "mirror image" of the applicable computer(s) that preserves the integrity of the original electronic evidence.
- The expert searches the "mirror image" to identify relevant data in accordance with the specifications that the parties have agreed upon.
- The expert discloses the responsive data to the respondent's attorney, who reviews the data for relevance and privilege.
- The respondent's attorney then produces to the requesting party the relevant, non-privileged data that the expert discovered.[130]

This procedure has been followed by United States District Courts in the Southern District of California in

---

[129] *Id.*
[130] Withers, *supra* note 1.

THE ROLE OF EXPERTS IN ELECTRONIC DISCOVERY

8

Playboy Enterprises, Inc. v. Welles,[131] and in the Southern District of Indiana in *Simon Property Group L.P. v. mySimon, Inc.*[132] In both cases, the court appointed a computer forensics expert in response to requests by the plaintiffs for the production of electronic evidence, and the court explicitly noted that the expert would act as an officer of the court and that any disclosure of information to the expert would not be deemed a waiver of the attorney-client privilege.[133] The experts were required to sign a protective order to preserve the confidentiality of privileged material.[134]

The above protocols assist the parties in setting clear goals for computer-based discovery, help limit the scope and cost of such discovery, and protect legitimate privilege and privacy concerns. They also provide a mechanism for allocating some of the costs. In each of the cases cited above, the requesting party paid the expenses of the neutral expert.[135]

Courts have examined and modified these protocols based on the facts of the particular case. For instance, in *Antioch Co. v. Scrapbook Borders, Inc.*,[136] a copyright infringement and unfair competition lawsuit, the court granted the plaintiff's motion to appoint a neutral expert before discovery had even begun because the defendants used e-mail as a form of communication for business use and may have stored relevant information that was being lost through normal use

---

[131] 60 F. Supp. 2d 1050, 1054-55 (S.D. Cal. 1999), *aff'd in part, rev'd in part on other grounds* 279 F.3d 796 (9th Cir. 2002).
[132] 194 F.R.D. 639, 641-42 (S.D. Ind. 2000).
[133] *See* Welles, 60 F. Supp. 2d at 1054-55; Simon, 194 F.R.D. at 641-42.
[134] Welles, 60 F. Supp. 2d at 1054-55; Simon, 194 F.R.D. at 642 (S.D. Ind. 2000). *See also* Travers v. McKinstry Co., No. Civ. 01-1206-J0, 2001 WL 34041790, at *1 (D. Or. Nov. 16, 2001)(appointing computer forensics expert as officer of court and noting that upon signing of appropriate protective order, all communications between expert and party requesting information must take place in presence of opposing counsel).
[135] *See* Withers, *supra* note 1.
[136] 210 F.R.D. 645, 646 (D. Minn. 2002).

of the computer equipment.[137] In formulating the procedures for the expert, the court in *Antioch* analyzed the procedures set forth in *Welles* and *Simon* and adopted "an amalgamation" of the procedures in those two cases.[138] The court required the plaintiff to select a computer forensics expert to produce a mirror image of the defendants' computer equipment.[139] Upon selecting an expert, the plaintiff had an obligation to notify the defendants of the expert, at which point the defendants were required to make their computer equipment available to the expert at their place of business at a mutually agreeable time.[140] The court ordered that the expert use its best efforts to avoid unnecessarily disrupting the normal activities or business operations of the defendants while inspecting, copying, and imaging the defendants' computer equipment.[141] Neither the plaintiff nor its counsel could inspect the computer equipment produced by the defendants, and the expert was required to maintain all information that it obtained in strict confidence.[142]

Within ten days of its inspection, the expert was required to provide both parties with a detailed description of the computer equipment produced by the defendants for inspection and to document the chain of custody for any electronic evidence drawn from the equipment.[143] The court directed that once the expert produced a mirror image of the defendants' hard drives, one copy be given to the court and a second copy be given to the defendants so they could sift

---

[137] In this regard, an expert retained by the plaintiff explained to the court that "data which is deleted from a computer is retained on the hard drive, but is constantly being overwritten by new data, through the normal use of the computer equipment." *Id.* at 651.
[138] *Id.* at 653.
[139] *Id.*
[140] *Id.*
[141] *Id.*
[142] *Id.*
[143] *Id.*

THE ROLE OF EXPERTS IN ELECTRONIC DISCOVERY

8

through the data in responding to the plaintiff's discovery requests and produce responsive documents and a privilege log.[144]

Other courts have adopted similar discovery protocols. In *Medtronic*,[145] another case involving trade secrets, patents and trade information, the defendant filed a motion to compel the production of substantial electronic evidence. In response, the court developed a detailed discovery plan for production of electronic documents and ordered the parties to select a neutral computer expert whose duties included "advising the parties with regard to any agreement on additional search terms; overseeing the flow and scheduling of production; coordinating deliverables between the parties and their vendors; [and] advising both parties, at either's request, on cost estimates and technical issues."[146] The court also found that the expert "shall be subject to all confidentiality requirements and protective orders set forth in this and in other orders in this case," and, if the expert designates any assistants, those assistants would also be subject to the same confidentiality obligations.[147] The parties were required to bear the costs of the computer expert's services equally.[148]

Courts will not always grant a party's request to appoint an expert to conduct electronic discovery or examine the authenticity of documents. In *Stallings-Daniel v. The Northern Trust Co.*,[149] the court denied the plaintiff's request for the appointment of an expert to investigate the defendant's e-mail files because the request was supported by nothing more than speculation. Accordingly, before requesting the

---

[144] *Id.* at 653-54.
[145] *Supra* note 32; 2003 WL 21468573 at *50 -*51.
[146] *Id.* at 50.
[147] *Id.*
[148] *Id.*
[149] No. 01 C 2290 2002 WL 385566, at *1 (N.D. Ill. March 12, 2002).

appointment of an expert, a party should be confident that it has a good faith basis for making the request.

As the above-referenced cases make clear, courts are becoming increasingly aware of the important role that experts can and should play with regard to electronic discovery. Attorneys involved in all facets of litigation should remain cognizant of how computer forensics experts can protect their client's interests throughout litigation.

GLOSSARY

Accessible Data – Information that is considered searchable and retrievable, such as information stored on a local hard drive or a server.

Active Data – Information that is stored either on a network server or locally on a hard drive and is currently available and readily accessible to end-users through a desktop or other computer connection.

Application Software – A program that performs a specific function directly for the user, also known as an "end-user program." This is in contrast to operating system software, which exists to support application software.[4]

Archive – A long-term storage area for copies of files or for files no longer in active use. Information stored in some archival systems, such as disks and optical drives, is considered "accessible data."[1]

Attachment – A file connected to an e-mail message.

Authentication – The act of proving that something, such as a document, is true or genuine, especially so it may be admitted as evidence.[2]

Back-Up Data – Data copied by network administrators to removable or remote media, such as disk or a tape, to provide data redundancy in the event of a system failure. The information stored in a back-up system is generally considered "inaccessible data."

Boolean Search – A form of search limited by specified distances between, and groupings of, words or numbers.

Buffer – A device or area used to store data temporarily and deliver it at a rate different from that at which it was received, as when a printer receives a document almost instantaneously and then prints it at a speed permitted by its machinery.

Burn – To imprint data onto a CD-ROM.

Bus – One of the sets of conductors connecting the various functional units in a computer.

C:/drive – *See* Hard Drive.

Cache – A small and fast memory that temporarily holds recently accessed data, designed to speed up subsequent access to the same data.[4]

CD-ROM – A compact disk that functions as read-only memory.[1]

CIO – Chief Information Officer.

Compress – To transform data to minimize the space required for its storage or transmission.[1]

Concept Search – A forensics tool that provides an efficient and accurate search of a hard drive by identifying word patterns and occurrences in documents and translating these patterns into concepts.

Cookies – Data files written onto a user's hard drive by a web server and later exchanged with the web server to identify the user each time the browser requests a page (*e.g.*, usernames and passwords).

Cost-shifting – Allocating the high cost of producing voluminous electronic records in response to extensive electronic discovery requests by having some percentage of the cost fall on the requesting party.

Data – Information on the computer system stored as bits and bytes in electronic memory.

Database – A collection of data arranged for ease and speed of search and retrieval.[1]

Digital Audio Tape (DAT) – A type of back-up medium that stores large quantities of data arranged in linear fashion.

Disk Drive – A machine that reads from, and writes data onto, a disk. While the disk rotates very fast, one or more "heads" read and write data.

Document Management Retention Policy (DMRP) – A policy that governs the review, retention and destruction of the paper and electronic documents that a company creates or receives.

Document – Under Rule 34 of the Federal Rules of Civil Procedure, includes "writings, drawing, graphs, charts, photographs, phonorecords and other data compilations from which information can be obtained, translated, if necessary, by the respondent through detection devices into reasonably usable form." Fed. R. Civ. P. 34(a).

DVD – A digital video disk, similar to a CD-Rom, used to store large amounts of data, especially audio-visual material.

Electronic Stickies – Electronic notes or reminders that authors and reviewers of documents can leave for each other.

E-mail – Electronic mail: the transmission of messages, usually text, from one person to another, by computer over communications networks.[4]

GLOSSARY

Embedded Data – Substantive information created by the user and hidden within the file itself. This includes, for example, the substance of previous edits, formatting commands, links to other files, hidden rows or columns in spreadsheets, and electronic stickies.

End-User Programs – *See* Application Software.

File – A collection of data or information that has a name, called the filename. Almost all information stored in a computer must be in a file.[3]

File Allocation Table (FAT) – Maintained by Windows-based file systems (called Master File Tables "MFTs" in certain Window systems). They enable the computer to know where saved documents are stored for later retrieval. FATs and MFTs also contain metadata.

File Extension – The portion of a filename, following the final point, which indicates the kind of data stored in the file (*e.g.*, .doc, .jpeg, .pdf).[4]

File Server – A computer and/or storage device dedicated to being the central repository of files.

Floppy Disk – A flexible plastic disk coated with magnetic material and covered by a protective jacket, used primarily to store data.[1]

Forensics – The use of science and technology to investigate and establish facts in criminal or civil courts of law.[1]

Group Shares – *See* Shared Drives.

Hard Drive – The mechanism that reads and writes data on the computer hard disk.[3]

Hardware - A computer and the associated physical equipment directly involved in the performance of data-processing or communications functions.[1]

Harvesting Protocol – A procedure for regulating data transmission between computers to sort each computer's files by file extension and then to extract only the files with those extensions.

Header – The part of an electronic mail message that precedes the body of the message and contains, among other things, the sender's name and e-mail address and the date and time the message was sent.[4]

Home Directory – Private space located on the hard drive(s) of the file server to which users can save files.

Inaccessible Data – Information that is not easily searchable or retrievable, such as the information stored on back-up magnetic tapes.

Incremental Back-up – The process of copying data from a server onto removable or remote media in full once during a specified time frame and supplementing that copy with additional copies of only files that have changed over a shorter time period. This process is used for large servers that contain too much data for the system to be repeatedly backed up in full.

Instant Message – Direct, real-time, person-to-person, textual communication over the internet.

IP Address – Internet Protocol Address. Establishes the format of the datagram (packet) and the address scheme. Analogous to putting an address on a postal delivery package.[3]

Jaz Drive – Iomega Corporation's drive that uses removable one or two gigabyte disk cartridges that contain conventional hard disks.[4]

Keyword Search – A search using a word as a reference point for finding other words or information.[1]

Litigation Hold – Mandated document retention once a company is put on notice that litigation is likely.

Master File Table (MFT) – *See* File Allocation Table (FAT).

Medium – An object or device, such as a disk, on which data is stored (plural: "media").[1]

Memory – Data storage on computer chips, as opposed to tapes or disks (which are media).

Metadata – Described as "data about data." It includes information that records, among other things, when a document was created, last accessed, last modified and last printed, and who created the document.

Mirror Image – An exact duplicate of the data on a computer hard drive. It is used by forensics experts to inspect the contents of the hard drive without endangering it.

MIS Department – Management Information System (MIS) Department, also known as Information Technology (IT) Department. Groups of technicians who have the day-to-day responsibility for designing and administrating the company's computer system.

Native Form – An original document that contains both metadata and embedded data.

GLOSSARY

Near-line Data – Data stored in removable media such as Floppy disks or CD-ROMs, which are fully searchable once inserted into a drive and can be automatically accessed by a mechanical system.

Network – The hardware and software that connects computers and allows them to share data.

> *Local Area Network (LAN)* – Computers located close together.
> *Wide Area Network (WAN)* – Computers located far apart, connected by telephone, cable lines or radio waves.

On-line Data – Active data that is accessible in the ordinary course of business.

Operating System – The system software on which all other software depends to make the computer functional. Operating systems perform basic tasks, such as recognizing input from the keyboard, sending output to the display screen, keeping track of files and directories on the disk, and controlling peripheral devices such as disk drives and printers.[3]

Optical Drives – A secondary storage medium for computers. Information is stored on high-density disks in the form of tiny pits read by laser.[3]

.Ost Files – Hidden files created by certain e-mail programs. They can be forensically converted into .pst files, which can be read to reveal large caches of past e-mail, calendar items and tasks.

Overwrite – To write new data on top of existing data so that it takes the place of the previous data.

PDA – Personal Digital Assistant. A lightweight, hand-held, usually pen-based computer used as a personal organizer.[1]

PDF - Portable Document Format. File format developed by Adobe Systems. PDF captures formatting information from a variety of desktop publishing applications, making it possible to send formatted documents and have them appear on the recipient's monitor or printer as intended.[4]

PDF'ing – Process of creating a PDF image file.

Perl Scripts – A specially tailored program used to cull documents of relevant users from a group share.

Privilege – A special legal right, exemption, or immunity granted to a person or class of persons.[2]

Protocol – A procedure for regulating data transmission between computers.

.Pst Files – Files converted from .ost files that reveal large caches of past e-mail, calendar items and tasks from certain e-mail programs.

QIC Tapes – Quarter Inch Cartridge Tapes. A type of back-up medium that stores large quantities of data arranged in linear fashion.

Record – As defined by the Uniform Rules of Evidence, a record is information that is inscribed on a tangible medium or that is stored in an electronic or other medium and is retrievable in perceivable form and includes items created on a computer, as through word processing or spreadsheet programs; records sent or received, such as e-mail; data stored through scanning or image processing of paper originals; and information compiled into databases. *See* Uniform Rules of Evidence (1999), Rule 101 and comment.

Remote Access – The ability to log onto a network from a distant location.[3]

Removable Media – Objects or devices, such as disks, tapes, and drives, on which data is stored and which can be moved to different locations for the purpose of data retrieval in the event of system failure.

Replicant Data – Duplicate files created by the operating system on the user's hard drive as back-ups in the event of malfunction or in the course of printing a paper copy.

Residual Data – Data that is retained on the hard drive after deletion. Though it is not readily retrievable through normal end-user operations, it will not be erased until it is overwritten.

Rotation – A cycle in which data on a server, typically smaller servers, are backed up in full each day for several weeks.

Sarbanes-Oxley (SOX) – A federal statute imposing harsh criminal penalties on any person who knowingly destroys, alters or conceals documents with the intent to impede, obstruct or influence the investigation or proper administration of any matter within the jurisdiction of any department or agency of the United States or in relation to or in contemplation of any such matter (15 U.S.C. Section 7201 et seq. (2002)).

GLOSSARY

Server – A computer that provides service (e.g., file, e-mail, web, and database) for other computers connected to it in a network.[4]

Client/Server Model – A computer serves as a central repository for data and programs that can be accessed over the network by other computers, called clients.
Peer-to-Peer Model – Any workstation on the network can act as the file server to which users will save documents they create or receive, as opposed to being saved on a central server.

Shared Drive – Home directories where users can post documents for others to view and modify.

Slack Space – The portion of the hard drive where deleted and unsaved data resides. Also known as "Swap Files."

Software – Computer instructions or programs.

Source Code – The language in which software is originally written, later translated into machine language format called object code.[3]

Spoliation – The destruction, failure to preserve, or significant alteration of evidence for use by another person in pending or future litigation.

Tiffing – Technology that creates an image file (Tiff), which is a snapshot of the surface of a document. It can be read only in specialized viewers such as Microsoft Imaging or Adobe Acrobat.

Travan Tapes – A type of back-up medium that stores large quantities of data arranged in linear fashion.

Unallocated Free Space – The portion of the hard drive where deleted and unsaved data reside.

USB – Universal Serial Bus. An interface that facilitates communication between a computer and external peripheral devices. A single USB port can be used to connect up to 127 peripheral devices, such as mice, keyboards, printers and microphones.

USB Thumb Drive – A compact, removable data storage device that attaches to a computer by way of a USB port.

Utilities – Programs that perform specific tasks related to the management of computer functions, resources, or files, such as password protection, memory management, virus protection, and file compression.[1]

Welles-Simon Protocol – A standardized procedure for protecting privileged and other confidential information during the forensic examination of a hard drive or back-up media.

Wipe Programs – Software designed to overwrite unallocated free space and slack space on a computer with zeros, ones, and other junk data for the purpose of erasing residual data.

Work Product – Tangible material or its intangible equivalent – in unwritten or oral form – that was either prepared by or for a lawyer or prepared for litigation, either planned or in progress.[2]

Zip Drive – A disk drive from Iomega Corporation that uses removable 100, 250, or 750 megabyte hard disks.

---

[1]   The American Heritage® Dictionary of the English Language, Fourth Edition, Houghton Mifflin Company, Copyright 2000.
[2]   Black's Law Dictionary Second Pocket Edition, West Group, Copyright 2001.
[3]   Webopedia: The only online dictionary and search engine you need for computer and Internet technology definitions., http://www.webopedia.com
[4]   The Free On-line Dictionary of Computing, http://www.foldoc.org/, Editor Denis Howe

APPENDIX A

PROPOSED AMENDMENTS TO THE FEDERAL RULES OF CIVIL PROCEDURE*

Rule 16. Pretrial Conferences; Scheduling; Management

*****

(b) Scheduling and Planning. Except in categories of actions exempted by district court rule as inappropriate, the district judge, or a magistrate judge when authorized by district court rule, shall, after receiving the report from the parties under Rule 26(f) or after consulting with the attorneys for the parties and any unrepresented parties by a scheduling conference, telephone, mail, or other suitable means, enter a scheduling order that limits the time

(1) to join other parties and to amend the pleadings;

(2) to file motions; and

(3) to complete discovery.

The scheduling order may also include

(4) modifications of the times for disclosures under Rules 26(a) and 26(e)(1) and of the extent of discovery to be permitted;

(5) provisions for disclosure or discovery of electronically stored information;

(6) adoption of the parties' agreement for protection against waiving privilege;

(7~~5~~) the date or dates for conferences before trial, a final pretrial conference, and trial; and

(8~~6~~) any other matters appropriate in the circumstances of the case.

---

* New material is underlined; matter to be omitted is lined through.

The order shall issue as soon as practicable but in any event within 90 days after the appearance of a defendant and within 120 days after the complaint has been served on a defendant. A schedule shall not be modified except upon a showing of good cause and by leave of the district judge or, when authorized by local rule, by a magistrate judge.

*****

Committee Note

The amendment to Rule 16(b) is designed to alert the court to the possible need to address the handling of discovery of electronically stored information early in the litigation if such discovery is expected to occur. Rule 26(f) is amended to direct the parties to discuss discovery of electronically stored information if such discovery is contemplated in the action. Form 35 is amended to call for a report to the court about the results of this discussion. In many instances, the court's involvement early in the litigation will help avoid difficulties that might otherwise arise.

Rule 16(b) is also amended to include among the topics that may be addressed in the scheduling order any agreements that the parties reach to facilitate discovery by minimizing the risk of waiver of privilege. Rule 26(f) is amended to add to the discovery plan the parties' proposal for the court to enter a case-management order adopting such an agreement. The parties may agree to various arrangements. For example, they may agree to initial provision of requested materials without waiver of privilege to enable the party seeking production to designate the materials desired for actual production, with the privilege review of only those materials to follow Alternatively, they may agree that if privileged information is inadvertently produced the producing party may by timely notice assert the privilege and obtain return of the materials without waiving the privilege. Other arrangements are possible. A case-management order to effectuate the parties' agreement may be helpful in avoiding delay and excessive cost in discovery. *See Manual for Complex Litigation* (4th) § 11.446. Rule 16(b)(6) recognizes the propriety of including such directives in the court's case management order. Court adoption of the chosen procedure by order advances enforcement of the agreement between the parties and adds protection against nonparty assertions that privilege has been waived. The rule does not provide the court with authority to enter such a case-management order without party agreement, or limit the court's authority to act on motion.

Rule 26. General Provisions Governing Discovery; Duty of Disclosure

*****

(b) Discovery Scope and Limits. Unless otherwise limited by order of the court in accordance with these rules, the scope of discovery is as follows:

*****

> **(2) Limitations.** By order, the court may alter the limits in these rules on the number of depositions and interrogatories or the length of depositions under Rule 30. By order or local rule, the court may also limit the number of requests under Rule 36. The frequency or extent of use of the

discovery methods otherwise permitted under these rules and by any local rule shall be limited by the court if it determines that: (i) the discovery sought is unreasonably cumulative or duplicative, or is obtainable from some other source that is more convenient, less burdensome, or less expensive; (ii) the party seeking discovery has had ample opportunity by discovery in the action to obtain the information sought; or (iii) the burden or expense of the proposed discovery outweighs its likely benefit, taking into account the needs of the case, the amount in controversy, the parties' resources, the importance of the issues at stake in the litigation, and the importance of the proposed discovery in resolving the issues. The court may act upon its own initiative after reasonable notice or pursuant to a motion under Rule 26(c). <u>A party need not provide discovery of electronically stored information that the party identifies as not reasonably accessible. On motion by the requesting party, the responding party must show that the information is not reasonably accessible. If that showing is made, the court may order discovery of the information for good cause and may specify terms and conditions for such discovery.</u>

*****

(5)   Claims of Privilege or Protection of Trial Preparation Materials.

(A)   *Privileged information withheld.* When a party withholds information otherwise discoverable under these rules by claiming that it is privileged or subject to protection as trial preparation material, the party shall make the claim expressly and shall describe the nature of the documents, communications, or things not produced or disclosed in a manner that, without revealing information itself privileged or protected, will enable other parties to assess the applicability of the privilege or protection.

(B)   *Privileged information produced.* When a party produces information without intending to waive a claim of privilege it may, within a reasonable time, notify any party that received the information of its claim of privilege. After being notified, a party must promptly return, sequester, or destroy the specified information and any copies. The producing party must comply with Rule 26(b)(5)(A) with regard to the information and preserve it pending a ruling by the court.

*****

(f)   Conference of Parties; Planning for Discovery. Except in categories of proceedings exempted from initial disclosure under

Rule 26(a)(1)(E) or when otherwise ordered, the parties must, as soon as practicable and in any event at least 21 days before a scheduling conference is held or a scheduling order is due under Rule 16(b), confer to consider the nature and basis of their claims and defenses and the possibilities for a prompt settlement or resolution of the case, to make or arrange for the disclosures required by Rule 26(a)(1), <u>to discuss any issues relating to preserving discoverable information</u>, and to develop a proposed discovery plan that indicates the parties' views and proposals concerning:

>   **(1)** what changes should be made in the timing, form, or requirement for disclosures under Rule 26(a), including a statement as to when disclosures under Rule 26(a)(1) were made or will be made;
>
>   **(2)** the subjects on which discovery may be needed, when discovery should be completed, and whether discovery should be conducted in phases or be limited to or focused upon particular issues;
>
>   **<u>(3)</u>** <u>any issues relating to disclosure or discovery of electronically stored information, including the form in which it should be produced;</u>
>
>   **<u>(4)</u>** <u>whether, on agreement of the parties, the court should enter an order protecting the right to assert privilege after production of privileged information;</u>
>
>   **(5~~3~~)** what changes should be made in the limitations on discovery imposed under these rules or by local rule, and what other limitations should be imposed; and

APPENDIX A

(64) any other orders that should be entered by the court under Rule 26(c) or under Rule 16(b) and (c).

The attorneys of record and all unrepresented parties that have appeared in the case are jointly responsible for arranging the conference, for attempting in good faith to agree on the proposed discovery plan, and for submitting to the court within 14 days after the conference a written report outlining the plan. A court may order that the parties or attorneys attend the conference in person. If necessary to comply with its expedited schedule for Rule 16(b) conferences, a court may by local rule (i) require that the conference between the parties occur fewer than 21 days before the scheduling conference is held or a scheduling order is due under Rule 16(b), and (ii) require that the written report outlining the discovery plan be filed fewer than 14 days after the conference between the parties, or excuse the parties from submitting a written report and permit them to report orally on their discovery plan at the Rule 16(b) conference.

*****

Committee Note

Subdivision (b)(2). The amendment to Rule 26(b)(2) is designed to address some of the distinctive features of electronically stored information, including the volume of that information, the variety of locations in which it might be found, and the difficulty of locating, retrieving, and producing certain electronically stored information. Many parties have significant quantities of electronically stored information that can be located, retrieved, or reviewed only with very substantial effort or expense. For example, some information may be stored solely for disaster-recovery purposes and be expensive and difficult to use for other purposes. Time-consuming and costly restoration of the data may be required and it may not be organized in a way that permits searching for information relevant to the action. Some information may be "legacy' data retained in obsolete systems; such data is no longer used and may be costly and burdensome to restore and retrieve. Other information may have been deleted in a way that makes it inaccessible without resort to expensive and uncertain forensic techniques, even though technology may provide the capability to retrieve and produce it through extraordinary efforts. Ordinarily such information would not be considered reasonably accessible.

In many instances, the volume of potentially responsive information that is reasonably accessible will be very large, and the effort and extra expense needed to obtain additional information may be substantial. The rule addresses this concern by providing that a responding party need not provide electronically stored information that it identifies as not reasonably accessible. If the requesting party moves to compel additional discovery under Rule 37(a), the responding party must show that the information is not reasonably accessible. Even if the information is not reasonably accessible, the court may nevertheless order discovery for good cause, subject to the provisions of Rule 26(b)(2)(i), (ii), and (iii).

The *Manual for Complex Litigation* (4th) § 11.446 illustrates the problems of volume that can arise with electronically stored information:

> The sheer volume of such data, when compared with conventional paper

APPENDIX A

documentation, can be staggering. A floppy disk, with 1.44 megabytes, is the equivalent of 720 typewritten pages of plain text. A CD-ROM, with 650 megabytes, can hold up to 325,000 typewritten pages. One gigabyte is the equivalent of 500,000 typewritten pages. Large corporate computer networks create backup data measured in terabytes, or 1,000,000 megabytes: each terabyte represents the equivalent of 500 billion typewritten pages of plain text.

With volumes of these dimensions, it is sensible to limit discovery to that which is within Rule 26(b)(1) and reasonably accessible, unless a court orders broader discovery based on a showing of good cause.

Whether given information is "reasonably accessible" may depend on a variety of circumstances. One referent would be whether the party itself routinely accesses or uses the information. If the party routinely uses the information–sometimes called "active data"–the information would ordinarily be considered reasonably accessible. The fact that the party does not routinely access the information does not necessarily mean that access requires substantial effort or cost.

Technological developments may change what is "reasonably accessible" by removing obstacles to using some electronically stored information. But technological change can also impede access by, for example, changing the systems necessary to retrieve and produce the information.

The amendment to Rule 26(b)(2) excuses a party responding to a discovery request from providing electronically stored information on the ground that it is not reasonably accessible. The responding party must identify the information it is neither reviewing nor producing on this ground. The specificity the responding party must use in identifying such electronically stored information will vary with the circumstances of the case. For example, the responding party may describe a certain type of information, such as information stored solely for disaster recovery purposes. In other cases, the difficulty of accessing the information–as with "legacy" data stored on obsolete systems–can be described. The goal is to inform the requesting party that some requested information has not been reviewed or provided on the ground that it is not reasonably accessible, the nature of this information, and the basis for the responding party's contention that it is not reasonably accessible. But if the responding party has actually accessed the requested information, it may not rely on this rule as an excuse from providing discovery, even if it incurred substantial expense in accessing the information.

If the requesting party moves to compel discovery, the responding party must show that the information sought is not reasonably accessible to invoke this rule. Such a motion would provide the occasion for the court to determine whether the information is reasonably accessible; if it is, this rule does not limit discovery, although other limitations–such as those in Rule 26(b)(2)(i), (ii), and (iii)–may apply. Similarly, if the responding party sought to be relieved from providing such information, as on a motion under Rule 26(c), it would have to demonstrate that the information is not reasonably accessible to invoke the protections of this rule.

The rule recognizes that, as with any discovery, the court may impose appropriate terms and conditions. Examples include sampling electronically stored information

APPENDIX A

to gauge the likelihood that relevant information will be obtained, the importance of that information, and the burdens and costs of production; limits on the amount of information to be produced; and provisions regarding the cost of production.

When the responding party demonstrates that the information is not reasonably accessible, the court may nevertheless order discovery if the requesting party shows good cause. The good-cause analysis would balance the requesting party's need for the information and the burden on the responding party. Courts addressing such concerns have properly referred to the limitations in Rule 26(b)(2)(i), (ii), and (iii) for guidance in deciding when and whether the effort involved in obtaining such information is warranted. Thus *Manual for Complex Litigation* (4th) § 11.446 invokes Rule 26(b)(2), stating that "the rule should be used to discourage costly, speculative, duplicative, or unduly burdensome discovery of computer data and systems." It adds: "More expensive forms of production, such as production of word-processing files with all associated metadata or production of data in specified nonstandard format, should be conditioned upon a showing of need or sharing expenses."

The proper application of those principles can be developed through judicial decisions in specific situations. Caselaw has already begun to develop principles for making such determinations. *See, e.g., Zubulake* v. *UBS Warburg LLC,* 217 F.R.D. 309 (S.D.N.Y. 2003); *Rowe Entertainment, Inc. v. William Morris Agency,* 205 F.R.D. 421 S.D.N.Y. 2002); *McPeek v. Ashcroft,* 202 F.R.D. 31 (D.D.C. 2001). Courts will adapt the principles of Rule 26(b)(2) to the specific circumstances of each case.

Subdivision (b)(5). The Committee has repeatedly been advised that privilege waiver, and the review required to avoid it, add to the costs and delay of discovery. Rule 26(b)(5)(A) provides a procedure for a party that has withheld information on grounds of privilege to make a privilege claim so that the requesting party can contest the claim and the court can resolve the dispute. Rule 26(b)(5)(B) is added to provide a procedure for a party that has produced privileged information without intending to waive the privilege to assert that claim and permit the matter to be presented to the court for its determination.

Rule 26(b)(5)(B) does not address whether there has been a privilege waiver. Rule 26(f) is amended to direct the parties to discuss privilege issues in their discovery plan, and Rule 16(b) is amended to alert the court to consider a case-management order to provide for protection against waiver of privilege. Orders entered under Rule 16(b)(6) may bear on whether a waiver has occurred. In addition, the courts have developed principles for determining whether waiver results from inadvertent production of privileged information. *See* 8 Fed. Prac. & Pro. § 2016.2 at 239-46. Rule 26(b)(5)(B) provides a procedure for addressing these issues.

Under Rule 26(b)(5)(B), a party that has produced privileged information must notify the parties who received the information of its claim of privilege within a "reasonable time." Many factors bear on whether the party gave notice within a reasonable time in a given case, including the date when the producing party learned of the production, the extent to which other parties had made use of the information in connection with the litigation, the difficulty of discerning that the material was privileged, and the magnitude of production.

APPENDIX A

The rule does not prescribe a particular method of notice. As with the question whether notice has been given in a reasonable time, the manner of notice should depend on the circumstances of the case. In many cases informal but very rapid and effective means of asserting a privilege claim as to produce information, followed by more formal notice, would be reasonable. Whatever the method, the notice should be as specific as possible about the information claimed to be privileged, and about the producing party's desire that the information be promptly returned, sequestered, or destroyed.

Each party that received the information must promptly return, sequester, or destroy it on being notified. The option of sequestering or destroying the information is included because the receiving party may have incorporated some of the information in protected trial-preparation materials. After receiving notice, a party must not use, disclose, or disseminate the information pending resolution of the privilege claim. A party that has disclosed or provided the information to a nonparty before receiving notice should attempt to obtain the return of the information or arrange for it to be destroyed.

Whether the information is returned or not, the producing party must assert its privilege in compliance with Rule 26(b)(5)(A) and preserve the information pending the court's ruling on whether the privilege is properly asserted and whether it was waived. As with claims of privilege made under Rule 26(b)(5)(A), there may be no ruling if the other parties do not contest the claim.

If the party that received the information contends that it is not privileged, or that the privilege has been waived, it may present the issue to the court by moving to compel production of the information.

Subdivision (f). Early attention to managing discovery of electronically stored information can be important. Rule 26(f) is amended to direct the parties to discuss these subjects during their discovery-planning conference. *See Manual for Complex Litigation* (4th) § 11.446 ("The judge should encourage the parties to discuss the scope of proposed computer-based discovery early in the case. . ."). The rule focuses on "issues related to disclosure or discovery of electronically stored information"; the discussion is not required in cases not involving electronic discovery, and the amendment imposes no additional requirements in those cases. When the parties do anticipate disclosure or discovery of electronically stored information, addressing the issues at the outset should often avoid problems that might otherwise arise later in the litigation, when they are more difficult to resolve.

When a case involves discovery of electronically stored information, the issues to be addressed during the Rule 26(f) conference depend on the nature and extent of the contemplated discovery and of the parties' information systems. It may be important for the parties to discuss those systems, and accordingly important for counsel to become familiar with those systems before the conference. With that information, the parties can develop a discovery plan that takes into account capabilities of their computer systems. In appropriate cases identification of, and early discovery from, individuals with special knowledge of a party's computer systems may be helpful.

The particular issues regarding electronically stored information that deserve attention during the discovery planning stage depend on the specifics of the given case. *See Manual for Complex Litigation* (4th) § 40.25(2) (listing topics for discussion in a proposed order regarding meet-and-confer

APPENDIX A

sessions). For example, the parties may specify the topics for such discovery and the time period for which discovery will be sought. They may identify the various sources of such information within a party's control that should be searched for electronically stored information. They may discuss whether the information is reasonably accessible to the party that has it, including the burden or cost of retrieving and reviewing the information. *See* Rule 26(b)(2). The form or format in which a party keeps such information may be considered, as well as the form in which it might be produced. "Early agreement between the parties regarding the forms of production will help eliminate waste and duplication." *Manual for Complex Litigation* (4th) § 11.446. Even if there is no agreement, discussion of this topic may prove useful. Rule 34(b) is amended to permit a party to specify the form in which it wants electronically stored information produced. An informed request is more likely to avoid difficulties than one made without adequate information.

Form 35 is also amended to add the parties' proposals regarding disclosure or discovery of electronically stored information to the list of topics to be included in the parties' report to the court. Any aspects of disclosing or discovering electronically stored information discussed under Rule 26(f) may be included in the report to the court. Any that call for court action, such as the extent of the search for information, directions on evidence preservation, or cost allocation, should be included. The court may then address the topic in its Rule 16(b) order.

Rule 26(f) is also amended to direct the parties to discuss any issues regarding preservation of discoverable information during their conference as they develop a discovery plan. The volume and dynamic nature of electronically stored information may complicate preservation obligations. The ordinary operation of computers involves both the automatic creation and the automatic deletion or overwriting of certain information. Complete cessation of that activity could paralyze a party's operations. *Cf. Manual for Complex Litigation* (4th) § 11.422 ("A blanket preservation order may be prohibitively expensive and unduly burdensome for parties dependent on computer systems for their day-to-day operations.") Rule 37(f) addresses these issues by limiting sanctions for loss of electronically stored information due to the routine operation of a party's electronic information system. The parties' discussion should aim toward specific provisions, balancing the need to preserve relevant evidence with the need to continue routine activities critical to ongoing business. Wholesale or broad suspension of the ordinary operation of computer disaster-recovery systems, in particular, is rarely warranted. Failure to attend to these issues early in the litigation increases uncertainty and raises a risk of later unproductive controversy. Although these issues have great importance with regard to electronically stored information, they are also important with hard copy and other tangible evidence. Accordingly, the rule change should prompt discussion about preservation of all evidence, not just electronically stored information.

Rule 26(f) is also amended to provide that the discovery plan may include any agreement that the court enter a case-management order facilitating discovery by protecting against privilege waiver. The Committee has repeatedly been advised about the discovery difficulties that can result from efforts to guard against waiver of privilege. Frequently parties find it necessary to spend large amounts of time reviewing materials requested through discovery to avoid waiving privilege. These efforts are necessary because materials subject to a claim of privilege are often difficult to identify,

APPENDIX A

and failure to withhold even one such item may result in waiver of privilege as to all other privileged materials on that subject patter. Not only may this effort impose substantial costs on the party producing the material, but the time required for the privilege review can substantially delay access for the party seeking discovery.

These problems can become more acute when discovery of electronically stored information is sought. The volume of such data, and the informality that attends use of e-mail and some other types of electronically stored information, may make privilege determinations more difficult, and privilege review correspondingly more expensive and time consuming. Other aspects of electronically stored information poses particular difficulties for privilege review. For example, production may be sought of information automatically included in electronic document files but not apparent to the creator of the document or to readers. Computer programs may retain draft language, editorial comments, and other deleted matter (sometimes referred to as "embedded data" or "embedded edits") in an electronic document file but not make them apparent to the reader. Information describing the history, tracking, or management of an electronic document (sometimes called "metadata") is usually not apparent to the reader viewing a hard copy or a screen image. Whether this information should be produced may be among the topics discussed in the Rule 26(f) conference. If it is, it may need to be reviewed to ensure that no privileged information is included, further complicating the task of privilege review.

The *Manual for Complex Litigation* notes these difficulties:

> A responding party's screening of vast quantities of unorganized computer data for privilege prior to production can be particularly onerous in those jurisdictions in which inadvertent production of privileged data may constitute a waiver of privilege as to a particular item of information, items related to the relevant issue, or the entire data collection. Fear of the consequences of inadvertent waiver may add cost and delay to the discovery process for all parties. Thus, judges often encourage counsel to stipulate to a "nonwaiver" agreement, which they can adopt as a case-management order.
>
> Such agreements protect responding parties from the most dire consequences of inadvertent waiver by allowing them to "take back" inadvertently produced privileged materials if discovered within a reasonable period, perhaps thirty days from production.

Manual for Complex Litigation (4th) § 11.446.

Parties may attempt to minimize these costs and delays by agreeing to protocols that minimize the risk of waiver. They may agree that the responding party will provide requested materials for initial examination without waiving any privilege–sometimes known as a "quick peek." The requesting party then designates the documents it wishes to have actually produced. This designation is the Rule 34 request. The responding party then responds in the usual

APPENDIX A

course, screening only those documents actually requested for formal production and asserting privilege claims as provided in Rule 26(b)(5)(A). On other occasions, parties enter agreements – sometimes called "clawback agreements" – providing that production without intent to waive privilege should not be a waiver so long as the producing party identifies the documents mistakenly produced, and that the documents should be returned under those circumstances. Other voluntary arrangements may be appropriate depending on the circumstances of each litigation.

As noted in the *Manual for Complex Litigation,* these agreements can facilitate prompt and economical discovery by reducing delay before the discovering party obtains access to documents, and reducing the cost and burden of review by the producing party. As the *Manual* also notes, a case-management order implementing such agreements can further facilitate the discovery process. Form 35 is amended to include a report to the court about any agreement regarding protections against inadvertent privilege forfeiture or waiver that the parties have reached, and Rule 16(b) is amended to emphasize the court's entry of an order recognizing and implementing such an agreement as a case-management order. The amendment to Rule 26(f) is modest; the entry of such a case-management order merely implements the parties' agreement. But if the parties agree to entry of such an order, their proposal should be included in the report to the court.

Rule 26(b)(5)(B) is added to provide an additional protection against privilege waiver by establishing a procedure for assertion of privilege after production, leaving the question of waiver to later determination by the court if production is still sought.

Rule 33. Interrogatories to Parties

*****

(d) **Option to Produce Business Records.** Where the answer to an interrogatory may be derived or ascertained from the business records, including electronically stored information, of the party upon whom the interrogatory has been served or from an examination, audit or inspection of such business records, including a compilation, abstract or summary thereof, and the burden of deriving or ascertaining the answer is substantially the same for the party serving the interrogatory as for the party served, it is a sufficient answer to such interrogatory to specify the records from which the answer may be derived or ascertained and to afford to the party serving the interrogatory reasonable opportunity to examine, audit or inspect such records and to make copies, compilations, abstracts or summaries. A specification shall be in sufficient detail to permit the interrogating party to locate and to identify, as readily as can the party served, the records from which the answer may be ascertained.

Committee Note

Rule 33(d) is amended to parallel Rule 34(a) by recognizing the importance of electronically stored information. The term "electronically stored information" has the same broad meaning in Rule 33(d) as in Rule 34(a). Much business information is stored only in electronic form; the Rule 33(d) option should be available with respect to such records as well.

APPENDIX A

Special difficulties may arise in using electronically stored formation, either due to its format or because it is dependent on a particular computer system. Rule 33(d) allows a responding party to substitute access to documents or electronically stored information for an answer only if the burden of deriving the answer will be substantially the same for either party. Rule 33(d) says that a party electing to respond to an interrogatory by providing electronically stored information must ensure that the interrogating party can locate and identify it "as readily as can the party served," and also provides that the responding party must give the interrogating party a "reasonable opportunity to examine, audit or inspect" the information. Depending on the circumstances of the case, satisfying these provisions with regard to electronically stored information may require the responding party to provide some combination of technical support, information on application software, access to the pertinent computer system, or other assistance. The key question is whether such support enables the interrogating party to use the electronically stored information as readily as the responding party.

Rule 34. Production of Documents, Electronically Stored Information, and Things and Entry Upon Land for Inspection and Other Purposes

(a) **Scope.** Any party may serve on any other party a request (1) to produce and permit the party making the request, or someone acting on the requestor's behalf, to inspect, ~~and~~ copy, <u>test, or sample</u> any designated <u>electronically stored information or any designated</u>

documents (including writings, drawings, graphs, charts, photographs, <u>sound recordings, images</u> ~~phonorecords~~, and other <u>data or</u> data compilations <u>in any medium –</u> from which information can be obtained, translated, if necessary, by the respondent through detection devices into reasonably usable form), or to inspect, ~~and~~ copy, test, or sample any <u>designated</u> tangible things which constitute or contain matters within the scope of Rule 26(b) and which are in the possession, custody or control of the party upon whom the request is served; or (2) to permit entry upon designated land or other property in the possession or control of the party upon whom the request is served for the purpose of inspection and measuring, surveying, photographing, testing, or sampling the property or any designated object or operation thereon, within the scope of Rule 26(b).

(b) **Procedure.** The request shall set forth, either by individual item or by category, the items to be inspected, and describe each with reasonable particularity. The request shall specify a reasonable time, place, and manner of making the inspection and performing the related acts. <u>The request may specify the form in which electronically stored information is to be produced.</u> Without leave of court or written stipulation, a request may not be served before the time specified in Rule 26(d).

The party upon whom the request is served shall serve a written response within 30 days after the service of the request. A shorter or longer time may be directed by the court or, in the absence of such an order, agreed to in writing by the parties, subject to Rule 29. The response shall state, with respect to each item or category, that inspection and related activities will be permitted as requested, unless the request is objected to, <u>including an objection to the requested form for producing electronically stored information, stating</u> ~~in which event~~ the reason for the objection ~~shall be stated~~. If objection is made to part of an item or category, the part shall be specified and inspection permitted of the remaining parts. The party submitting the request may move for an order under Rule 37(a) with respect to any objection to or other failure to respond to the request or any part thereof, or any failure to permit inspection as requested.

<u>Unless the parties otherwise agree, or the court otherwise orders,</u>

<u>(i)</u>a~~A~~ party who produces documents for inspection shall produce them as they are kept in the usual course of business or shall organize and label them to correspond with the categories in the request<u>; and</u>

<u>(ii) if a request for electronically stored information does not specify the form of production, a responding party must produce the information in a form in which it is ordinarily maintained, or in an electronically searchable form. The party need only produce such information in one form.</u>

*****

Committee Note

Subdivision (a). As originally adopted, Rule 34 focused on discovery of "documents" and "things." In 1970,

Rule 34(a) was amended to authorize discovery of data compilations in anticipation that the use of computerized information would grow in importance. Since that time, the growth in electronically stored information and in the variety of systems for creating and storing such information have been dramatic. It is difficult to say that all forms of electronically stored information fit within the traditional concept of a "document." Accordingly, Rule 34(a) is amended to acknowledge explicitly the expanded importance and variety of electronically stored information subject to discovery. The title of Rule 34 is modified to acknowledge that discovery of electronically stored information stands on equal footing with discovery of documents. Although discovery of electronically stored information has been handled under the term "document," this change avoids the need to stretch that word to encompass such discovery. At the same time, a Rule 34 request for production of "documents" should be understood to include electronically stored information unless discovery in the action has clearly distinguished between electronically stored information and "documents."

The wide variety of computer systems currently in use, and the rapidity of technological change, counsel against a limiting or precise definition of electronically stored information. The definition in Rule 34(a)(1) is expansive, including any type of information that can be stored electronically. A common example that is sought through discovery is electronic communications, such as e-mail. A reference to "images" is added to clarify their inclusion in the listing already provided. The reference to "data or data compilations" includes any databases currently in use or developed in the future. The rule covers information stored "in any medium," to encompass future developments in computer technology.

APPENDIX A

Rule 34(a)(1) is intended to be broad enough to cover all current types of computer-based information, and flexible enough to encompass future changes and developments.

References elsewhere in the rules to "electronically stored information" should be understood to invoke this expansive definition. A companion change is made to Rule 33(d), making it explicit that parties choosing to respond to an interrogatory by permitting access to responsive records may do so by providing access to electronically stored information. More generally, the definition in Rule 34(a)(1) is invoked in number of other amendments, such as those to Rules 26(b)(2), 26(b)(5)(B), 26(f), 34(b), 37(f), and 45. In each of these rules, electronically stored information has the same broad meaning it has under Rule 34(a)(1).

The definition of electronically stored information is broad, but whether material within this definition should be produced, and in what form, are separate questions that must be addressed under Rule 26(b)(2), Rule 26(c), and Rule 34(b).

Rule 34(a)(1) is also amended to make clear that parties may request an opportunity to test or sample materials sought under the rule in addition to inspecting and copying them. That opportunity may be important for both electronically stored information and hard-copy materials. The current rule is not clear that such testing or sampling is authorized; the amendment expressly provides that such discovery is permitted. As with any other form of discovery, issues of burden and intrusiveness raised by requests to test or sample can be addressed under Rules 26(b)(2) and 26(c).

Rule 34(a)(1) is further amended to make clear that tangible things must–like documents and land sought through discovery–be designated in the request.

Subdivision (b). The amendment to Rule 34(b) permits the requesting party to designate the form in which it wants electronically stored information produced. The form of production is more important to the exchange of electronically stored information than of hard-copy materials, although one format a requesting party could designate would be hard copy. Specification of the desired form may facilitate the orderly, efficient, and cost-effective discovery of electronically stored information. The parties should exchange information about the form of production well before production actually occurs, such as during the early opportunity provided by the Rule 26(f) conference. Rule 26(f) now calls for discussion of form of production during that conference.

The rule does not require the requesting party to choose a form of production; this party may not have a preference, or may not know what form the producing party uses to maintain its electronically stored information. If the request does not specify a form of production for electronically stored information, Rule 34(b) provides that the responding party must – unless the court orders otherwise or the parties otherwise agree – choose between options analogous to those provided for hard copy materials. The responding party may produce the information in a form in which it ordinarily maintains the information. If it ordinarily maintains the information in more than one form, it may select any such form. But the responding party is not required to produce the information in a form in which it is maintained. Instead, the responding party may produce the information in a form it selects for the purpose of production, providing the form is electronically searchable. Although this option is not precisely the same as the option to produce hard-copy materials organized and labeled to correspond to the requests, it should be functionally analogous because it will enable the party seeking production to locate pertinent information.

APPENDIX A

If the requesting party does specify a form of production, Rule 34(b) permits the responding party to object. The grounds for objection depend on the circumstances of the case. When such an objection is made, Rule 37(a)(2)(B) requires the parties to confer about the subject in an effort to resolve the matter before a motion to compel is filed. If they cannot agree, the court will have to resolve the issue. The court is not limited to the form initially chosen by the requesting party, or to the alternatives in Rule 34(b)(2), in ordering an appropriate form or forms for production. The court may consider whether a form is electronically searchable in resolving objections to the form of production.

Rule 34(b) also provides that electronically stored information ordinarily need be produced in only one form, but production in an additional form may be ordered for good cause. One such ground might be that the party seeking production cannot use the information in the form in which it was produced. Advance communication about the form that will be used for production might avoid that difficulty.

Rule 37. Failure to Make Disclosure or Cooperate in Discovery; Sanctions

*****

<u>(f)</u>   <u>**Electronically Stored Information.**</u>   <u>Unless a party violated an order in the action requiring it to preserve electronically stored information, a court may not impose sanctions under these rules on the party for failing to provide such information if:</u>

<u>(1)</u>   <u>the party took reasonable steps to preserve the information after it knew or should have known the</u>

information was discoverable in the action; and

(2) the failure resulted from loss of the information because of the routine operation of the party's electronic information system.*

Committee Note

Subdivision (f) is new. It addresses a distinctive feature of computer operations, the routine deletion of information that attends ordinary use. Rule 26(f) is amended to direct the parties to address issues of preserving discoverable information in cases in which they are likely to arise. In many instances, their discussion may result in an agreed protocol for preserving electronically stored information and management of the routine operation of a

---

* The Committee is continuing to examine the degree of cupability that will preclude eligibility for a safe harbor from sanctions in this narrow area, where electronically stored information is lost or destroyed as a result of the routine operation of a party's computer system. Some have voiced concerns that the formulation set out above is inadequate to address the uncertainties created by the dynamic nature of computer systems and the information they generate and store. Comments from the bench and bar on whether the culpability or fault that takes a party outside any safe harbor should be something higher than negligence are important to a full understanding of the issues.

An example of a version of Rule 37(f) framed in terms of intentional or reckless failure to preserve information lost as a result of the ordinary operation of a party's computer system is set out below, as a way to focus comment and suggestions:

(f) Electronically Stored Information. A court may not impose sanctions under these rules on a party for failing to provide electronically stored information deleted or lost as a result of the routine operation of the party's electronic information system unless:
(1) the party intentionally or recklessly failed to preserve the information; or
(2) the party violated an order issued in the action requiring the preservation of the information.

party's information system to avoid loss of such information. Rule 37(f) provides that, unless a court order requiring preservation of electronically stored information is violated, the court may not impose sanctions under these rules on a party when such information is lost because of the routine operation of its electronic information system if the party took reasonable steps to preserve discoverable information.

Rule 37(f) applies only with regard to information lost due to the "routine operation of the party's electronic information system." The reference to the routine operation of the party's electronic information system is an open-ended attempt to describe the ways in which a specific piece of electronically stored information disappears without a conscious human direction to destroy that specific information. No attempt is made to catalogue the system features that, now or in the future, may cause such loss of information. Familiar examples from present systems include programs that recycle storage media, automatic overwriting of information that has been "deleted," and programs that automatically discard information that has not been accessed within a defined period. The purpose is to recognize that it is proper to design efficient electronic information storage systems that serve the user's needs. Different considerations would apply if a system were deliberately designed to destroy litigation-related material.

Rule 37(f) addresses only sanctions under the Civil Rules and applies only to the loss of electronically stored information after commencement of the action in which discovery is sought. It does not define the scope of a duty to preserve and does not address the loss of electronically stored information that may occur before an action is commenced. Rule 37(f) does not, however, require that there be an actual discovery request. It requires that a party take reasonable steps to preserve electronically stored information when the party knew or should have known it was discoverable in the action. Such steps are often called a litigation hold.

The reasonableness of the steps taken to preserve electronically stored information must be measured in at least three dimensions. The outer limit is set by the Rule 26(b)(1) scope of discovery. A second limit is set by the new Rule 26(b)(2) provision that electronically stored is information not reasonably accessible must be provided only on court order for good cause. In most instances, a party acts reasonably by identifying and preserving reasonably accessible electronically stored information that is discoverable without court order. In some instances, reasonable care may require preservation of electronically stored information that is not reasonably accessible if the party knew or should have known that it was discoverable in the action and could not be obtained elsewhere. Preservation may be less burdensome than access, and is necessary to support discovery under Rule 26(b)(2) if good cause is shown. The third limit depends on what the party knows about the nature of the litigation. That knowledge should inform its judgment about what subjects are pertinent to the action and which people and systems are likely to have relevant information. Once the subjects and information systems are identified, e-mail records and electronic "files" of key individuals and departments will be the most obvious candidates for preservation. Other candidates for preservation will be more specific to the litigation and information system. Preservation steps should include consideration of system design features that may lead to automatic loss of discoverable information, a problem further addressed in Rule 37(f). In assessing the steps taken by the party, the court should bear in mind what the party knew or reasonably should have known when it took steps to preserve information.

APPENDIX A

Often, taking no steps at all would not suffice, but the specific steps to be taken would vary widely depending on the nature of the party's electronic information system and the nature of the litigation.

One consideration that may sometimes be important in evaluating the reasonableness of steps taken is the existence of a statutory or regulatory provision for preserving information, if it required retention of the information sought through discovery. *See, e.g.,* 15 U.S.C. § 78u-4(b)(3)(C); Securities & Exchange Comm'n Rule 17a-4. Although violation of such a provision does not automatically preclude the protections of Rule 37(f), the court may take account of the statutory or regulatory violation in determining whether the party took reasonable steps to preserve the information for litigation. Whether or not Rule 37(f) is satisfied, violation of such a statutory or regulatory requirement for preservation may subject the violator to sanctions in another proceeding – either administrative or judicial – but the court may not impose sanctions in the action if it concludes that the party's steps satisfy Rule 37(f)(1).

Rule 37(f) does not apply if the party's failure to provide information resulted from its violation of an order in the action requiring preservation of the information. An order that directs preservation of information on identified topics ordinarily should be understood to include electronically stored information. Should such information be lost even though a party took "reasonable steps" to comply with the order, the court may impose sanctions. If such an order was violated in ways that are unrelated to the party's current inability to provide the electronically stored information at issue, the violation does not deprive the party of the protections of Rule 37(f). The determination whether to impose a sanction, and the choice of sanction, will be affected by the party's reasonable attempts to comply.

If Rule 37(f) does not apply, the question whether sanctions should actually be imposed on a party, and the nature of any sanction to be imposed, is for the court. The court has broad discretion to determine whether sanctions are appropriate and to select a proper sanction. *See, e.g.,* Rule 37(b). The fact that information is lost in circumstances that do not satisfy Rule 37(f) does not imply that a court should impose sanctions.

Failure to preserve electronically stored information may not totally destroy the information, but may make it difficult to retrieve or restore. Even determining whether the information can be made available may require great effort and expense. Rule 26(b)(2) governs determinations whether electronically stored information that is not reasonably accessible should be provided in discovery. If the information is not reasonably accessible because a party has failed to take reasonable steps to preserve the information, it may be appropriate to direct the party to take steps to restore or retrieve information that the court might otherwise not direct.

Rule 45. Subpoena

(a) **Form; Issuance.**

    (1) Every subpoena shall

        (A) state the name of the court from which it is issued; and

        (B) state the title of the action, the name of the court in which it is pending, and its civil action number; and

APPENDIX A

(C) command each person to whom it is directed to attend and give testimony or to produce and permit inspection, ~~and~~ copying, testing, or sampling of designated books, documents, electronically stored information, or tangible things in the possession, custody or control of that person, or to permit inspection of premises, at a time and place therein specified; and

(D) set forth the text of subdivisions (c) and (d) of this rule.

A command to produce evidence or to permit inspection, copying, testing, or sampling may be joined with a command to appear at trial or hearing or at deposition, or may be issued separately. A subpoena may specify the form in which electronically stored information is to be produced.

(2) A subpoena commanding attendance at a trial or hearing shall issue from the court for the district in which the hearing or trial is to be held. A subpoena for attendance at a deposition shall issue from the court for the district designated by the notice of deposition as the district in which the deposition is to be taken. If separate from a subpoena commanding the attendance of a person, a subpoena for production, ~~or~~ inspection, copying, testing, or sampling shall issue from the court for the district in which the production or inspection is to be made.

(3) The clerk shall issue a subpoena, signed but

otherwise in blank, to a party requesting it, who shall complete it before service. An attorney as officer of the court may also issue and sign a subpoena on behalf of

> **(A)** a court in which the attorney is authorized to practice; or
>
> **(B)** a court for a district in which a deposition or production is compelled by the subpoena, if the deposition or production pertains to an action pending in a court in which the attorney is authorized to practice.

(b) **Service.**

> **(1)** A subpoena may be served by any person who is not a party and is not less than 18 years of age. Service of a subpoena upon a person named therein shall be made by delivering a copy thereof to such person and, if the person's attendance is commanded, by tendering to that person the fees for one day's attendance and the mileage allowed by law. When the subpoena is issued on behalf of the United States or an officer or agency thereof, fees and mileage need not be tendered. Prior notice of any commanded production of documents and things or inspection of premises before trial shall be served on each party in the manner prescribed by Rule 5(b).
>
> **(2)** Subject to the provisions of clause (ii) of subparagraph (c)(3)(A) of this rule, a subpoena may be served at any place within the district of the court by which

APPENDIX A

it is issued, or at any place without the district that is within 100 miles of the place of the deposition, hearing, trial, production, ~~or~~ inspection, copying, testing, or sampling specified in the subpoena or at any place within the state where a state statute or rule of court permits service of a subpoena issued by a state court of general jurisdiction sitting in the place of the deposition, hearing, trial, production, ~~or~~ inspection, copying, testing, or sampling specified in the subpoena. When a statute of the United States provides therefor, the court upon proper application and cause shown may authorize the service of a subpoena at any other place. A subpoena directed to a witness in a foreign country who is a national or resident of the United States shall issue under the circumstances and in the manner and be served as provided in Title 28, U.S.C. § 1783.

(3) Proof of service when necessary shall be made by filing with the clerk of the court by which the subpoena is issued a statement of the date and manner of service and of the names of the persons served, certified by the person who made the service.

(c) **Protection of Persons Subject to Subpoenas.**

(1) A party or an attorney responsible for the issuance and service of a subpoena shall take reasonable steps to avoid imposing undue burden or expense on a person subject to that subpoena. The court on behalf of which the subpoena was issued shall

enforce this duty and impose upon the party or attorney in breach of this duty an appropriate sanction, which may include, but is not limited to, lost earnings and a reasonable attorney's fee.

(2) **(A)** A person commanded to produce and permit inspection, ~~and~~ copying, testing, or sampling of designated electronically stored information, books, papers, documents or tangible things, or inspection of premises need not appear in person at the place of production or inspection unless commanded to appear for deposition, hearing or trial.

(B) Subject to paragraph (d)(2) of this rule, a person commanded to produce and permit inspection, ~~and~~ coping, testing, or sampling may, within 14 days after service of the subpoena or before the time specified for compliance if such time is less than 14 days after service, serve upon the party or attorney designated in the subpoena written objection to providing ~~inspection or copying of~~ any or all of the designated materials or of the premises – or to providing information in the form requested. If objection is made, the party serving the subpoena shall not be entitled to inspect, ~~and~~ copy, test, or sample the materials or inspect the premises except pursuant to an order of the court by which the subpoena was issued. If

APPENDIX A

objection has been made, the party serving the subpoena may, upon notice to the person commanded to produce, move at any time for an order to compel the production<u>, inspection, copying, testing, or sampling</u>. Such an order to compel ~~production~~ shall protect any person who is not a party or an officer of a party from significant expense resulting from the inspection and copying commanded.

(3) (A) On timely motion, the court by which a subpoena was issued shall quash or modify the subpoena if it

(i) fails to allow reasonable time for compliance;

(ii) requires a person who is not a party or an officer of a party to travel to a place more than 100 miles from the place where that person resides, is employed or regularly transacts business in person, except that, subject to the provisions of clause (c)(3)(B)(iii) of this rule, such a person may in order to attend trial be commanded to travel from any such place within the state in which the trial is held, or

(iii) requires disclosure of privileged or

other protected matter and no exception or waiver applies, or

(iv) subjects a person to undue burden.

(B) If a subpoena

(i) requires disclosure of a trade secret or other confidential research, development, or commercial information, or

(ii) requires disclosure of an unretained expert's opinion or information not describing specific events or occurrences in dispute and resulting from the expert's study made not at the request of any party, or

(iii) requires a person who is not a party or an officer of a party to incur substantial expense to travel more than 100 miles to attend trial, the court may, to protect a person subject to or affected by the subpoena, quash or modify the subpoena or, if the party in whose behalf the subpoena is issued shows a substantial need for the testimony or material that cannot be otherwise met without undue hardship and assures that the person to whom the subpoena is addressed will be reasonably compensated, the court may

APPENDIX A

order appearance or production only upon specified conditions.

(d) **Duties in Responding to Subpoena.**

(1) <u>(A)</u> A person responding to a subpoena to produce documents shall produce them as they are kept in the usual course of business or shall organize and label them to correspond with the categories in the demand.

<u>(B) If a subpoena does not specify the form for producing electronically stored information, a person responding to a subpoena must produce the information in a form in which the person ordinarily maintains it or in an electronically searchable form. The person producing electronically stored information need only produce it in one form.</u>

<u>(C) A person responding to a subpoena need not provide discovery of electronically stored information that the person identifies as not reasonably accessible. On motion by the requesting party, the responding party must show that the information sought is not reasonably accessible. If that showing is made, the court may order discovery of the information for good cause.</u>

(2) <u>(A)</u> When information subject to a subpoena is withheld on a claim that it is privileged or subject

to protection as trial preparation materials, the claim shall be made expressly and shall be supported by a description of the nature of the documents, communications, or things not produced that is sufficient to enable the demanding party to contest the claim.

(B) When a person produces information without intending to waive a claim of privilege it may, within a reasonable time, notify any party that received the information of its claim of privilege. After being notified, any party must promptly return, sequester, or destroy the specified information and all copies. The person who produced the information must comply with Rule 45(d)(2)(A) with regard to the information and preserve it pending a ruling by the court.

(e) **Contempt.** Failure of any person without adequate excuse to obey a subpoena served upon that person may be deemed a contempt of the court from which the subpoena issued. An adequate cause for failure to obey exists when a subpoena purports to require a non-party to attend or produce at a place not within the limits provided by clause (ii) of subparagraph (c)(3)(A).

Committee Note

Rule 45 is amended to conform the provisions for subpoenas to changes in other discovery rules, largely related to discovery of electronically stored information. Rule 34 is

APPENDIX A

amended to provide in greater detail for the production of electronically stored information. Rule 45(a)(1)(C) is amended to recognize that electronically stored information, as defined in Rule 34(a), can also be sought by subpoena. As under Rule 34(b), Rule 45(a)(1)(D) is amended to provide that the subpoena can designate a form for production of electronic data. Rule 45(c)(2) is amended, like Rule 34(b), to authorize the person served with a subpoena to object to the requested form. In addition, as under Rule 34(b), Rule 45(d)(1)(B) is amended to provide that the person served with the subpoena must produce electronically stored information either in a form in which it is usually maintained or in an electronically searchable form, and that the person producing electronically stored information should not have to produce it in more than one form unless so ordered by the court for good cause.

    As with discovery of electronically stored information from parties, complying with a subpoena for such information may impose burdens on the responding person. The Rule 45(c) protections should guard against undue impositions on nonparties. For example, Rule 45(c)(1) directs that a party serving a subpoena "shall take reasonable steps to avoid imposing undue burden or expense on a person subject to the subpoena," and Rule 45(c)(2)(B) permits the person served with the subpoena to object to it and directs that an order requiring compliance "shall protect a person who is neither a party nor a party's officer from significant expense resulting from compliance." Rule 45(d)(1)(C) is added to provide that the responding person need only provide reasonably accessible electronically stored information, unless the court orders additional discovery for good cause. A parallel provision is added to Rule 26(b)(2). In many cases, advance discussion about the extent, manner, and form of producing electronically stored information should alleviate such concerns.

Rule 45(a)(1)(B) is also amended, as is Rule 34(a), to provide that a subpoena is available to permit testing and sampling as well as inspection and copying. As in Rule 34, this change recognizes that on occasion the opportunity to perform testing or sampling may be important, both for documents and for electronically stored information. Because testing or sampling may present particular issues of burden or intrusion for the person served with the subpoena, however, the protective provisions of Rule 45(c) should be enforced with vigilance when such demands are made.

Rule 45(d)(2) is amended, as is Rule 26(b)(5), to add a procedure for assertion of privilege after inadvertent production of privileged information.

Throughout Rule 45, further amendments have been made to conform the rule to the changes described above.

Form 35. Report of Parties' Planning Meeting
*****

3. Discovery Plan. The parties jointly propose to the court the following discovery plan: [Use separate paragraphs or subparagraphs as necessary if parties disagree.]

Discovery will be needed on the following subjects: _____(brief description of subjects on which discovery will be needed)

_____

<u>Disclosure or discovery of electronically stored information should be handled as follows: (brief description of parties' proposals)</u>

APPENDIX A

<u>The parties have agreed to a privilege protection order, as follows: (brief description of provisions of proposed order)</u>

All discovery commenced in time to be completed by _____ (date) _____. [Discovery on _____ (issue for early discovery) _____ to be completed by _____ (date) _____.]

TABLE OF AUTHORITIES

ABC Home Health Servs. v. IBM Corp.,
   158 F.R.D. 180 (S.D. Ga. 1994) Ch.5 (n.11)

Abdallah v. Coca-Cola Co.,
   No. Civ.A. 1:98CV3679-RW, 1999 WL 527835
   (N.D. Ga. July 16,1999) Ch.5 (n.14)

Anti-Monopoly, Inc. v. Hasbro, Inc.,
   No. 94 CIV. 2121(LMM)(AJP), 1995 WL 649934
   (S.D.N.Y. Nov. 3, 1995) Ch.3 (nn.4,17,21)

Antioch Co. v. Scrapbook Borders, Inc.,
   210 F.R.D. 645 (D. Minn. 2002) Ch.2 (n.38)
   Ch.3 (nn.20,28), Ch.6 (nn.6,36,37,43), Ch.7 (nn.11,16)

Applied Telematics, Inc. v. Sprint Communications Co.,
   No. Civ.A. 94-46031996 WL 539595
   (E.D. Pa. Sept. 18, 1996) Ch.2 (n.22)

Arambura v. Boeing Co.,
   112 F.3d 1398 (10th Cir. 1997) Ch.5 (n.70)

Arista Records, Inc.v. Sakfield Holding Co. S.L.,
   314 F.Supp.2d 27 (D.D.C. 2004) Ch.5 (n.82)

Armstrong v. Executive Office of the President,
   1 F.3d 1274 (D.C. Cir. 1993),
   rev'd on other grounds 90 F.3d 553 (1996) Ch.8 (n.76)

Barnhill v. United States,
   11 F.3d 1360 (7th Cir. 1993) Ch.5 (n.5)

Bd. Of Educ. Of Evanston Tp. High Sch. Dist. No. 202 v. Admiral Heating & Ventilating, Inc.,
   104 F.R.D. 23 (N.D. Ill. 1984) Ch.3 (n.11)

Belcher v. Bassett Furniture Indus.,
   588 F.2d 904 (4th Cir. 1978) Ch.4 (n.15)

Black & Veatch Int'l Co. v. Foster Wheeler Energy Corp.,
   No. 00-2402-JAR, 2002 WL 1071932 (D. Kan. May 10, 2002) .Ch.3 (n.17)

Brown Bag Software v. Symantec Corp.,
   960 F.2d 1465 (9th Cir. 1992) Ch.6 (n.4)

Brush v. Harkins,
   9 F.R.D. 681 (W.D. Mo. 1950) Ch.4 (n.29)

Builders Ass'n of Greater Chicago v. City of Chicago,
   215 F.R.D. 550 (N.D. Ill. 2003) Ch.7 (n.16)

Byers v. Illinois State Police,
   No. 99 C 8105, 2002 WL 1264004 (N.D. Ill. June 3, 2002)
   (Magistrate Judge) Ch.3 (nn.18,26), Ch.7 (nn.8,10,27,29,40-41)

Byrnie v. Town of Cromwell,
    243 F.3d 93 (2d Cir. 2000) Ch.5 (nn.19,50,52,58,59,62,79)

Cabinetware, Inc. v. Sullivan,
    No. Civ. S. 90-313 LKK, 1991WL 327959
    (E.D. Cal. July 15, 1991) Ch.5 (nn.53,68)

Caldera, Inc. v. Microsoft Corp.,
    72 F. Supp. 2d 1295 (D. Utah 1999) Ch.7 (n.8)

Calzaturficio S.C.A.R.P.A. s.p.a. v. Fabiano Shoe Co.,
    201 F.R.D. 33 (D. Mass. 2001) Ch.4 (n.23)

Camco, Inc. v. Baker Oil Tools, Inc., 45 F.R.D. 384
    (S.D. Texas 1968) Ch.3 (n.9)

Cantaline v. Raymark Indus., Inc., 103 F.R.D. 447
    (S.D. Fla. 1984) Ch.4 (nn.43,44)

Capellupo v. FMC Corp.,
    126 F.R.D. 545 (D. Minn. 1989) Ch.2 (n.12,22)

Carlton Group, Ltd. v. Tobin,
    No. 02 Civ.5065 SAS, 2003 WL 21782650
    (S.D.N.Y. July 31, 2003) Ch.8 (nn.5-14)

Carlucci v. Piper Aircraft Corp.,
    102 F.R.D. 472 (S.D. Fla. 1984) .Ch.2 (nn.12,22)

Centurion Indus., Inc., v. Warren Steurer & Assocs.,
    665 F.2d 323 (10th Cir. 1981) Ch.4 (n.6)

Chao v. 3RE.com, Inc.,
    No. 01-2350-MlV, 2003 WL 21946597
    (W.D. Tenn. July 28, 2003) Ch.7 (n.16)

China Ocean Shipping Group Co. v. Simone Metals, Inc.,
    No. 97 C 2694, 1999 WL 966443 (N.D. Ill. Sept. 30, 1999) Ch.5 (n.29)

Coates v. Johnson & Johnson,
    756 F.2d 524 (7th Cir. 1985) Ch.2 (n.12)

Cohn v. Taco Bell Corp.,
    No. 92 C 5852, 1995 WL 519968 (N.D. Ill. Aug. 30, 1995) Ch.5 (n.10)

Computer Assocs. Int'l, Inc. v. Am. Fundware, Inc.,
    133 F.R.D. 166 (D. Colo. 1990) Ch.5 (nn.5,43,60,67,68,71,80)

Computer Assocs. Int'l, Inc. v. Quest Software Inc.,
    No. 02 C 4721, 2003 WL 21277129 (N.D. Ill. June 3, 2003) . . .Ch.6 (n.40)
    Ch.8 (nn.93-97)

Concord Boat Corp. v. Brunswick Corp.,
    169 F.R.D. 44 (S.D.N.Y. 1996) .Ch.4 (nn.5,6,31,42)

TABLE OF AUTHORITIES

Crown Life Ins. Co. v. Craig,
 995 F.2d 1376 (7th Cir. 1993) Ch.3 (n.4), Ch.5 (n.66)

Daewoo Elecs. Co., Ltd. v. United States,
 650 F. Supp. 1003 (Ct. of Intl. Trade 1986) Ch.7 (n.12)

Danis v. USN Communications, Inc.,
 No. 98 C 7482, 2000 WL 1694325
 (N.D. Ill. Oct. 23, 2000) Ch.5 (nn.2,4,7,9,20,26-30,34
 40-42,49,54,59,62,64,68,81,83), Ch.8 (87-89)

Dodge, Warren & Peters Ins. Servs., Inc. v. Riley,
 105 Cal. App. 4th 1414 (Cal. Ct. App. 2003) Ch.8 (nn.118-120)

Dow Chem. Co. v. Allen,
 672 F.2d 1262 (7th Cir. 1982) Ch.4 (n.6)

Ex parte Wal-Mart, Inc.,
 809 So. 2d 818 (Ala. 2001) Ch.8 (n.17)

F.D.I.C. v. Singh,
 140 F.R.D. 252 (D. Me. 1992) Ch.6 (n.11)

Fennell v. First Step Designs, Ltd.,
 83 F.3d 526 (1st Cir. 1996) Ch.6 (n.34)

Fireworks Spectacular, Inc. v. Premier Pyrotechnics, Inc.,
 107 F. Supp. 2d 1307 (D. Kan. 2000) Ch.6 (nn.2,23)

First USA Bank, N.A. v. PayPal, Inc.,
 No. 03-1558, 2003 WL 22071558 (Fed. Cir. Aug. 21, 2003) Ch.6 (n.40)

Food Lion, Inc. v. United Food and Commercial Worker's Int'l Union,
 103 F.3d 1007 (D.C. Cir. 1997) Ch.4 (n.25)

Four Seasons v. Consorcio Barr,
 267 F. Supp. 2d 1268 (S.D. Fla. 2003) Ch.8 (nn.44,50,56-65,98)

F.T.C. v. Texaco, Inc.,
 517 F.2d 137 (D.C. Cir. 1975), *cert. denied* 431 U.S. 974 (1977) Ch.4 (n.29)

F.T.C. v. U.S. Grant Resources,
 No. Civ.A. 04-596, 2004 WL 1396315
 (E.D.La. June 18, 2004) . . . . .Ch. 4 (n.45)

Gates Rubber Co. v. Bando Chem. Indus., Ltd.,
 167 F.R.D. 90 . . . . .Ch.6 (nn.30-31,33), Ch.8 (n.102)

Gates Rubber Co. v. Bando Chem. Indus., Ltd.,
 9 F.3d 823 (10th Cir. 1993) Ch.6 (n.23)

Gray v. Bicknell,
 86 F.3d 1472 (8th Cir. 1996) Ch.6 (n.14)

Hoechst Diafoil Co. v. Nan Ya Plastics Corp.,
   174 F.3d 411 (4th Cir. 1999) Ch.6 (n.23)

Illinois Tool Works, Inc. v. Metro Mark Prods., Ltd.,
   43 F. Supp. 2d 951 (N.D. Ill. 1999) Ch.5 (n.84)

In re Brand Name Prescription Drugs Antitrust Litig.,
   Nos. 94 C 897, MDL 997, 1995
   WL 360526 (N.D. Ill. June 15, 1995) Ch.7 (n.12), Ch.8 (n.17)

In re Bristol-Meyers Squibb Sec. Litig.,
   205 F.R.D. 437 (D. N.J. 2002) . . .Ch.3 (nn.7-8,21,23), Ch.7 (nn.5,16,25,32)

In re Exxon Valdez,
   142 F.R.D. 380 (D.D.C. 1992) Ch.4 (n.45)

In re Ford Motor Co.,
   345 F.3d 1315 (11th Cir. 2003) Ch.3 (n.28), Ch.6 (nn.6,7,34)

In re Kagan,
   351 F.3d 1157 (D.C. Cir. 2003) Ch.6 (n.24)

In re Lernout & Hauspie Sec. Litig.,
   222 F.R.D. 29 (D.Mass. 2004) Ch.6 (n.14)

In re Livent, Inc. Noteholders Sec. Litig.,
   No. 98 Civ. 7161 VMDFE, 2003
   WL 23254 (S.D.N.Y. Jan. 2, 2003) Ch.7 (n.16)

In re Potash Antitrust Litig.,
   No. 3-93-197, MDL No. 981, 1994 WL 1108312
   (D. Minn. Dec. 5, 1994) Ch.5 (n.14)

In re Prudential Ins. Co. of Am. Sales Practices Litig.,
   169 F.R.D. 598, (D.N.J. 1997), *rev'd on other grounds* 133 F.3d 225 (3rd
   Cir. 1998) ("Prudential") Ch.2 (nn.12,22,54,58), Ch.5 (nn.26,39)

In re Sealed Case,
   877 F.2d 976 (D.C. Cir. 1989) Ch.6 (n.11)

In re Triton Energy, Ltd. Sec. Litig.,
   No. 5:98CV256, 2002
   WL 32114464 (E.D. Tex. March 7, 2002) Ch.6 (nn.35,40,42)

In re Trost,
   164 B.R. 740 (W.D. Mich. 1994) Ch.4 (n.8)

Jones v. Goord,
   No. 95 CIV. 8026(GEL), 2002 WL 1007614
   (S.D.N.Y. May 16, 2002) Ch.3 (nn.16-17,25,28)

Keir v. Unumprovident Corp.,
   No. 02 Civ. 8781(DLC), 2003 WL 21997747
   (S.D.N.Y. Aug. 22, 2003) Ch.5 (n.44)

TABLE OF AUTHORITIES

Kewanee Oil Co. v. Bicron Corp.,
 416 U.S. 470 (1974) Ch.6 (n.2)

Koplin v. Rosel Well Perforators, Inc.,
 734 P.2d 1177 (Kan. 1987) Ch.4 (n.26)

Kronisch v. United States,
 150 F.3d 112 (2d Cir. 1998) Ch.5 (nn.6,62,70)

Kucula Enterprises, Ltd. v. Auto Wax Co., Inc.,
 No. 02 C 1403, 2003
 WL 21230605 (N. D. Ill. May 27, 2003) Ch.6 (n.31), Ch.8 (nn.51-65)

Lauren Corp. v, Century Geophysical Corp.,
 953 P.2d 200 (Colo. Ct. App. 1998) Ch.5 (nn.78,85)

Lewy v. Remington Arms Co.,
 836 F.2d 1104 (8th Cir. 1988) Ch.2 (nn.28-33)

Linder v. Calero-Portocarrero,
 180 F.R.D. 168 (D.C. Cir. 1998) Ch.6 (n.8)

Linnen v, A.H. Robins Co., Inc.,
 No. 97-2307, 1999 WL 462015 (Mass. Super. June 16, 1999) Ch.2
 (nn.22,61), Ch.5 (n.37, 39)

Lois Sportswear, U.S.A., Inc. v. Levi Strauss & Co.,
 104 F.R.D. 103 (S.D.N.Y. 1985) Ch.6 (n.5)

Long Island Diagnostic Imaging, P.C. v. Stony Brook Diagnostic Assocs.,
 728 N.Y.S.2d 781 (2d Dep't. 2001) Ch.5 (n.34)

Mallinckrodt Chem. Works v. Goldman, Sachs & Co.,
 58 F.R.D. 348 (S.D.N.Y. 1973) Ch.3 (n.9)

Mann v. Univ. of Cincinnati,
 824 F.Supp. 1190 (S.D. Ohio), *aff'd* 152 F.R.D. 119
 (S.D. Ohio 1993) Ch.4 (n.42)

Mathias v. Jacobs,
 197 F.R.D. 29 (S.D.N.Y. 2000), *vacated on other grounds* 2001 WL
 1149017 (S.D.N.Y. 2001) Ch.5 (n.35)

McCabe v. Ernst & Young LLP,
 221 F.R.D. 423 (D.N.J. 2004) Ch.4 (n.44)

McPeek v. Ashcroft,
 202 F.R.D. 31 (D.D.C. 2002) ("McPeek I") ..Ch. 2 (n.61), Ch.3 (nn.26-27)
 Ch.5 (n.17), Ch.7 (nn.9,21,33)

McPeek v. Ashcroft,
 212 F.R.D. 33 (D.D.C. 2003) ("McPeek II") Ch.2 (n.39)
 Ch.3 (n.5)(Magistrate Judge), Ch.3 (nn.24, 26), Ch.7 (n.33)

Medtronic Sofamor Danek, Inc. v. Michelson,
   No. 01-2373-MIV, 2003 WL 21468573 (W.D. Tenn. May 13, 2003) . . .Ch.6
   (nn.40,44), Ch.7 (nn.35-39,42), Ch.8 (n.114), Ch.8 (p.165)

Metro. Opera Ass'n. v. Local 100, Hotel Employees & Rest. Employees Int'l
Union,
   212 F.R.D. 178 (S.D.N.Y. 2003) Ch.2 (n.22)
   Ch.5 (nn.20,23-25,49)

Minn. Mining & Mfg. Co. v. Pribyl,
   259 F.3d 587 (7th Cir. 2001) Ch.5 (n.33)

Monotype Corp. PLC v. Int'l Typeface Corp.,
   43 F.3d 443 (9th Cir. 1994) Ch.8 (n.66)

Morris v. Union Pac. R.R.,
   373 F.3d 896 (8th Cir. 2004) Ch.5 (n.59)

Munshani v. Signal Lake Venture Fund II, LP,
   No. 005529BLS, 2001 WL 1526954
   (Mass. Super. Oct. 9, 2001) Ch.8 (nn.121-126)

Murphy Oil U.S.A., Inc. v. Fluor Daniel, Inc.,
   No. Civ.A. 99-3564, 2002 WL 246439, (E.D. La. Feb. 19, 2002) Ch.2
   (n.14)

Nat'l Assn. of Radiation Survivors v. Turnage,
   115 F.R.D. 543 (N.D. Cal. 1987) Ch.5 (nn.20,61,83)

Nat'l Wildlife Fed'n v. EPA,
   286 F.3d 554 (D.C. Cir. 2002) Ch.6 (nn.9, 11,24)

Nicholas J. Murlas Living Trust v. Mobil Oil Co.,
   93 C 6956, 1995 WL 124186 (N.D. Ill. March 20, 1995) Ch.3 (n.28)

OpenTV v. Liberate Tech.,
   219 F.R.D. 474 (N.D. Cal. 2003) Ch.7 (nn.23,24)

Oppenheimer Fund, Inc. v. Sanders,
   437 U.S. 340 (1978) Ch.7 (nn.1,2)

Owens v. Morgan Stanley & Co., Inc.,
   No. 96 CIV. 9747(DLC), 1997 WL 793004
   (S.D.N.Y. Dec. 24, 1997) Ch.7 (n.8)

Proctor & Gamble Co. v. Haugen,
   179 F.R.D. 622 (D. Utah 1998), *aff'd in part, rev'd in part*
   222 F.3d 1262 (10th Cir. 2000) Ch.2 (n.22), Ch.5 (n.70)

Pennar Software Corp. v, Fortune 500 Sys. Ltd.,
   No. 01-01734 EDL, 2001 WL 1319162
   (N.D. Cal. Oct. 25, 2001) Ch.5 (nn.5,73)

TABLE OF AUTHORITIES

Playboy Enterprises, Inc. v. Welles,
    60 F. Supp. 2d 1050 (N.D. Cal. 1053) Ch.3 (nn.19-20)
    Ch.4 (nn.14,37-41), Ch.6 (nn.6,25,35,38,40-41), Ch.7 (n.11), Ch.8 (n.131)

Positive Software Solutions, Inc. v. New Century Mortgage Co.,
    259 F. Supp. 2d 561 (N.D. Tex. 2003) Ch.6 (n.34)

Public Citizen v. Carlin, 2 F. Supp. 2d 1 (D.D.C. 1997),
    rev'd on other grounds 184 F.3d 900 (1999) Ch.8 (n.75)

QZO, Inc. v. Moyer,
    594 S.E.2d 541 (S.C. Ct. App. 2004) Ch.5 (n.68)

Rambus, Inc. v. Infineon Technologies AG,
    220 F.R.D. 264 (E.D.Va. 2004) Ch.2 (n.33)

Reed v. Bennett,
    193 F.R.D. 689 (D. Kan. 2000) Ch.4 (n.23)

Residential Funding Corp. v. DeGeorge Fin. Corp.,
    306 F.3d 99 (2d Cir. 2002) Ch.5 (nn.5,59,79)

Richards v. Jain,
    168 F. Supp. 2d 1195 (W.D. Wash. 2001) Ch.6 (nn.9,17)

RKI, Inc. v. Grimes,
    177 F. Supp. 2d 859 (N.D. Ill. 2001) Ch.5 (n.32)

Rowe Entm't, Inc. v. William Morris Agency, Inc.,
    205 F.R.D. 421 (S.D.N.Y. 2002) Ch.2 (n.17)
    Ch.3 (nn.19,22,27-28), Ch.6 (nn.5,36,40-41,44-45), Ch.7
    (nn.3,9,14,16,21,27,29,42)

Sattar v. Motorola, Inc.,
    138 F.3d 1164 (7th Cir. 1998) Ch.4 (nn.14,18), Ch.7 (n.8)

S.E.C. v. Cassano,
    189 F.R.D. 83 (S.D.N.Y. 1999) Ch.6 (n.19)

S.E.C. v. Lavin,
    111 F.3d 921 (D.C. Cir. 1997) Ch.6 (n.11)

S. Diagnostic Ass'n v. Bencosme,
    833 So. 2d 801 (Fla. Dist. Ct. App. 2002) Ch.5 (n.16), Ch.8 (n.17)

Shamis v. Ambassador Factors Corp.,
    34 F. Supp. 2d 879 (S.D.N.Y. 1999) Ch.2 (n.54)

Simon Property Group, L.P. v. mySimon, Inc.,
    194 F.R.D. 639 (S.D. Ind. 2000) . . . . .Ch.2 (n.38), Ch.3 (nn. 20,28)
    Ch.6 (nn.6,26,39,41,43), Ch.7 (n.11), Ch.8 (nn.139-141)

Stallings-Daniel v. N. Trust Co.,
    No. 01 C 2290, 2002 WL 385566 (N.D. Ill. March 12, 2002) . . .Ch.3 (n.28)
    Ch.8 (n.149)

Standard Chlorine of Del., Inc. v. Sinibaldi,
    821 F. Supp. 232 (D. Del. 1992) Ch.4 (n.43)

State v. Cook,
    777 N.E.2d 882 (Ohio App. 2002) Ch.8 (nn.33,69)

Stevenson v. Union Pac. R.R. Co.,
    354 F.3d 739 (8th Cir. 2004) Ch.2 (n.56), Ch.5 (n.5)

Strasser v. Yalamanchi,
    669 So. 2d 1142 (Fla. Dist. Ct. App. 1996) Ch.4 (n.8)

Super Film of Am., Inc. v. UCB Films, Inc.,
    219 F.R.D. 649 (D. Kan. 2004) Ch.3 (nn.7,19,26)

Syposs v. United States,
    181 F.R.D. 224 (W.D.N.Y. 1998) Ch.4 (n.29)

Telecom Int'l Am., Ltd. v. AT&T Corp.,
    189 F.R.D. 76 (S.D.N.Y. 1999) Ch.5 (nn.6,10-12)

Telectron, Inc. v. Overhead Door Corp.,
    116 F.R.D. 107 (S.D. Fla. 1987) Ch.2 (n.22), Ch.5 (nn.55-56)

T.N. Taube Corp. v. Marine Midland Mortgage Corp.,
    136 F.R.D. 449 (W.D.N.C. 1991) Ch.3 (n.12)

Travers v. McKinstry Co.,
    No. CIV. 01-1206-JO, 2001 WL 34041790 (D. Or. Nov. 16, 2001) Ch.8
    (n.134)

Trigon Ins. Co. v. United States, 204 F.R.D. 277 (E.D. Va. 2001) Ch.5
    (nn.5,55,65,73,76,77,82), Ch.8 (n.127-129)

Tulip Computers Int'l B.V. v. Dell Computer Corp.,
    No. CIV.A. 00-981-RRM, 2002 WL 818061 (D. Del. Apr. 30, 2002) . .Ch.3
    (n.28), Ch.6 (nn.36,40), Ch.8 (n.34)

Turner v. Hudson Transit Lines, Inc.,
    142 F.R.D. 68 (S.D.N.Y. 1991) Ch.5 (nn.1,7,10,22,79)

Uncle Henry's, Inc. v. Plaut Consulting, Inc.,
    240 F. Supp. 2d 63 (D. Me. 2003) Ch.8 (n.66)

United States v. Bowers,
    920 F.2d 220 (4th Cir. 1990) Ch.8 (n.66)

United States v. Catabran,
    836 F.2d 453 (9th Cir. 1988) Ch.8 (nn.66,69)

TABLE OF AUTHORITIES

United States v. Columbia Broad. Sys., Inc.,
 666 F.2d 364 (9th Cir. 1982) Ch.4 (nn.5,40)

United States ex rel Koch v. Koch Indus.,
 197 F.R.D. 463 (N.D. Okla. 1998) Ch.5 (nn.1,6,13,36,47-48,59,75)

United States ex rel. Schwartz v. TRW, Inc.,
 No. CV 96-3065-RSWL, 2002
 WL 31688812 (C.D. Cal. Nov. 13, 2002) Ch.4 (n.31)

United States v. Hutson,
 821 F.2d 1015 (5th Cir. 1987) Ch.8 (n.67)

United States v. Jasper,
 No. 00 CR. 0825(PKL), 2003 U.S. Dist. LEXIS 12619 (S.D.N.Y. July 22,
 2003) Ch.7 (n.16)

United States v. Philip Morris USA Inc.,
 327 F.Supp.2d 21 (D.D.C 2004) ....Ch. 5 (n.66)

United States v. Stewart,
 294 F.Supp.2d 490 (S.D.N.Y. 2003) Ch.6 (n.1)

United States v. Rigas,
 281 F. Supp. 2d 733 (S.D.N.Y. 2003) Ch.6 (nn.1,13,15-18)

United States v. Siddiqui,
 235 F.3d 1318 (11th Cir. 2000) Ch.8 (n.66)

United States v. Taylor,
 166 F.R.D. 356 (M.D.N.C. 1996),
 aff'd 166 F.R.D. 367 (M.D.N.C. 1996) Ch.4 (n.24)

United States v. Triumph Capital Group, Inc.,
 211 F.R.D. 31 (D. Conn. 2002) Ch.6 (nn.10,30,32), Ch.8 (n.32)

United States v. Zolin,
 809 F.2d 1411 (9th Cir. 1987), *aff'd in part, vacated in part on other grounds,* 491 U.S. 554 (1989) Ch.6 (n.12)

U.S. Steel Corp. v. United States,
 730 F.2d 1465 (Fed. Cir. 1984) Ch.6 (n.4)

Vick v. Texas Employment Comm'n,
 514 F.2d 734, 737 (5th Cir. 1975) Ch.2 (nn.12,59)

West v. Goodyear Tire & Rubber Co.,
 167 F.3d 776 (2d Cir. 1999) Ch.5 (n.50)

Willard v. Caterpillar Inc.,
    40 Cal. App. 4th 892, 48 Cal. Rptr. 2d 607 (1995) Ch.2 (n.12)

William T. Thompson Co. v. Gen. Nutrition Corp.,
    593 F. Supp. 1443 (C.D. Cal. 1984) Ch.2 (n.55)
    Ch.5 (nn.11-12,15,30,63,85)

Wright v. AmSouth Bancorp.,
    320 F.3d 1198 (11th Cir. 2003) Ch.3 (nn.5,28), Ch.5 (n.16)

Xpedior Creditor Trust v. Credit Suisse First Boston (USA), Inc.,
    No. 02 CIV. 9149(SAS), 2003 WL 22283835
    (S.D.N.Y. Oct. 2, 2003) Ch.7 (nn.21,32)
    Ch.8 (n.27)(Judge Scheindlin)

York v. Hartford Underwriters Ins. Co.,
    No. 01-CV-590-B(J), 2002
    WL 31465306 (N.D. Okla. Nov. 4, 2002) Ch.3 (n.16)

Zubulake v. UBS Warburg LLC,
    217 F.R.D. 309 (S.D.N.Y. May 13, 2003)
    ("Zubulake I") Ch.2 (nn.16,18,19-21,38)
    Ch.3 (nn.19,23-24)(Judge Scheindlin), Ch.7 (nn.3,5-6,9,15-16,18-21,23,26-
    29,33-34), Ch.8 (nn.26-29)(Judge Scheindlin)

Zubulake v. UBS Warburg, LLC,
    216 F.R.D. 280 (S.D.N.Y. July 24, 2003) ("Zubulake III") Ch.2 (n.16)
    Ch.7 (nn.18,33), Ch.8 (nn.30-31)

Zubulake v. UBS Warburg LLC,
    No. 02 CIV. 1243(SAS), 2003 WL 22410619 (S.D.N.Y. Oct. 22, 2003)
    ("Zubulake IV") Ch.2 (n.16), Ch.7 (n.18)

Zubulake v. UBS Warburg LLC,
    No. 02 CIV. 1243(SAS), 2004 WL 1620866 (S.D.N.Y. July 20, 2004)
    ("Zubulake V") Ch.2 (n.16), Ch.3 (n.43), Ch.5 (n.86), Ch.7 (n.18)

Statutes & Rules:

Federal Statutes:

18 U.S.C. § 1512 (2003) Ch.2 (n.4)

18 U.S.C. §1519 (2003) Ch.2 (n.25)

18 U.S.C. §1520 (2003) Ch.2 (n.24)

29 U.S.C. §§ 1027, 1059 . . . . .Ch.2 (n.8)

29 CFR § 825.500 . . . . .Ch.2 (n.9)

29 CFR § 1627.3 . . . . .Ch.2 (n.7)

TABLE OF AUTHORITIES

Sarbanes-Oxley Act ("Corporate and Criminal Fraud Accountability Act of 2002"), 15 U.S.C. §§ 7201-7266 (2002) Ch.2 (nn.10,24)

Securities Exchange Act of 1934 §17(a) Ch.2 (p.21)

Uniform Trade Secrets Act § 1(2)(ii)(C) Ch.6 (nn.2,22)

Uniform Trade Secrets Act §1(4)(ii) Ch.6 (n.21)

Federal Rules:

Fed. R. Civ. P. 8(a) Ch.5 (n.8)

Fed. R. Civ. P. 26(a) Ch.3 (pp.48,57)

Fed. R. Civ. P. 26(a), 1993 Revision, Advisory Committee Notes Ch.3 (n.7)

Fed. R. Civ. P. 26(a)(1)(B) Ch.3 (p.49)

Fed. R. Civ. P. 26(b)(1) Ch.3 (n.3), Ch.6 (n.3)

Fed. R. Civ. P. 26(b)(2) Ch.3 (n.2), Ch.3 (p.55), Ch.7 (n.13), Ch.8 (n.15)

Fed. R. Civ. P. 26(c) Ch.3 (p.55), Ch.7 (n.1)

Fed. R. Civ. P. 26(c)(7) Ch.6 (n.4)

Fed. R. Civ. P. 26(e)(1) Ch.3 (n.6)

Fed. R. Civ. P. 26(f) Ch.3 (p.49), Ch.3 (pp.57-58)

Fed. R. Civ. P. 30 ....Ch.4 (p.74), Ch.4 (nn.20,27)

Fed. R. Civ. P. 30(b)(1) Ch.4 (n.21)

Fed. R. Civ. P. 30(b)(2) Ch.4 (n.21)

Fed. R. Civ. P. 30(b)(6) Ch.4 (nn.21-22), Ch.4 (p.74)

Fed. R. Civ. P. 33(d) Ch.3 (p.50)

Fed. P. Civ. P. 34 ....Ch.3 (p.47), Ch.4 (p.67), Ch.6 (p.103)

Fed. R. Civ. P. 34, Advisory Committee Notes, 1970 Amendment Ch.3 (n.4) Ch.4 (n.10), Ch.8 (n.15)

Fed. R. Civ. P. 34(a) Ch.2 (n.36), Ch.3 (p.49), Ch.4 (n.10)

Fed. R. Civ. P. 34(b) Ch.3 (n.10)

Fed. R. Civ. P. 34 (c), Advisory Committee Note, 1980 Amendment .Ch.3 (n.11)

Fed. R. Civ. P. 45 ....Ch.4 (p.70), Ch.4 (p.76), Ch.4 (p.78)

Fed. R. Civ. P. 45(a)(1)(C) Ch.4 (n.7)

Fed. R. Civ. P. 45(c)(2)(A) Ch.4 (n.19)
Fed. R. Civ. P. 45(c)(2)(B) Ch.4 (n.5), Ch.4 (nn.28,30,36)
Fed. R. Civ. P. 45(c)(3)(A)-(B) Ch.4 (nn.32-34)
Fed. R. Civ. P. 45(d)(1) Ch.4 (n.11)
Fed. R. Civ. P. 45(d)(2) Ch.4 (n.35)
Fed. R. Civ. P. 53 ....Ch.8 (p.159)
Fed. R. Civ. P. 53(b) Ch.8 (nn.114-115)
Fed. R. Evid. 706 ....Ch.8 (n.113)
Fed. R. Evid. 803(6) Ch.8 (n.67)
Fed. R. Evid. 901(a) Ch.8 (n.66)
U.S. Dist. Ct. Rules, E.D. Ark. And W.D. Ark, LR 26.1 .Ch.3 (n.30), Ch.8 (n.86)
U.S. Dist. Ct. Rules, D.N.J., L.Civ.R. 26.1(b)(2) Ch.3 (n.30)
U.S. Dist. Ct. Rules, D.N.J., L.Civ.R. 26.1(d) Ch.3 (nn.30-33), Ch.8 (n.79)
D.Wy. L. Civ. Rule 26.1(d) Ch.3 (n.30), Ch.8 (n.79)

State Rules:

Cal. Code Civ. P. § 2017 ....Ch.8 (n.79)
Ill. Sup. Ct. R. 201(b) Ch.8 (n.79)
Ill. Sup. Ct. R. 214 ....Ch.8 (n.79)
Md. R. Civ. P. 2-504.3 ....Ch.8 (n.79)
Tex. R. Civ. P. § 196.4 ....Ch.3 (n.30), Ch.8 (n.79)

Miscellaneous:

Draft Amendments to ABA Civil Discovery Standards,
Standard 29 (Nov. 2003) ....Ch.5 (n.31)(with quotation)
Exchange Act Rule 17a-4 ....Ch.2 (p.21)
Mississippi Supreme Court Order 13 (May 29, 2003) Ch.3 (n.30)
Model Rule of Professional Conduct 3.4(a) Ch.5 (n.51)
NASD Rule 3110 ....Ch.2 (p.21)
NYSE Rule 440 ....Ch.2 (p.21)
Uniform Rules of Evidence (1999) Rule 101 and comment Ch.2 (n.37)

TABLE OF AUTHORITIES

Secondary Sources:

Abrams, Steven M. & Weis, Philip C., *Knowledge of Computer Forensics is Becoming Essential For Attorneys In The* Information *Age*, 75-FEB N.J. St. B.J. 8 (Feb. 2003) Ch.8 (nn.2,35,37,50,69,104,114)

Ainsworth, Earl, *E-Discovery, Five Steps to Success*, Guide to Internet Service 2003-2004, Supplement to New Jersey Lawyer Ch.8 (n.111)

Arent, Lisa M., Brownstone, Robert D., Fenwick, William A., *E-Discovery: Preserving, Requesting and Producing Electronic Information*, 19 Santa Clara Computer & High Tech. L.J. 131 (Dec. 2002) ...Ch.8 (nn.19,22,107)

Arkin, Stanley S. and Sullivan, Charles S., *Document Destruction Under Sarbanes-Oxley*, N.Y.L.J. (September 15, 2003) Ch.2 (n.27)

Arruda, Michael E., Prinzing, Margaret R. & Rana, Shruti A., *Documents? What Documents? Some Guidelines About a Document Retention Policy and its Implementation*, ABA's Business Law Today, Vol. 12, Number 3 (January/February 2003), *available at* http://www.abanet.org/buslaw/blt/2003-01-02/arruda.html ..Ch.2 (nn.53,57)

Ballon, Ian C., E-*Commerce & Internet Law: Treatise with Forms* (Glaser Legal Works 2001), photo reprint in part *Email & Electronic Communications* Advanced Corporate Compliance Workshop 2003, San Francisco, CA (July 10-11, 2003) Ch.2 (nn.42,55,63)

Brown, Mary Kay, & Weiner, Paul D., *Digital Dangers*: *A Primer on Electronic Evidence in the Wake of Enron*, 74 PA Bar Assn. Quarterly 1 (Jan. 2003) Ch.8 (nn.44,46,48-49)

Byron, Ellen, *Computer Forensics Sleuths Help Find Fraud*, The Wall Street Journal, March 18, 2003 .... Ch.8 (nn.70,98,109,112)

Carpenter, Sheila J. & Patterson, Shaunda A., *Discovery of Electronic Documents*, 29-SUM Brief 64 (2000) Ch.5 (n.6)

Carroll, John L., *Discovery Disputes & Electronic Media*, America, ALI-ABA Course of Study, 421 (American Law Institute-American Bar Association Continuing Legal Education, 2001), *available on* WESTLAW at SG405 ALI-ABA421 .... Ch.8 (n.47)

Cendali, Dale M., Rodihan, Susan, & Dorsett, Emily, *Electronic Discovery*, Seventh Annual Internet Law Institute, 615 (Practicing Law Institute ed. 2003), *available on* WESTLAW at 755 PLI/Pat 615 .... Ch.8 (n.38)

Cotton, Christopher V., *Document Retention Programs for Electronic Records: Applying a Reasonableness Standard to the Electronic Era*, 24 Iowa J. Corp. L. 417 (Winter 1999) (citations omitted). Ch.2 (nn.5-6)

Craine, Kevin, *Here Come the Lawyers. Is Your IT Department Ready?* ...Ch.4 (n.3)

Digital Forensics: Tales From the Computer Hard Drive, NJ Lawyer: The Weekly Newspaper, June 23, 2003 .... Ch.8 (nn.21,36)

Dort, Kenneth K. & Spatz, Roger R., *Discovery in the Digital Era: Considerations for Corporate Counsel*, 20 NO. 9 Computer & Internet Law. 11, September 2003 .... Ch.2 (nn.40,43-46,51-52)

Ehlers, Elizabeth Bacon, et al., *E-Discovery*, Business, Law and the Internet (Illinois Institute for Continuing Legal Education, March 2002), *available on* WESTLAW at BLI IL-CLE 2-1, 2.35 .... Ch.8 (nn.18,117)

Feldman, Joan, *The Basics of Computer Forensics*, 12 Practical Litigator 17 (March 2001) Ch.6 (nn.28-30)

Feldman, Joan, *Cyber-Sleuthing: Obtaining Facts from Electronic Copies of Defendants' Documents, Recovering Deleted Files, & the Like*, ATLA Annual Convention Reference Materials (July 2003), *available on* WESTLAW at 2 Ann. 2003 ATLA-CLE 1811 .... Ch.8 (n.69)

Feldman, Joan E. & Kohn, Rodger I., *The Essentials of Computer Discovery*, Seventh Annual Internet Law Institute (PLI Patents, Copyrights, Trademarks, & Literary Property Course Handbook Series No. GO-018F, 2003), *available on* WESTLAW at 755 PLI/Pat 649 .... Ch.8 (n.72)

Feldman, Joan, *The Expert's Role In Computer-Based Discovery*, Association of Trial Lawyers of America, Winter 2003 Convention Reference Materials (Feb. 2003), *available on* WESTLAW at Winter 2003 ATLA-CLE 157 .... Ch.8 (nn.3,41,91-92,99-100)

Hart, Jacob P. & Plum, Anna Marie, *Litigating the Production of Electronic Media: "Disk-Covery" Issues for the 21st Century*, SG007 ALI-ABA 169 (2001) Ch.4 (n.3)

Hirsch, Ladd A., *Document Retention & Destruction: Issues in a Post Sarbanes-Oxley World*, University of Houston Law Foundation (November 2002) Ch.2 (n.35)

Howell, Beryl A. & Friedberg, Eric M., *21st Century Forensics: Searching for the "Smoking Gun" in Computer Hard Drives*, The Prosecutor (Nov./Dec. 2003) Ch.8 (nn.36,40,43)

http://www.krollontrack.com/eEvidence/eDiscovery/MarketStatistics, .Ch.4 (n.3)

Johnson-Laird, Andrew, *Smoking Guns & Spinning Disks*, 11 No. 8 Computer Law 1 (Aug. 1994) Ch.8 (nn.19,39,101, 103)

Johnson, Michelle, Esq., *Electronic Evidence at Trial: Authentication, Experts & Focus, Digital Discovery & e-Evidence*, Vol. 1, No. 8 (Sept. 2001) Ch.8 (nn.105,107)

TABLE OF AUTHORITIES

Klein, A., *Federal Rules of Civil Procedure: Depositions & Discovery, Commentary* (National Institute for Trial Advocacy 2003) Ch.3 (n.14)

Lange, Michelle C.S., *New Act has Major Impact on Electronic Evidence; Several Provisions of Sarbanes-Oxley Govern Document Retention Policies*, 26 N.J.L.J. 11, p. C8 (November 4, 2002) Ch.2 (n.2)

Llewellyn, Virginia, *Planning with Clients for Effective Electronic Discovery*, 14 NO. 4 Prac. Litigator 7 (July 2003) Ch.2 (nn.15,62)

Marcus, Richard L., *Confronting the Future: Coping with Discovery of Electronic Material* 64 Law & Contemporary Problems 253 (Spring/Summer 2001) Ch.4 (n.13), Ch.8 (nn.108,110)

Messina, Joseph P. & Trinkle, Daniel B. *Document Retention Policies After Anderson*, Boston Bar Journal (September – October 2002) Ch.2 (n.34)

Michalowicz, Michael J., *Computer Harassment? Top Data-Forensics Sleuths, Steps to Take When Problems Arise*, N.J. Lawyer: The Weekly Newspaper, April 21, 2003 at A3 ....Ch.8 (n.106)

Moore's Federal Practice 3d, §37A.12 [5][d] Ch.2 (nn.12,59)

Moore's Federal Practice 3d, §37A.12[5][e] Ch.2 (n.61)

Morris, Frank C. Jr., *The Electronic Platform: Email & Other Privacy Issues in the Workplace*, 20 NO. 8 Computer & Internet Law. 1 (August 2003), summarizing Beware Workplace E-mail: Survey Says Expert Tells How to Reduce Risk and Avoid Court Dates, 2001 Electronic Policies & Practice Surveys, *available at* http://www.epolicyinstitute.com/survey/index.html Ch.2 (n.13)

Murphy, Devin, *The Discovery of Electronic Data in Litigation: What Practitioners & Their Clients Need to Know*, 27 Wm. Mitchell L. Rev. 1825 (2001) ....Ch.8 (n. 4)

Nimsger, Kristin M. Esq., et al., *Electronic Discovery in Technology Litigation*, 23rd Annual Institute on Computer Law 297 (Practicing Law Institute ed. 2003), *available on* WESTLAW at PLI/Pat 297 ....Ch.8 (nn.42,68)

Redgrave & Nimsger, *Electronic Discovery & Inadvertent Production of Privileged Documents*, 49 Federal Lawyer 37 (July 2002) ..Ch.6 (nn.17,20)

Redish, Martin H., *Electronic Discovery & the Litigation Matrix*, 51 Duke L. J. 561 (Nov. 2001) Ch.8 (n.74)

Rosenberg, *Electronic Discovery Proves Effective Legal Weapon*, Oklahoma City Journal Press (April 21, 1997), 1997 WL 14390671 ....Ch.7 (n.4)

Rosenthal, Lesley Friedman, *Electronic Discovery Can Unearth Treasure Trove of Information or Potential Land Mines*, 75-Sept. N.Y. St. B.J. 32 (Sept. 2003) Ch.8 (nn.51,90)

Scheindlin, Hon. Shira A. & Rabkin, Jeffrey, *Electronic Discovery in Federal Civil Litigation: Is Rule 34 Up To The Task?* 41 B.C. L. Rev. 327 (2000) . . .Ch.3 (nn.4,13,15,23,25), Ch.4 (nn.1,8), Ch.5 (nn.29-30), Ch.6 (nn.7,17)

Scheindlin, Hon. Shira A. & Rabkin, Jeffrey, *Retaining, Destroying & Producing E-Data: Part 2*, N.Y.L.J., May 9, 2002 ....Ch.8 (nn.20,24,77-78,90)

Securities and Exchange Commission Press Release 2002-173, dated December 3, 2002, *available at* http://www/sec/gov/news/press/2002-173.htm . . .Ch.2 (n.11)

The Sedona Principles: Best Practices, Recommendations & Principles for Addressing Electronic Document Production (Sedona Conference Working Group Series 2004), *available at* http://www.sedonaconference.org . . .Ch.2 (nn.47-50,60-61,64-65), Ch.3 (n.29), Ch.8 (n.16)

Sen. Rep. No. 107-146 at 14 ....Ch.2 (n.26)

Sloan, Peter, *Retention, Preservation, & Spoliation of Electronic Data*, Ontrack Datatrail (2000) Ch.5 (nn.38,40)

Smith, Elliot Blair, *Wall St. Bloodhounds Track IMs for Clues*, USA Today, Sept. 18, 2003 ....Ch.8 (nn.80-82)

Smith, Kevin D. & Becker, Laura J., *Recent Developments Affecting Self-Insurers & Risk Managers*, 36 Tort & Ins. L.J. 593 (2001) Ch.4 (n.26)

Snyder, James A,. & Morelock, Angela, *Electronic Data Discovery: Litigation Gold Mine or Nightmare?* 58 J. Mo. B. 18 (Jan/Feb. 2002) Ch.8 (nn.45,47,70)

Strong, John, et al., *McCormick on Evidence*, Vol. II. (5th ed. 1999) Ch.8 (n.73)

Thompson, Todd, *The Paper Trail Has Gone Digital: Discovery in the Age of Electronic Information*, 71-MAR J. Kan. B.A. 16 (March, 2002) Ch.5 (nn.69,72)

Traynor, Michael & Ploeger, Lori, *Hot Topics In Electronic Discovery*, 712 PLI/Pat 51, 61 (2002) ....Ch.4 (nn.3-5,9,12,16), Ch.8 (n 92)

Tressel, Ruth A. & Noonan, Daniel J., *Using Technology To Fend Off Future Legal Crises*, ACCA Docket 21, NO. 7 (July/August 2003) Ch.2 (n.41)

Wall, Christopher D. & Lange, Michele C.S., *Recent Developments in Electronic Discovery*, Washington Lawyer (March 2003) Ch.8 (n.84)

Weinstein's Federal Evidence § 5.03.42 [2] Ch.6 (n.2)

Weinstein's Federal Evidence § 5.03.42 [3] Ch.6 (n.11)

TABLE OF AUTHORITIES

Weinstein's Federal Evidence § 5.03.42 [4] Ch.6 (n.13)

Winthrop, Pillsbury, *Electronic Data Discovery: Duty to Preserve Evidence*, Bulletin No. 03-13 (Nov. 26, 2003) Ch.5 (nn.43-44,49,73)

Withers, Kenneth J., *Computer-Based Discovery In Federal Civil Litigation*, 2000 Fed. Cts. L. Rev. 2 § II.G.1 (2000) Ch.4 (nn.17, 18) Ch.5 (nn.21-22,45-46), Ch.8 (nn.1,25,116,130,135)

INDEX

Active Data 7,113,127,144
Adverse Inference 95
Archive
    Disk 15
    E-mail 4,9
Authentication of Evidence 148
Back-Up
    Data 12-16,72,113
    Incremental 13
    Media 5-6,13,15
    Program 15
    Protocol/Policy 13-14
    Rotation 13,15
    Tape 13-15,25,39,91,127
Boolean Search 144
Cache . . . .*See* Memory
Compress 8,15
Computer
    Desktop 5,6,17
    Laptop 6,17
Computer Forensics Expert . . . .*See* Experts
Concept Search 144
Confidentiality
    Data 55,73,77,134,154
    Trade Secrets 77,104,110-111,146
Cost-Shifting 24,121
Data
    Accessible 25,127-128
    Active 7-8,113,144
    Back-up 12-16,113,115
    Deleted 16-17,72,113-114
    Embedded 8,12,72
    Files 71
    Inaccessible 8,25,127,128
    Metadata 9-12,145-146
    Near line 127
    Online 127
    Privileged/Confidential 73,134,154
    Reasonably Usable Form 71
    Replicant 113
    Residual 16-17,72,113,115
Data Compilation . . . .*See* Discovery
Desktop
    Computer 5-6,17
    C:/drive or Hard drive 4,71-72,88

Discovery
    Data Compilation 50-51
    Electronic Form 50-56
    Generally 47
    Non-Parties 67
    Request 139
    Rules 56-57
    Shared Costs 24-25,121
    Subpoena 70,75,79
    Two-Tiered 60

Document
    Destruction 20-22,30
    Generally 49-50,70,86,89
    Native 12
    Retention 20-22,30,39,85,87

Document Management Retention Program (DMRP)
    Generally 19-46
    Implementation 35
    Reasonableness 31,38

Drive
    Hard 4,71-72,88
    Jaz 5,13
    Optical 15
    Shared 4
    Zip 35
    USB Thumb 5

E-mail 4,8,11,25,67,88,115
    Archive 4,39
    Directory 39
    Back-up tapes 4,90-91
    Retention 44-45
    Server 8

Embedded Data 7,12,72

Evidence
    Authentication 151
    Preservation 28,39,75,82-90
    Spoliation 27,81,91

Experts
    Authentication of Evidence 148
    Costs 158
    Court Appointed 159
    Forensics Experts Generally 11,135-158
    Litigation 137
    Responding to Discovery Requests 154
    Role of Consultants 135
    Selection 156
    Shaping Discovery Requests 139

INDEX

Federal Rules of Civil Procedure
  Amendments 58
  Cost-Shifting 24,121,125
  Discovery 74,112
  Document Demand 70,76
  Generally 82
File
  Data 71
  Extensions 8
  File Allocation Table (FAT)/ Master File Table (MFT) 9-11
  Privileged/ Confidential 134
  Servers 4-5,9
Forensics
  Computer 135
  Expert ....*See* Experts
  Software 114,124
  Tools 5
  Utilities 17
Free Space 14,144-145
Group Share (or Shared Drive) 4,6,9
Hard Drive (or c:/drive) 4,71-72,88
Hardware
  Inspection 73
  Mirror Image 73
Harvesting
  Generally 8-9,70
  Protocol 8
Header
  Internet 11
Home Computer (Desktop Computer) 5-6,44
Home Directory 4,6
Information Technology (IT) ....*See* MIS
Instant Message 152
Internet Based File Server 5-6
Internet Headers 11
Information Technology (IT) ....*See* MIS
Laptop Computer 6,17
Litigation Hold Procedure (Legal Hold) 39-42,44
Local Area Network (LAN) 3
Master File Table 9-11
Media
  Back-up 5-6,13,15,16
  Removable 5,6
Memory
  Cache 17
  Free Space 144

239

Memory (con't)
    Slack Space 17
    Unallocated Free Space 17
Metadata 7,9-12,145
Mirror Image 73,115,143
MIS Department (also IT Department) 3,43,44,75
Motions
    Discovery 83
    Protective Orders 55,83,116-118
    To Compel 74
Near-Line Data 127
Network
    Local Area Network 3
    Forensic Tools 5
    Generally 3-4
    Wide Area Network 3
Online Data 127
Operating System 16
Overwrite
    Generally 15-16,124
    Programs 17
PDF'ing 5
Perl Script 5
Personal Digital Assistant (PDA) 5-6,44
Privilege
    Attorney-Client 105
    Information 55-56,77
    Waiver 103,109-110
    Work Product 105-106
Protective Orders 55-56,84,116-117
Protocol
    Back-up 13-14
    Harvesting 8
    Welles-Simon 112,116-119,162-163
Remote Access 5
Removable Media 5-6
Rowe Factors (Rowe Test) 25
Sarbanes-Oxley 20-21,29
Sanctions 15,20,22,63,83,92,146
    Safe Harbor 63
Scheindlin, Hon. Shira A. 48,51,54-55,67,113,123,126,140-141,151,154
Search
    Boolean 144
    Concept 144
    Harvest Protocol 8

INDEX

Search (con't)
    Keyword 143
    Perl Script 5
Sedona Principles 45
Server 3,13
    Client/ Server Model 4
    E-mail 8
    File 4-5,9
    Generally 4-5
    Internet Based 5
    Peer-to-Peer Model 4
Shared Cost of Discovery 24,77-78,121
Slack Space (Swap Files) 17,114
Software
    Application (End-User Program) 6,112
    Forensic 114,124
    Generally 6-7
    Operating System (System Software) 6
Special Master 159
Spoliation
    Adverse Inference 95
    Consequences 22,92,94
    Elements 93
    Generally 27,81,91
Tapes
    Back-up 13-15,25,39,39,91,127
    Digital Audio Tape (DAT) 15
    Quarter Inch Cartridge (QIC) 15
    Travan 15
Tiffing 5
Trade Secret ....*See* Confidentiality
Unallocated Free Space 17
Utilities
    Forensic 17
Welles-Simon Protocol ....*See* Protocol
Wipe Program 17
Work Product ....*See* Privilege
Zubulake Factors 26

Notes:

Notes:

Notes:

Notes:

Notes: